Ransom Kha

HE NEVER
LEFT ME ALONE

May God bless you
as you read this book.
Ransom Khanye
07.09.2020

SACUENI
2020

ISBN 978-973-0-31682-7

CONTENTS

FOREWORD

I felt a huge burden getting lifted off me as I wrote a page or so of this book each day for five continuous months. I wrote it to encourage people who are grieving. I also wrote to help those who are not grieving but are in the presence of those grieving to understand what grief feels like. Unfortunately, grief is not universal for everyone. Yet the handful of people I knew who were grieving at the time of my writing, commented on my writing. In their comments, some confirmed that they could identify with some of what I was writing.

I also wrote a lot of stories about lessons I learned during and after my time of trying to assist my ill wife recover from cancer. I learned about many different natural remedies and I have shared much of what I learned within the pages of this book. I also got through many difficult situations that I write about. I write very strongly about my personal religious beliefs. I write about my many travels and about my transitioning from being a widower to a married man again. So effectively you will find in the pages of my book all about death and grief followed by romance and what you may even refer to as comic content as you go through the journey of my life.

I want to say a few words about pain. From time to time I still do feel pain. It is pain that comes from the memories of my loss. I lost a lot more than just a wife. So do not think I am in pain and forever grieving for my late wife. Also do not think that I love the pain, as one insensitive person once told me that I want to stay in mourning because that is how I get attention from people! God forbid that I should want to stay in pain so I can get attention! Also, please do not presume to tell me that I have no right to feel pain because I moved on with my life. Should I have stayed alone and wept myself to death?

I lost my own life that I used to live, cherish and enjoy. I lost the happiness that characterised my daily life. I lost the goals and ambitions from the plans of a future I had been preparing for. Nobody in this life should ever even try to make me feel sorry, embarrassed or ashamed for feeling this pain of loss. Do I feel it constantly or continuously? NO. But once in a while pain comes upon me, and as rarely as it does happen, I should never ever be made to feel guilty as though I have done something wrong. To those who want to tell me how I should be I am sorry because I would not be myself if I were the way others tell me to be. My next book will thus focus exclusively on being silent in order to comfort the grieving.

Christ has done a remarkable work of healing me and I know the pain is not as severe anymore because of the healing. So I say to anyone and everyone who cares about others, please do not judge and condemn others. I have done a lot to get myself out of pain and grief. If you can create or recreate a human being then, and only then can you tell another person how they ought to feel. But remember, you can only live your own life. Be nice to others even if, and especially because, you do not understand them. God loves and cares for them too.

May you be blessed by learning something from what I went through. May your reading bring you some insights and new perspectives that you would not have otherwise.

ACKNOWLEDGEMENTS

Firstly, I thank my wife Erika who at first feared this project would consume me and take me away from her and into my past but later found it to be interesting and useful reading for other people. The writing of this book took off a lot of stress that otherwise needed to come out.

There were at least 53 people who daily received a WhatsApp message with a story that was part of the book in development. For the support and encouragement and feedback I received from you all, I am thankful. To my family members in the Khanye WhatsApp family chat, sisters and nephews and nieces, thank you for the continuous encouragement. I also thank the Mokalakes who were also reading along and expressing their views and concerns along my writing of the book.

I particularly thank Harvey Henderson for extensively combing through almost each and every article I wrote. The criticism was very constructive and helpful in showing me different perspectives.

I also thank Sam Mahlangu who not only gave me critical feedback but who long urged me to write a book.

Lastly but not least, Camelia Putureanu, who was the very first person to try to persuade me to write a book. It has been many years since she urged me to, yet I have never forgotten how much she believed that I could do it. Thanks Cami.

1 MORE QUESTIONS THAN ANSWERS

Blessed be God, even the Father of our Lord Jesus Christ, the Father of mercies, and the God of all comfort; Who comforteth us in all our tribulation, that we may be able to comfort them which are in any trouble, by the comfort wherewith we ourselves are comforted of God. (2 Corinthians 1:3-4)

I can be almost certain that in the most horrible pain that you are experiencing at the time of your loss, your mind is full of questions! It would be futile for me or anyone to try to give the answers to the questions because those questions as far as I know have no humanly known answers.

As someone who has been in deep grief, I am taking this moment to reflect as I think of someone who may also be going through the same. You are probably reading this because of your own very painful loss or someone close to you has lost a loved one to death. Either way, I hope my own experience can serve to encourage you through your pain.

Firstly, I should reassure you that the questions you have are okay to have. I had them too, when I lost my loved ones! I also lost my dad in November 2015. I lost my sister as well in April 2004. I am not even promising that I will provide the answers for you but I am just saying that you are not alone in that realm of thought.

The most likely questions you may have are:

Why it was your loved one who had to die?

Why now?

Why did God not heal them or prevent them from dying?

The fact that you feel this way means that you really loved them. It also means that their premature departure has left a vacuum full of pain for you.

It is not a simple thing to just accept death and move on. As long as the pain remains you will always have these questions and nobody will ever succeed to answer them for you.

Why am I so sure? I speak not only from personal experience but also from scriptural examples.

Picture Job for instance. He was no doubt a good man of God. And yet even he was filled with questions. He took all his many questions directly to God.

Did God even answer his questions? No, He didn't! Instead God hit him with the existential question. He asked him: "Where were you when I made the heavens and the earth?" God essentially told him, "Be quiet Job". He said be still and know that I am God. He simply implied this... "I am God and you cannot even understand anything even if I did explain it to you!"

REFLECTION:

We can never understand the issues surrounding death. We will all have to wait until we reach heaven to know some reasons behind our pain.

BLESSING:

So today I pray that your soul will be filled with the Spirit of God and be still.

God loved your special one more than you or any human could. God's heart is pained too as you feel the pain that you feel. May you find your peace in Jesus!

2 A BAG FOR LIFE

And the LORD God formed man of the dust of the ground, and breathed into his nostrils the breath of life; and man became a living soul. (Genesis 2:7)

A few days just after the death of my first wife I went to buy some items in one local supermarket in Swindon. I walked from aisle to aisle while putting the groceries into my shopping trolley.

The difference between me and most other shoppers in the supermarket was that my heart was bleeding with pain. I was there bodily but yet mentally I was far removed. My mind could not understand how everyone was seemingly so peaceful, so calm so serene when I was so distraught.

The music that was playing in the shop was so insensitive to how I felt. It was careless and louder than it could have been. The happy children who were running around seemed so disrespectful of my state and pain (of which they had absolutely no way of knowing).

In that shop, absolutely nobody knew or cared that I had just lost the mother of my two small children. Nobody knew how I was asking myself many questions about what I could have done better to help my wife remain alive.

Still distressing over these stressful thoughts I reached the checkout till to pay. The jolly young lady at the till innocently doing her job unknowingly fired one lethal shot at me. She asked me, "Would you like a bag for life?" Boy that just did it! A bag for life? I just lost a life and here is this girl casually offering me a bag for life!

Of course that was not what she meant but in my frame of mind it was such a senseless question. How could buying that bag bring any life to my wife or to anyone that needs to cling to dear life?

REFLECTION:

A bag for life has no life to give. Only God has life and only He can restore it after we kick the bucket of life.

BLESSING:

Only God sees your pain as well as understands it. May He continue to soothe you and comfort you today and everyday. He is the resurrection and the life! Have a blessed day!

3 I HAVE APPOINTMENTS TO KEEP

For they are the spirits of devils, working miracles, [which] go forth unto the kings of the earth and of the whole world, to gather them to the battle of that great day of God Almighty. (Revelation 16:14)

Often times we ponder over the meaning of life. But we certainly dwell more on wondering about beyond this life. What shall happen when we die? Will we go straight to heaven as soon as our eyes close in death as taught by some people? Or if our lives have been badly lived and we deserve hell fire will we go straight to hell as suggested by some? Yet some have exercised their mental genius to come up with the concepts of purgatory and even a state of limbo.

So just what does happen at death? I am pacified to know that the dead know nothing. Their very memory is forgotten the moment they die. There is no free spirit roaming around without a body remaining to comfort or torture me.

Incidentally, Satan did visit me several times as I slept in my room a month or so after my wife died. Three or four times I spoke to Mandy after she had already died. She came back to me in such sweet dreams and made me so happy but yet nonetheless surprised to see her.

So, still in dreamland, I challenged her by saying to her, "Mandy you are supposed to be dead, what are you doing here?" She answered me and said "God decided that I was not supposed to die and He sent me back to you. And so I came back."

Nice try Satan! (Ecclesiastes 9:5) Even Mandy herself, both of whose parents had already rested in the Lord, said many times to me that she had made appointments with her parents and she wanted to keep the appointments and meet them in heaven one day. And that appointment in heaven will only become a reality after Jesus comes to take his children to heaven. (1 Thessalonians 4:16) Otherwise there would be no need for the second coming because then we would all just go straight to heaven by death and quickly be with Jesus. Who would He need to come for if we are all there already? Why would anyone need to be resurrected when they have already gone to heaven? Jesus did not call Lazarus down from heaven after he had died, but out of the grave. (John 11:43).

REFLECTION:

True, after death the next thing will be the resurrection but that shall happen only at the second coming of Jesus. So blessed is he who dies in the Lord as he will be resurrected to be given a new immortal body and life eternal. (Revelation 14:13)

BLESSING:

May God give you peace as you remain grounded in truth. Let not Satanic attacks ever have any power over you just because you are mourning. The Lord is with you!

4 THE SOUND OF SILENCE

I will sing of the mercies of the Lord for ever: with my mouth will I make known thy faithfulness to all generations. (Psalm 89:1)

Many a time it is never part of our imagination that the beautiful sounds of the present could be something that we may seek and miss tomorrow. In fact it may not even strike us as important as it really actually is until it is permanently withdrawn. Then what adds insult to injury is that the cause of that withdrawal is death.

After spending a wonderful decade of singing duets and harmonising together in congregational songs, the last thing I could have ever imagined was the pain brought by the absence of Mandy's voice.

'Sing mummy', urged our daughter several times during family worship time at a time her mother was so unwell that she could no longer sing. I explained to her that mummy's voice could not come out well in a song anymore because she was sick. At that time it was really sad because she was being asked to sing but could not. It was sad yes but only temporary I thought because she would become well again and be able to sing.

The real pain only came in full force when I went to attend church services after her death. There I discovered that I too could no longer sing! Not because I had lost my voice but because I had lost my accompanying voice. In my mind, as I tried to sing I could hear the voice of harmonisation that could and would have been there when Mandy was singing next to me. The attempts to sing now resulted in weeping. Not only could I not sing anymore but I even failed to remain in the congregation as they sang. So I left during each song and went outside until I thought the singing was over.

To know that Jesus himself was familiar with grief and that even as I was experiencing the pain of grief Jesus was ever present in my time of trouble brought me some degree of comfort. This knowledge and understanding did not take the pain away. Only a hope of the promised resurrection when Jesus comes again could sustain me and keep me going.

REFLECTION:

Years went by and slowly I regained the courage to face the sound of the silence of the missing harmony in song. I became able to sing again and praise the God who created the heavens and the earth with thanksgiving.

BLESSING:

I hope that whenever you too will pass through the sound of silence you will hear a voice saying, "My child be still and know that I am God". May you be blessed today.

5 THE LAST TRUMP

In a moment, in the twinkling of an eye, at the last trump: for the trumpet shall sound, and the dead shall be raised incorruptible, and we shall be changed. (1 Corinthians 15:52)

I had spent more than 24 hours in the hospital and I was full of fatigue and exhaustion. A friend finally persuaded me to go home and sleep a little. They assured me they would stay by her side until I returned. With much reluctance I went home and left John, a nurse by profession and Georginah, my sister in law in the private ward my wife was laying in.

When I reached home I fell down on my knees and cried out to God. I begged Him to do a miracle and restore Mandy's health. Then I took a much needed shower before getting about an hour of sleep. Which sleep was really just a horizontal body in bed but an active restless head.

When I reached the hospital I was told a doctor had been there and that she wanted to speak to me. She came back and called me out of the room to talk to me privately. She said to me that the sounds of Mandy's cries were now the sounds made by someone who is clinging to dear life in their final moments. She asked if I wanted them to turn off her life support or leave it still going. I told her to do whatever they can to keep her alive and that I was going to talk to my God.

I went back inside the room and stood next to Mandy's bed and talked to her. She wasn't responding much but that didn't stop me. I told her I was going to pray and she nodded. Holding her hand, I prayed and committed her life to God. I prayed for a miracle healing against the hopeless situation everyone was giving up on. My faith was not shaken and I sincerely believed a miracle could happen for her. I prayed out loud and later my sister in law was to tell me that I was a bit too loud!

On the chair behind me was a netbook softly playing some songs. Just as soon as my prayer ended a familiar favorite of ours started playing. With her hand still in mine I joined in and sang the song for her from start to finish. For the song, I was conscious that I was not singing very softly. But I sang from my heart. The song I sang was the song, "He'll Do It Again".

It was not long after I finished singing that the beeping sounds from the life support machines increased in tempo. Her breathing became slower and slower and then it stopped while the machine beep changed into one continuous long tone.

REFLECTION:

Mandy went to sleep and rested from all the cares of this world. I have no doubt in my mind that she died in the Lord. I look forward to the resurrection day much more than I ever did before because I do want to meet her again. In a twinkling of an eye we shall all be changed.

BLESSING:

My peace comes from this hope that the dead shall be raised. Today, may you find your peace in this too.

6 THE DREADED PLAYLIST

And he hath put a new song in my mouth, even praise unto our God: many shall see it, and fear, and shall trust in the LORD. (Psalms 40:3)

There are times when we collect our favourite music and compile it all into one group of songs or playlist for convenience and ease of accessibility. Computers can make the use of playlists easier. By using playlists we can repeatedly play the same songs without even raising a finger.

During the months of dealing with Mandy's cancer treatment, we developed a certain playlist of favourite music by various artists. This playlist consisted of at least over 100 songs in total and took some careful and thoughtful effort in selecting songs.

I have previously referred to the music that played in the background from a netbook that was on a chair inside of Mandy's private ward. The music was actually from the playlist I am referring to here now. Eventually, as most would probably agree, after listening several times to a playlist one develops a mental index of the sequence on the playlist and at the end of any song on the playlist they know which song comes next.

So it happened that the songs that played in sequence at the last moments of Mandy's life inadvertently also left an indelible mark on my mind. Little did I imagine that even years later whenever I would play the songs from that playlist I would literally relive those moments again just as if they were happening again.

Several times I tried to be courageous and to revisit the songs again. But as long as I played the songs in the sequence that I created in 2009 then I remembered everything minute by minute as though it were happening again. Not only did I remember but I reacted bodily with mental pain to the familiar sounds of the life support machines that were in the room that I heard the songs from. I felt the same stress and tension and tearfulness as back then. I also remembered which song was playing as I prayed. I remembered how, as she was now dying, Mandy was breathing at every point of the songs that played. I remembered the rapid beeps from the machine that monitored her heartbeat as her heart weakened slower and slower to its final stop and the shrill of the long continuous sound that ensued.

The songs continued to play in the ward just as they had always done before. They marked the most painful time just after Mandy died and lay there still and lifeless.

Thankfully the songs on the playlist, apart from a few, were not the most common ones. And I did not hear them at all ever since I did not play that playlist anymore.

REFLECTION:

I have an abundance of new songs that I play, sing along to and meditate upon. I do not need to hear the old playlist anymore as I do not want to remain re-living the stress of the moment of death. May it bring hope and comfort to someone to know that even sharing this memory now does not cause me the pain it could have done years ago. I thank God for His power and performing the remarkable act of healing.

BLESSING:

If you are hurting today please take courage and know that in His time and in a way unique to you, God will heal you too. Be blessed today.

7 WE SHALL NOT RESUSCITATE

Jesus said unto her, I am the resurrection, and the life: he that believeth in me, though he were dead, yet shall he live: And whosoever liveth and believeth in me shall never die. Believest thou this? (John 11:25-26)

On the Saturday night before the death of Mandy I was having some great moments in her hospital ward of positively trying to strengthen and encourage her. I was busy telling her stories and reminding her of all the lovely things we had been through together. I was trying to make her laugh and smile and forget the present circumstances and focus on the future.

It was during these moments that some doctor came and interrupted us. They said they had been discussing something important with other staff and they wanted to speak to me. So I had to leave my wife alone to listen to some music while I was going to a meeting.

The meeting was held in some doctor's office. When we reached the office there were two other senior officials of the hospital to whom I was introduced. I was told their names and work titles of importance that were not really of much interest to me. Besides, the meeting was not a discussion with me but just a formality for the hospital to explain their plans to me. I guess they remained in a group to be witnesses to each other that they had told me what they needed to in case I took legal action against the hospital later. So they began by outlining the condition of Mandy's illness and the stage at which the cancer had reached in its development on her. They really only wanted to tell me their final decision which was that they had already informed their staff not to take Mandy into the intensive care unit even as her condition worsened. They wanted me to know that according to the situation they would not even do anything should her heart stop. "We will not resuscitate her" was the decision they had called me to tell me.

Despite the decision to not attempt to save life I left the office thinking God will resurrect. But I was actually more of the thought that even in that dire moment when humans see no hope, God can still do wonders and miraculously heal her. I returned to Mandy and told her that they do not know our God can do wonders. Let's think about and plan how we will bring all our families together and celebrate our 10th wedding anniversary.

REFLECTION:

On the day of resurrection there will be many conversations to be continued I am sure. Even though humans will not even try to resuscitate, which can fail anyway, God will certainly resurrect.

BLESSING:

Take courage and comfort from knowing that he that believeth though he were dead yet shall live. May God bless you.

8 SPILLED BLOOD

If it be possible, as much as lieth in you, live peaceably with all men. Dearly beloved, avenge not yourselves, but rather give place unto wrath: for it is written, Vengeance is mine; I will repay, saith the Lord. (Romans 12:18-19)

The intravenous drip that was providing fluids that were supplying some glucose and other minerals suddenly stopped flowing during the night of Saturday 12th December 2009. We called for a nurse to inform them of the situation so they could correct it. But it turned out to be a much more involved and pedantic task than we could have even imagined.

Firstly the nurse tried to reseat the drip and check it for any blockages. Then upon finding no blockage she changed the drip. As there was still no change she decided that maybe Mandy's vein was blocked. So she would just move the needle to another vein. And that was the beginning of the physical needle-pricking torture for Mandy and mental trauma for me as an onlooker.

The moving of the needle to another vein meant another prick on the skin for Mandy. After that prick the vein was missed and the drip was still not installed. A second attempt was made, which was another prick and that was not successful either. So the nurse said she would go and call someone who specialises in this area and who can find veins very easily. But that could not happen until Sunday morning around 11am or so.

When the anaesthetician arrived, who happened to be the expert in finding veins and installing needles, I told him to be careful because Mandy was really afraid of needles and she had already been pricked so much. Notwithstanding my plea, he unsuccessfully tried twice to insert the needle into the vein on Mandy's arms. With each trial it was more groaning and pain for her. Ultimately he said he would put the drip through the groin as that was a more sure location for the required vein. This time when he pricked on the groin Mandy screamed and the needle that was being used drew some urine! The vein expert had just managed to prick her bladder with a needle! Yet he was still not successful in locating any vein and at this time he decided he would need to hand the process over to some surgeon colleagues from the theatre.

It was around 1pm when the surgical team would arrive. Complete with some 3 trainee doctors and a superintendent. I took the responsible husband's task to explain to them that my wife had been through a lot of torture already at the hands of the colleagues who had been trying to fit a drip already before. I implored them that they should therefore be very gentle and careful with her. What I got was a very angry reaction from the most senior doctor who was on duty that day. She told me that she was the only one available and if I did not let her do her job then only on Monday would other doctors become available. She further insisted that as a family member I should leave the room so they would be able to carry out their surgical operation work without my interference. I said I would not leave my wife alone and she replied and said then they would not do the work they were meant to while I was in the room. She asked me what I wanted to do and I asked Mandy who told me to just leave. So I did.

I was outside the ward in the corridors for more than an hour. During that hour, I wept so much from distress about what had just been discussed and also what I had witnessed with all the pricking and screaming of Mandy's. About 20 minutes after I had been sent outside I was followed by one kind young trainee doctor who came and apologised to me for the way their senior had treated me. Seeing that I was weeping, he said he was with me in thought and did not understand why his colleague was so mean and rough. He added that the other doctors actually agreed with what I had said but the senior doctor overruled them and was always mean even to other patients and their families.

When they finally called me back into the ward it was after well over an hour. But what I found pierced my heart right to the core. There was so much spilled blood all around Mandy on the bed which had just been left uncleaned. She was as it were literally left lying in a pool of blood. I had to call a nurse to clean up the mess and our friend was on duty in that ward that day and she came and cleaned up her friend's blood.

REFLECTION:

All these things happened a few hours before Mandy's death. The torture I had to endure was not just watching her die peacefully in bed. I had a lot of mental torture also just before she died. Nonetheless I resisted the added torture of trying to sue the hospital and fight them for what I felt was unacceptable treatment. After all, fighting them would not bring back

Mandy. And whoever treats others badly will have their sins catching up with them one day.

BLESSING:

I hope that this traumatic experience makes whatever pain you have today feel less distressed today about your own situation. May God help you to get over your own pain and heal you!

9 WHERE IS THEIR MOTHER?

As one whom his mother comforteth, so will I comfort you; and ye shall be comforted in Jerusalem. (Isaiah 66:13)

Whenever I travel internationally, unless I am not with the children, I always need to carry a lot more documentation than just passports. In addition to passports, which I must have anyway, I must also carry expired passports of my late wife plus her death certificate. In January 2010 as we needed to change flights at the Johannesburg international airport we also needed to pass through immigration before proceeding to our boarding gate. The airline we were booked with was South African Airways for 14th January travel to London Heathrow airport and we stood in line to have our documents checked.

When my turn came, I handed over my emergency travel document. "Where is your visa?" I was asked. I produced my expired passport with a valid visa clearly showing my "Indefinite Leave to remain" stamp. "Where is the mother of these children? You need a letter of consent from her for them to travel with you but without her. Please step aside to speak to another member of staff."

That member of staff was said to be working for the home office in London and he told me that I was not allowed to travel with my children without a letter from their mother to authorise me, according to the law. I told him that we were just coming from her burial and going back home so I could resume work and so kids could go back to school. He demanded my passport, again. I gave him the same emergency travel document and he wanted to see evidence that I had also applied for a passport when I obtained the emergency travel document.

But I had made no such application. He demanded the reason and I told him that I was going to apply for a British passport. He wanted to see proof that the children were actually mine. I showed him their birth certificates. Then he demanded proof of their mother's death. I showed him her death certificate. By this time what had been a long queue was almost finished and most of the other passengers had boarded buses to be taken to the aircraft. Yet the man was in no hurry to let us go. He quizzed me about where I work and what job I was doing before I protested that we were now about to miss our flight.

Finally, he reluctantly let us go. Such was my frustrating journey back to England. No kindness or mercy was shown to the grieving children and to their father!

REFLECTION:

Sometimes in life we meet with heartless and mean people. Even when they know we are bereaved. Just keep going and do not let them bring you further down.

BLESSING:

May God give you courage and strength to keep going even through obstacles. Be blessed today.

10 THE FOOD IS NOT REALLY NICE DADDY

Fear thou not; for I am with thee: be not dismayed; for I am thy God: I will strengthen thee; yea, I will help thee; yea, I will uphold thee with the right hand of my righteousness. (Isaiah 41:10)

On January 15th of 2010 a family of 3 arrived back in Swindon, England. This was a new structure of family which no longer had a mother as we had just come back from the burial of Mandy in Africa. Tired from a journey of over 14 hours that involved an hour's flight, and another 10 hours flight plus the typical long international flight check in times, we had reached a cold home that was also full of chaos. It was chaotic in that it was untidy. We had been gone from it over a month before when we left for the funeral in Botswana, Mandy's country of birth.

I turned the heating on and with the kids took the car to the supermarket to get some food supplies. Upon our return I prepared some food for us to eat. The food preparation was such a lengthy and arduous chore for me because I had been out of action from the kitchen now for nearly a decade. Mandy had disallowed my involvement in cooking just after we got married. So now my cooking skills were nearly non-existent. Compounding the difficulty was the reality that we were now just three in the house and not four as before. That thought hurt, really bad, and I wept over it covertly as I wanted to be positive for the little ones.

After endless hours of my cooking it was now time to eat. So we sat down at the kitchen table and said grace before having our meal which consisted of plant based ingredients that have now escaped my memory. What does not escape from my memory though is how slowly the kids were eating. Asking the question, "Don't you like the food?" Had two different answers from the two year old Vuyiso than from the five year old Vuyo. Vuyo tried to be diplomatic and said it was nice but not like mummy's food. Vuyiso on the other hand said it straight, "It's not really nice daddy!"

The pain I felt was multifaceted. It was about the missing wife who had cooked delicious meals, her absence hurt but her cooking was also missed. And my failure to make tasty food for her children was devastating.

REFLECTION:

I think the meal switched over to bread in the end before tidying up and preparations for bedtime. I had to look up recipes and relearn how to cook. And that night, while the little ones slept, I occupied myself with culinary education which soon paid off and made me a good cook again till this day.

BLESSING:

May the Lord make His face shine upon you and give you peace and healing today.

11 A BED FOR THREE

Be strong and of a good courage, fear not, nor be afraid of them: for the Lord thy God, he it is that doth go with thee; he will not fail thee, nor forsake thee. (Deuteronomy 31:6)

Our house in Swindon has 3 bedrooms. They are of different sizes and shapes too, considering the window and wardrobe structures. The second largest room has a view to the rear garden and busy pedestrian walkway that is always bustling with kids and parents on their daily school runs. It was this second room that we had turned into Mandy's room for the last month or so before she died. A room that we had thought would be her recovery room.

In that room we had had a specialised hospital bed brought in. The bed had remote controls for raising or lowering it and tilting it to various angles of inclination for comfort. It also had wheels so it could be pushed around but also lockable to hold it firm in a location. Additionally the mattress of this bed was inflatable and highly comfortable.

The room with the hospital bed was, in reality, Vuyo's room. But under the present circumstances there was no way I was going to let him sleep in his room alone. Firstly the furnishings were unsuitable for him. And secondly I would feel cruel for me to abandon my now motherless child in a room by himself overnight.

The other room, Vuyiso's room was the smallest in the house yet the coldest one too. Because of the coldness and also because of her being a motherless child I would also not have allowed her to sleep alone in her room.

The room that was left available was the master bedroom with a queen size bed in it. That was the bed on which I bundled up with my children and was comforted by their presence while I believe my presence did bring them also some degree of comfort in their loss. From here we had a view of the front garden, the footpath and the walkway as well as part of Eldene school and the Crumpled Horn pub around the shops.

REFLECTION:

So it was that in the first few weeks after returning from the funeral we all slept in one room and in one bed and talked and sang and prayed and cried together every night. Not as dramatic an event as the other experiences but certainly emotionally significant for me. It was part of my healing process.

BLESSING:

May this brief insight make a positive contribution to your recovery journey today. And may God pacify your soul today.

12 HAS JESUS COME BACK YET? A 3 YEAR OLD CHILD ASKS

And if I go and prepare a place for you, I will come again, and receive you unto myself; that where I am, there ye may be also. (John 14:3)

Just a few months after her mother died, my daughter Vuyiso was full of hope of the resurrection. She had just turned 3 and was at that age where everything daddy told her was unquestionable.

Somehow the back door that leads into the house via the kitchen had not latched-on properly and tightly enough to remain shut when a gale of wind pushed it open. As it opened it made an audibly loud sound. Anyone could have thought that someone had just opened the door and entered the house.

"Has Jesus come back yet?" eagerly and earnestly asked Vuyiso. For a moment I missed her point but then I quickly remembered the motivation behind her eagerness.

Having learned and understood that the only time she could ever hope to see her mother again would be when Jesus comes again, the arrival of Jesus needed to happen quickly. After all that arrival would herald the re-union with her mother.

As soon as I figured out the idea behind the expectation of Jesus' arrival, albeit via the kitchen door, I had to explain a bit more to her about the nature and form of Jesus's second coming. The Bible says He will not come alone but with many many angels (Daniel 7:13). And He will not come silently but with a loud noise (Mark 13:26). And He will not come secretly because all eyes shall see Him (Revelation 1:7). So there will be no need for anyone to ask anyone else if Jesus has come yet.

And so, disappointing though the news was, I had to present it to Vuyiso that Jesus had not yet returned.

REFLECTION:

There are undoubtedly many who like Vuyiso are eager for the return of Jesus not only to be with Jesus but to be reunited with their loved ones who are now in their graves. Be of good cheer and hold on to the promise by Jesus who, before going to heaven did say, "I will come again" (John 14:3).

BLESSING:

May you remain steadfast in your faith in the promise of Jesus. God bless you today.

13 A PHONE CALL FROM THE OFFICE

I will call upon the LORD, who is worthy to be praised: so shall I be saved from mine enemies. (Psalm 18:3)

Just a few days after Mandy's death, I went to my office at the university of Oxford's Biochemistry department. The purpose for my trip to the office was to get my documents that were necessary for me to get a travel document since my passport had already expired.

Upon my arrival I had several different possible location points where the documents could have been that I could search. There were bookshelves that I checked from, but from which I could not find what I was looking for.

My desk had six or eight drawers that I also searched but yet still could not locate the documents. I was now getting quite anxious and distressed as I was failing to find the desperately needed papers.

Finally I took a seat, picked the phone on my desk and dialled my home number without any deep thought. As the phone started ringing at home I quickly hung up! The person that I was trying to ring, my wife, would not be able to answer the phone this time around and remind me of where the documents were. It was not that she would not but she could not as she had died just a few days prior.

The realisation that all my calls to her from the office would never happen again brought much pain. I was to feel this same pain and repeat the same error without thinking for some few more weeks in the future as I came to the office. The habit of ringing her for quick questions and plans and updates was going to take a while to wear off because I was so used to it.

REFLECTION:

Although it took me quite a few more impossible call attempts, I eventually learned to make more of my calls heavenward to the one who will always be there and who does not sleep nor slumber.

BLESSING:

I pray today that the Lord may answer you when you call Him. Have a blessed day.

14 A DOUBLE TRAGEDY

For to me to live is Christ, and to die is gain. (Philippians 1:21)

Mandy's elder brother, Edison was a very kind and loving brother whose kindness I personally experienced during the time I knew him. He used to pay us many surprise visits at our home in Broadhurst, Gaborone, Botswana. He was always laughing and joking and was really pleasant to be around.

I recall that on our wedding date he provided us with some stunning brown coloured traditional African attire for our changing clothes (In Botswana, it is a custom for the bride and groom to change their attire at least 3 times on their wedding day and come back and parade before the guests in the outfits). Mandy had told me about how her brother used to work in some mines in South Africa and often used to bring her presents when he was visiting home. He was a very kind and loving big brother.

As we left Botswana for the first time on 30th June 2002, Edison was one of the saddest people ever who shed tears because we were leaving. Most of the times he used to work on field trips and was quite difficult to get hold of and speak to. But whenever we did manage to speak to him, it was always such a delight to speak to him.

Around late October of 2009 we had sent news to Botswana to Mandy's family that Mandy had now been pronounced terminally ill since the breast cancer was said to have metastasized and to have spread to multiple organs in her body, including her liver. Apparently when Edison heard the news of his youngest and most favourite sister's terminal sickness he collapsed and fell to the ground from shock. He was sent to a hospital where he continued to suffer from what we were told was a severe headache for an entire month. He apparently could not even speak or eat during all the time that he was in hospital.

About two weeks or so before Mandy's death we got a phone call from Mandy's eldest brother Tomson. The news of that phone call was to inform us that sadly Edison did not make it through his sickness. And so it was that the one who loved his sister so much that upon hearing she was in danger of death had now died as a result of the shocking news.

To say Mandy was devastated would be an understatement. She was literally shattered and we could almost predict that Mandy was now truly never going to make it either. Finally we buried her about a week or so after the funeral of her brother. Their graves are close to each other in their home village of Moshupa, Botswana.

REFLECTION:

So the Mokalake family lost not one but two siblings in December of 2009. If anyone would want answers from God it would have to be the family that lost two of its members just like that. But God in His mercy, has been taking care of the remaining family. The understanding of why things like this happen has not been given. But we know that even when Jesus was on earth He didn't heal everyone who had faith in Him and desired healing. So we must leave it to the almighty to make us understand, at the second coming of Jesus.

BLESSING:

May God soothe your pain in spite of the lack of understanding of why the pain has been allowed to happen in the very first place. Be blessed today.

15 BRAVELY SINGING AND FULL OF HOPE

O sing unto the Lord a new song; for he hath done marvellous things: his right hand, and his holy arm, hath gotten him the victory. (Psalm 98:1)

A new chapter had dawned when it was no longer the Khanye quartet attending church services every Saturday at Whitby Grove but just three of us. It also was not going to be the same voices presenting the special song from the Khanye family. Things were never going to be the same again ever. It was a different time to be alive for us and circumstances were definitely changed.

So it was that I felt the need for me and my children to share messages of hope in song with the grief stricken congregation of Swindon church. Somehow I had the determination to sustain the well known and established family tradition of regularly bringing an offering in song to church. But the meaning of the song at this point in time was critically important.

"I am Drinking From My Saucer" was a song that I found a meaning of hope from. It says I am drinking from my saucer because my cup has overflowed. At a time of loss it really took a bit of a stretch of the imagination to think that my cup had overflowed. But yet I did like to sing that I already had been blessed enough in the life I had lived until that point, as the lyrics said. So 'Drinking From My Saucer " became one new favourite tune.

For one of the Sabbaths I ordered the backing track for the song that says "Thank you Lord". The song reminded me and the church that as long as there is a roof above our heads, a good place to sleep, food on the table and shoes on our feet we have all the reasons we need to thank the Lord for His blessings on us.

REFLECTION:

I trained the kids and we stood up and sang songs of hope at a time where all hope seemed to be lost. With song, we encouraged others, though the loss was far greater on us than on them.

BLESSING:

May you too find encouragement for your situation today. Remember there is always something worse than your present situation and nothing is permanent - Not even your loss. Have a blessed day.

16 EVERYONE SEEMS TO HAVE THEIR SPOUSE

The Lord bless thee, and keep thee: The Lord make his face shine upon thee, and be gracious unto thee: The Lord lift up his countenance upon thee, and give thee peace. (Numbers 6:24-26)

Sometimes it is only when you lose something that you suddenly come to realise its value and importance. In fact it can indeed be by observing your surroundings that you can come to realise that there is something out there that you do not have but that others do. This realisation would probably not be so pronounced if it were not backed by the fact that whatever you lack now is something you had before but lost due to some circumstances.

So it happened that when I was newly widowed, I suddenly started to see couples everywhere I looked. In my mind it didn't matter so much that there existed plenty others who were not couples. Seeing young couples made me think that I really should be like them. Even the fact that some of the couples I saw were much older brought feelings of pain as I thought of how I had also expected to grow old alongside my spouse.

When I went to attend church services I saw husbands and wives sitting together. I saw little children of the same age as mine enjoying sitting on their mothers and fathers' laps. I saw the couples helping each other to take care of the kids and one of the two taking the kids out to their bathroom visits, just as it used to be for me.

When I went shopping I envyingly saw couples lifting their little ones between themselves. Sometimes they held hands and formed a family chain joined by hands. This all brought a feeling of nostalgia in me. I had enjoyed those kinds of moments too in the past but they were all gone now.

The happy families, just by virtue of being there were unknowingly a source of pain for me. No, I was not unhappy for them or with them nor did I even blame them but my situation seemed to be heightened by their joy. Indeed it was a bitter sweet experience that life was showing me.

REFLECTION:

It very well may happen for you too that it may seem that all the others are living your dream life. Your actual life may appear to have been shattered and to have become meaningless right now. But hang on in there because just as a rose bush may look dead through the autumn and winter, come spring time and roses will bloom again. Seasons are always changing and God is faithful to usher in the next season. He will make the sun shine again after the rain. He has made all things beautiful in its time. Thankfully I did meet my new wife Erika and never again did I feel pained by seeing couples anymore.

BLESSING:

May God shine his face upon you and give you peace.

17 SHAMEFULLY DISCOVERING MY "TOILET CLEANER"

Peace I leave with you, my peace I give unto you: not as the world giveth, give I unto you. Let not your heart be troubled, neither let it be afraid. (John 14:27)

Self-discovery is not a very easy process. It is also perhaps one of the most uncomfortable things that perhaps we all love to hate. Living in the illusion that we are probably doing as best as we can seems the most comfortable and desirable place to be.

It was a few weeks after returning from Mandy's funeral that it dawned on me for the first time in my life how unhelpful I had been to her. Not that she had not told me this herself but either just laziness or arrogance or chauvinism blinded me and kept me from doing the right thing.

I felt entitled to my rest because after all I had been to work all day and I was very tired. I had a wife who was at home and who could do the things that needed to be done at home with the exception of heavy work, lifting things and repairs to broken stuff on and in the house. Such was my mentality both consciously and unconsciously.

As such I hardly knew where the storage place of a vacuum cleaner and a broom was. I also had no clue how to operate the washing machine. It was all my wife's responsibility I thought without any problem on my mind about this. I even forgot about how to cook a meal.

It may not take much imagination, therefore that I soon discovered how hard it was to do all the cleaning, all the child bathing, cooking and yet function normally.

Some brothers and sisters took turns to come and give me the much needed help in the house because I was grieving and partly incapacitated at the time. But though I was truly grateful for their help, not all their ways of working were according to my preference.

What hit me really hard and sent me sobbing with pain in my heart was discovering that in all the 10 years that I had been married I had never cleaned the toilet! It was when I saw the toilet getting dirtier and dirtier that I realised that it needed cleaning and that I did not even know where the cleaning materials were stored and even how they were used. I felt so guilty that I wept. I could not even bear the repugnant thought of what I had done to my wife all those years. I had turned her into my toilet cleaner effectively.

It was too late now to change how I had been to her. But perhaps I could become a better person from now. I became alert to my own flaws and planned to be a better human, going forward to deal with my guilt.

REFLECTION:

Friend, perhaps you too may also feel guilty about some things you probably could have done better? There is always a chance to turn over a new leaf even though the person you wronged is no longer there.

BLESSING:

May God help you to forgive yourself and may He give you the will to be and to do better in your life as you carry on living. May the peace by the God of heaven be yours today.

18 NO MUMMY TODAY? NOT TOO WELL?

And said, If thou wilt diligently hearken to the voice of the Lord thy God, and wilt do that which is right in his sight, and wilt give ear to his commandments, and keep all his statutes, I will put none of these diseases upon thee, which I have brought upon the Egyptians: for I am the Lord that healeth thee. (Exodus 15:26)

One February Sabbath morning the two children and I walked towards the church at Whitby Grove. We had arrived a bit too late to secure a parking space inside the church yard and so we had parked on the street that leads to Rodbourne so we would walk to the church.

Along the walk we met a lovely family that we had not seen ever since the time we had first met them at the family camp in Devonshire the previous October. After saying the greeting, the man asked with a lovely smile on his face, "No mummy today? Not too well?"

It is almost too easy to assume that just because we make a big effort to notify as many people as possible and ask them to tell others that someone has died, then everyone knows about it. But that assumption could not be further from the truth. The man asking had obviously not heard about Mandy's death and was just asking out of the kindness of his heart since the last time he had seen her, he had learned that she was unwell.

"She died in December", I choked away as I informed him in response." O, I am awfully sorry to hear that. I didn't know. I never heard about it,`` he said. "May God comfort you and help you take care of the little ones," he concluded as we were entering the church building. I felt that the man was really sad to hear the news. But he remained composed and calm because perhaps he realised how fragile I myself was at that particular moment.

This was not the last time I was going to meet with someone who was not aware of Mandy's death. And each time I had to keep informing them that she had died it kept hurting me over and over just to say it. But I suppose that was part of the process of informing myself too, until it no longer hurt to say it. Probably the lessening of the pain meant that I was now beginning to believe it and accept it too.

REFLECTION:

Years have passed now and I now hardly feel the pain I felt in the past when I told someone about the death. It is still not a pleasant thing to talk about but yet it is good to say that God has done a lot of healing this far.

BLESSING:

He will also heal your pain and enable you to feel stronger than you may feel right now. "I am the Lord that healeth thee," He says. May you feel His healing today.

19 A LEAF DADDY, A LEAF

In the midst of the street of it, and on either side of the river, was there the tree of life, which bare twelve manner of fruits, and yielded her fruit every month: and the leaves of the tree were for the healing of the nations. (Revelation 22:2)

A lot was going on at the height of Mandy's illness. I had watched her condition get worse and worse to the extent that even though I remained adamant and full of faith that she was going to be well again the prognosis was all against me.

So I rang her eldest sister, Georginah and told her about the prevailing situation which was not very good at all. It took more than one phone call to convince her that the illness was really serious and getting worse. Then it took quite some persuading for her to even consider coming to England. She was more for the idea of Mandy going to Botswana to recoup and recover from home.

The biggest problem was that sister Georginah had never been in an aircraft before in her life and so was anxious. The second biggest problem was that the obtaining of a UK visa for her to travel and help me take care of her sister would not be easy. Eventually both issues were overcome and she landed at Heathrow airport's terminal 5 one cold morning.

The sisters' reunion was a very happy one in spite of the dire circumstances. The elder sister was very helpful not only with taking care of her ailing sibling but with looking after her young nephew and niece. As the disease grew worse and Mandy got weaker, I was granted leave from work in order to be able to stay by my family.

Both our children were going to school and kindergarten respectively every morning. My sister in law was the one walking them both to Eldene primary school where the kindergarten was also located. At some point however, as I was no longer going to work, I was now the one walking the kids to school and kindergarten.

"A leaf daddy, a leaf!" Shouted 2 year old Vuyiso to me one morning as she picked a leaf from the ground and showed me one morning as I took her to kindergarten.

It was as though I was waking up from some deep sleep when I realised that I was so inattentive even to nature around me. I was just walking like some vehicle on autopilot without even interacting with my own daughter. My brain was loaded to the full with stress about my sick wife about whom the doctors had said there was no hope of recovery.

The stress brought by the burden of the disease had taken over my mind. For much longer, I was to remain entranced with the refusal to accept that death was imminent. At the same time I was moving from day to day with no perception of things and people about me. This was all just before Mandy actually died. Yet my mind and body had been overtaken by the stress of the disease.

REFLECTION:

Are you overwhelmed by some situation right now? Are you consumed by some thoughts day and night that you are like a car on cruise control? Jesus says come ye that labour and are heavy laden and I will give you rest. Take time away from your thoughts and meditate in nature on God's creation. Spend time today focusing on Jesus who offers to shepherd you even as you traverse through the valley of the shadow of death.

BLESSING:

Be blessed, strengthened and encouraged today.

20 THERE ARE NO SHORTCUTS IN GRIEVING

As for man, his days are like grass; As a flower of the field, so he flourishes. For the wind passes over it, and it is gone, And its place remembers it no more. (Psalm 103:15-16)

Because I had lived with stress for a while during Mandy's illness, I thought I was just okay when I lost her to death. Little did I realise that I was severely traumatised. I only just realised a few months later that I even suffered what could be some permanent brain injury as a result of the trauma.

My ability to memorise for examinations seemingly was also diminished significantly. Yet I had no idea about this until I dismally failed to recall some things that I had memorised so well for a critical examination.

Since bereavement, I seem permanently much slower at doing things. I generally do not seem to have the same energy levels and enthusiasm as I used to have in the past. It could be that I may have tried to take shortcuts in seeking to end my grief rather quickly. Some psychology experts have suggested that "the reassuring thing about grieving is that the process will not be cheated. It will take as much time as it needs."

So with some relative enlightenment about the process of grief we can begin to appreciate the futility of attempts to introduce quick fixes in trying to speak recovery to those afflicted by the pain of losing their loved ones to death. Never has the grieving process been made to move quicker by people saying, "Get over it now, you have cried enough." It is a process that takes longer in some people than in others. Yet with time most people do feel better and better.

REFLECTION:

It may still be early days for you in grief. It may feel as though there is no hope for the future. But if the examples of other people are anything to go by, then there is hope for you too. I know this may be the hardest thing to imagine now but I have been there myself. God is with you and never leaves you and He will remain with you till you too can testify and tell someone else how you once were.

BLESSING:

May God's wonderful peace sweep over you today and give you courage.

21 THE SEARCH FOR AN AU PAIR

Be strong and of a good courage, fear not, nor be afraid of them: for the Lord thy God, he it is that doth go with thee; he will not fail thee, nor forsake thee. (Deuteronomy 31:6)

By degrees, I realised that it was going to be impossible to try to carry on working in Oxford while living in Swindon and leaving my children behind every morning to return to them only in the evening. At first I was assisted by my sister in law Georginah who came all the way from Botswana to take care of the children.

It was during the time she was around that we discussed the way forward that seemed feasible and practicable. Her stay would not be indefinite and I was not just about to give up my work to take care of the kids.

So the idea of searching for an au pair took shape. There was a need to get registered with different websites before starting the painstaking search efforts for someone who would be sensitive to our situation and also able to come and live in our home.

Many of the au pairs advertised had their own conditions stipulated about their expectations and needs. Many also seemed to be from other countries than the UK. Ultimately I entered into discussions with several different people whom I tried vetting very carefully until I found one university student from Spain who seemed to have a good grasp of English but wanted the chance to improve her spoken English by living in the UK for a while.

Upon reaching some advanced plans for her coming I decided it was time to speak via Skype and 'meet' before buying her a flight ticket. The call revealed something really awkward. The girl could hardly speak English in spite of how well she wrote. As I asked her some simple questions she responded by saying, 'waiting' (by this she was asking me to wait) then typed them onto some translation software or her own responses in Spanish were to be read by her in English after my waiting.

I did some basic security checks and police checks on her and also verified her identity before giving her a contract and letting her come over. She was only 19 years old after all and was indeed more terrified of her trip than I could be of any mischief she could have been plotting. I was kind of under pressure to get someone quickly so I could return to work fully and I could not afford to delay much further.

So landed L, the Spanish AuPair at Bristol airport from Castellón de la Plana to become my child minder with whom communication would be quite difficult. She could read and understand English fairly well but pronounced all 'g's as 'h' for things like big she would say 'bih' and got us all smiling. Otherwise she was a very pleasant child who loved the children and made them laugh and play. She took them to the park and did crafts with them and made them enjoy the presence of a happy individual in the home. I had to give her some cooking basic training but she also used a recipe book because she had not really cooked much before. Sadly L would only stay for just 3 months as pre-agreed as she needed to return to university.

REFLECTION:

Adjusting back to 'normal' life was not going to be easy. But life was going to keep going on with or without my adjusting. And for the small steps I managed to take at that time I was thankful to God.

BLESSING:

You may also find yourself needing to make some necessary adjustments to your life. Some may not be easy but necessary. Take it easy, but take it! God will go with you through all the unfamiliar realms and see you through. Have a blessed day today.

22 SOMEBODY CRIED FOR ME

Rejoice with them that do rejoice, and weep with them that weep. (Romans 12:15)

Jesus wept. (John 11:35)

Time to say farewell has always revealed to me those people who truly love me. In 2002 as we left Gaborone, Botswana to relocate to the UK we had some friends who came to see us and say goodbye at the Grand Palm hotel where we stayed for our last week. Among the many friends who came by, one struck me as that friend who sticks closer than a brother. Not only did Toby say that he was sad that we were leaving, but he also shed a tear which we noticed.

How do I know someone really cares for me by seeing their tears? Around the year 2005, our very good friends Ivo and Angelika from Estonia were relocating to their country. I remember myself weeping uncontrollably when we sang a Portuguese farewell song for them and as I saw the memorable photographs that we had taken together. They were truly dear friends and I wept because I was sad they were leaving.

In the year 2018, it was time for us to leave Baicoi, Romania and return to the UK. We had a very good relationship with our very kind church pastor Dorin Sisu and he came to say farewell to us. He prayed for us and said some encouraging words before departing. But what really touched us was also noticing a tear of sadness in his eye because we were leaving.

Tears shed by a friend for me have always touched me very deeply. And I never forget those who have ever cried for me in all the situations I have ever been in. The impact has been greater especially when I least expected the people would be so sad for me. Though I may be surprised at first because at times I have not known myself to have been that dear to the person weeping for me, I am humbled and I learn that instance that someone cares about me. It instantly makes me know and accept that the person is special to me, forever.

I had a visit once, in April of 2004 from the pastor of Swindon Adventist church. I had just returned from the funeral of my younger sister Tobekile. The pastor came one evening to ask me about how the funeral and the journey had all gone. I did all my story telling and I did not even expect that he would be deeply affected by my grief at all when I noticed a tear in his eyes. I was truly touched and I had new respect for the man of God who cried for me for a sister of mine whom he had never even met. He also gave me a gift from the church which was a financial contribution towards my flight costs.

I also will never forget how when I reached Gweru from the airport in Harare, my brother in law, DC, came and gave me a hug just as I stepped out of the car and he wept and wept whilst hugging me!

REFLECTION:

The tears of a friend for a friend go a long way to cement the friendship. They are also a very soothing reassurance that somebody cares about us. Maybe you too have someone whom you remember shedding a tear for your pain. Other people I have spoken to also confirm that they felt loved and cared for when they noticed someone shedding a tear on their behalf. I hope you too can feel the hand of God in the wiping of your tears and comforting you in your sorrow via someone else's tears for you.

BLESSING:

Today may you feel God's love and care flowing to you via those who care about you. Have a wonderful day.

23 YOU ARE STILL YOUNG, YOU WILL FIND ANOTHER WIFE

For the wisdom of their wise men shall perish, and the understanding of their prudent men shall be hid. (Isaiah 29: 14)

Oftentimes when people see someone broken with grief they naturally want to help them somehow. As human beings we are always drawn together by the pain and suffering of the other ones than not.

Unfortunately we are not all naturally gifted with the wisdom and ability to do and say the right things at all times, in spite of our good intentions. Sometimes quite the opposite of our good intentions result from our words or actions.

At a time that my grief was raw, not long after having lost my wife to death from cancer I encountered some very painful remarks that were uttered with the best of intentions to console me. Regardless of the good intention, the sum effect of the remarks was dreadful.

Someone perhaps thought they were stating the obvious and hence it would likely bring me joy for them to say, "You are still young. You will find another wife."

That was not the most soothing of statements to make to one who had no desire for their spouse to die. The trouble was not only that my mind was too far from searching for someone else. The trouble was that there seemed to be absolutely no regard or thought about the fact that I was crying for the deceased. The deceased had no apparent value in the minds of those making such remarks. But they forgot to think that to me that same deceased had meant everything.

This sort of remark would keep recurring from different people and in different places. And each time it did, it hurt to think how little the deceased had any impact on other people's minds. It was as if she had been a commodity that could just be replaced by the next one. There seemed to be no realisation that if one deceased person were so easily replaceable and so easily forgotten then so would be the next.

REFLECTION:

God cares about us even when we are hurting and He is especially by our side in our moments of pain. It is easy for people to add more pain without even intending to. Just by mere careless words, people can hurt us. But we need to accept that most people really have no idea about what they are doing when they say hurtful things.

BLESSING:

May God give you the patience you need to withstand some painful remarks you may hear. Be blessed today as you continue your journey to recovery.

24 A CRIMINAL INVESTIGATION DEPARTMENT INVESTIGATION

Let your conversation be without covetousness; and be content with such things as ye have: for he hath said, I will never leave thee, nor forsake thee. (Hebrews 13:5)

The fact that the hospital staff had made a decision not to resuscitate, for which they had called me out of Mandy's room to inform me, was bad enough. They had taken away almost a whole hour of what turned out to be our very last 24 hours together just to defend their decision not to send Mandy to the intensive care unit or attempt to resuscitate her if the need would arise. Later they subjected her to lots of pain with their hit and miss attempts to put a needle into her vein, which they took turns to try and failed. Finally, when they did a surgical operation to insert the needle they had left her lying in her own blood without even cleaning it. Then when I was away for a little needed rest they had administered morphine on her which I think accelerated her death and which I would not have agreed to had I been around when it was offered to her.

After all of those very stressful things, Mandy had finally died. She was now at peace. But my stresses had only just begun.

Firstly, I received a phone call informing me that I was to go to the hospital to 'identify' her body. That was rather strange because she had died in the same hospital that was now calling me to go and identify her body.

Apparently the hospital had claimed that it did not know the cause of her death and a post mortem had to be carried out.

When I got to the hospital, where I was accompanied by my brother in law, there were two members of the CID department waiting to see me. Apparently they needed information about Mandy's treatment regime. They needed to establish how Mandy had died and I needed to help them with their investigation. As such I was to contact them in the next 24 hours with details about Mandy's treatment.

Meanwhile I was required to report to the police headquarters at Gable Cross off the A420 road leading from Swindon to Oxford and meet the coroner.

I had already been planning the funeral and I had decided to take Mandy's body back to her country Botswana for burial. People had already gathered at Mandy's family's home in Moshupa, Botswana and were waiting to hear just when we would be arriving with the body for burial.

I also considered that all the people in the UK who would not be able to go to the funeral in Africa would appreciate a body viewing moment and also a service of remembrance, and pay their last respects for her. I planned the service for Sunday. But when I contacted the hospital to arrange the said viewing I was told the body was not even in Swindon. It had been taken away for an autopsy in Bristol. They could not even confirm when they would be able to let me take it for burial. Besides, December 2009 had had so much snow that some roads had been closed. So the coroner was not even sure when they could send the body back with the snow issues affecting roads. The memorial service therefore had to go on without any viewing of the body.

I submitted the details of Mandy's treatment to the Criminal Investigation Department officers. I met with the coroner. The autopsy was completed and I appointed some undertakers and paid them and they issued certification for burial out of the UK and provided me with a sealed metal-lined coffin whose destination had to be the undertakers in Botswana but only after I had a confirmation from an airline that they would carry the body as cargo.

Who would have thought that someone who spent days and nights of sleepless searching for help for his wife would at last be subjected to criminal investigations? Also, the stress of needing papers done by me for someone who had died in hospital, a hospital which claimed it did not know what killed her, was a bit much.

REFLECTION:

In spite of all the drama. In spite of all the distress. In the end we left the snowy UK with its sub zero temperatures to land in Gaborone whose temperature was 46 degrees Celsius on our arrival day. God prevailed for me. The coroner proved that cancer with metastasis was the cause of death and I hope that the coroner also informed the hospital since the hospital could not figure it out themselves.

BLESSING:

Though the issues of this world may torment you, there is a limit to how far they can go. God never leaves you and never forsakes you. Even if they could kill your body, they can never destroy your soul. Trust in Him today.

25 TAKING ALL THE BLAME

Henceforth I call you not servants; for the servant knoweth not what his lord doeth: but I have called you friends; for all things that I have heard of my Father I have made known unto you. (John 15:15)

One older and wiser friend, Ray, once remarked, "If the sky were blue, and you said that the sky is blue, there is always going to be someone who disagrees with you simply because it is you who said it."

When it was time to make a choice of the treatment method that Mandy would use, a number of people assumed that I had made the choice for her. They even confronted me about it and challenged me to try to persuade me to take their wiser options. What many never actually got to know was that Mandy herself took her decision and then educated me about her reasons why. All that I did was to pledge and uphold my support for her choices throughout with whatever she wanted to do.

It so happened that Mandy found out for herself about natural remedies for cancer treatment. She even obtained two DVDs by Dr Lorraine Day, a stage 4 cancer survivor from the USA. The two DVDs were titled, "Cancer Doesn't Scare Me Anymore" and "You Can't Improve on God". After Mandy got me to watch the DVDs I was confident that she had made the right decision to choose natural treatment rather than conventional treatment. I presumptuously believed that, without any doubt, God was going to heal Mandy from cancer and especially because she had chosen God's natural remedies as her method of treatment.

We then spent thousands of pounds in the purchasing of all the herbs and equipment plus for paying the experts for consultation and guidance. We also intensified our praying and fasting life and invited friends and family across the globe to join in from wherever they were.

The biggest problem that we came up against was that the treatment did not yield the desired and expected results. Instead, Mandy started to get worse the moment she was given some test results by a General Practitioner who wept as she told Mandy that the cancer had spread to the liver. That triggered the blame from friends. But most of the blame was directed exclusively at me.

Not so many people got to know or to hear directly from Mandy herself about why she had chosen her treatment methods. She had some very tough and compelling arguments for her choices which not even our friends who are doctors could move her from. And so, taking her side, I began my journey of learning about herbs and diet and lifestyle as they relate to wellness as I had never done before. That journey was only disturbed but not terminated by her death.

The best comfort that I ever got was that Mandy's family themselves never blamed me for any of the decisions I took with or about Mandy. They knew just how we were as a couple and they could never be blackmailed to believe that I had ill-treated her even till her death. They knew that people were blaming me and told me that even if others did blame me, I should know that they themselves did not. That was what mattered the most.

Yet I still lost so many friends. I know they loved Mandy and they blamed me for her death. But none of them loved her more than I did. So with the pain of losing my wife I suffered the added pain of also losing many friends.

REFLECTION:

Sometimes bad things happen and spiral into a loop. The angry people blaming a bleeding hurting widower with two little children remind me of the biblical Job's friends who tried to convince him that he had done wrong. They even got angry with him as they tried to get him to confess. But he stood his ground as he had done nothing wrong.

ENCOURAGEMENT:

You too may have some things flung at you to convince you that you are guilty when you are not. You may even feel that there are many things that you could have and should have done better. You may even have people turning away from you that were your friends before. Do not despair. You are never alone as God himself is your friend who never leaves His own. Hold on to Him.

26 THE LOSS IS MORE THAN JUST YOURS

Then David and the people that were with him lifted up their voice and wept, until they had no more power to weep. (1 Samuel 30:4)

Is grief really a private thing or should it be? Given the decade of reflection after the death of my first wife I think I have had plenty of time for introspection. Yet I accept that every individual will have a unique experience so there will be variations about the issue from person to person. Though I believe this can apply to every bereavement situation, for now I want to direct my focus specifically towards the one who has lost their spouse. One of the most comforting and compassionate things you will ever see and feel is the empathetic grief of another for your loss. It has a lasting impact and it can show just how much someone cares about you.

What is very easy to miss however is this, there are possibly so many other people who are grossly affected by the loss also. You may never ever know just how many people will suffer in silence for the same loss that is eating you up. It is just that they do not have the same right and privilege that you have to weep and mourn exactly the way the pain makes you do. Note that I do not suggest that you should weep and mourn any less at all. But I am just pointing out that you really and truly are not alone in feeling pain.

Your loved one may have had friends. The friends are also hurting for the loss. The deceased may have living parents and those parents are devastated too. Then they also may have one or more siblings. Those siblings' pain is also a huge pain.

If only someone could have shown me the pain others were also experiencing, maybe I would have grieved differently. I do not know how differently I would have grieved if that would have happened. I think maybe I was too consumed by what the loss meant just to me and my children. It is even possible that some people did try to show how hurt they were also but my mind was possibly too deep in feeling the pain just on me to recognize the pain felt by any other person.

So what I am saying is simply this, there are others who loved your spouse too. They may also be hurting so deeply and for so long too but you may never know anything about it. For some it will take you some years just to find this out. It is possible that you may never find out about other people who were also affected by the death.

REFLECTION:

This entire excerpt was born out of reflection. Over a length of time I have realised how in my late wife's death so many people lost someone who was dear to them also. Nevermind that it was referred to as my loss. It was also as much their loss as it was mine. "Sorry for your loss" should really be rephrased to "We have suffered a deep loss". The bereaved being given space to grieve privately robs them of the chance to experience empathy by those who feel that the loss is very much theirs too.

BLESSING:

May you find comfort in knowing that your pain may not be yours alone. May God use this understanding to heal your hurts.

27 WHY I STOPPED EATING SEEDLESS GRAPES

And God said, Behold, I have given you every herb bearing seed, which is upon the face of all the earth, and every tree, in the which is the fruit of a tree yielding seed; to you it shall be for meat. (Genesis 1:29)

It was on a cold December morning on Manchester road in the Swindon town centre that I finally found seeded grapes. I shed tears of joy and half of sorrow as I had searched for seeded grapes for the greater part of ten months and could not find them. So this was really a delightful moment but also a sad one to think it may have been too late for their intended usage.

We had found out how grape seeds were powerful antioxidants and hence anti cancer agents. We had even discovered how expensively priced the substance called "grape seed extract" was. Naturally we wanted to have the grapes with seeds in themselves but found none sold in the supermarkets. From the supermarkets we could only find seedless grapes. We wondered if it was just a conspiracy theory or a reality that the seedless grapes were a result of some genetic engineering processes carried out in laboratories. In the book of Genesis, the Bible tells us that God had created herbs which bear seeds.

So I bought the grapes from the corner shop and happily took them home to my ailing wife. Sadly she could hardly eat anything anymore. Not even the seeded grapes.

One could be excused to think that because the use of natural remedies did not help cure Mandy's cancer I would abandon the whole idea. The opposite is actually true.

I actually furthered my learning in the area. I obtained a diploma in Holistic Nutrition. I bought volumes of books about natural treatments and watched a myriad of documentaries on the subject. I helped many people with various conditions that some had tried for years to resolve without success. I was convinced that natural remedies actually do work and in many cases definitively heal some conditions.

After learning for myself about lifestyle, diet and diseases I could not remain as I used to be. I could also not just keep quiet about what I know when I care about my friends and family.

REFLECTION:

It is not very easy to share with people because unfortunately there are many who are not open minded and who are not endowed with ever inquiring minds. Most people would rather not know anything because they rely on doctors to take care of them. The problem is that many times when some symptoms finally show up, even the doctors may not be able to help as it is already too late.

BLESSING:

So my dear friend you too have a choice. Learn more for yourself about your body and your health. Study literature about natural remedies and scientific research to back it and decide for yourself what you think. At least attempt to find out why grapes no longer have seeds in them anymore, in these modern times. May God bless you and give you happiness and contentment in whatever direction you choose for yourself.

28 TURNING THE WORLD INTO MY OYSTER

But they that wait upon the Lord shall renew their strength; they shall mount up with wings as eagles; they shall run, and not be weary; and they shall walk, and not faint. (Isaiah 40:31)

As it so happened that my life had been affected by the loss of my wife, I felt the need to make some adjustment to my life. I realised that I had become so affected that I could not function normally anymore. After all, what had been my normal routine and day to day life had just drastically changed.

I would get up early in the morning so as to travel for an hour and reach Oxford by 8am. Then I would set off on my way back home around 4:30pm to reach home at about 6pm with rush hour traffic. The difference that I was now experiencing was that this time around the journeys and work days were not the same as before.

I would weep all the way to the office. Then I would pretty much weep all day in the office. Then finally I would also weep all the way back home.

Something had to change. I probably needed a change of environment I thought. But where could I go? What would happen about my income if I could not work anymore? How would I take care of my children? How would I pay the mortgage?

I began by searching for all the cheaper to live countries in the world. I looked at Mexico, India, Thailand, Bulgaria, Romania and Hungary, among many other options. I joined different internet Christian groups and began making virtual global friendships. After chatting back and forth using yahoo messenger and reading about various countries I decided to go for a fact finding mission to Romania.

I bought 3 flight tickets from Wizz air from London Luton airport UK to Baneasa airport in Bucharest, Romania for June 2010. I had gleaned that I could enrol onto a very affordable English taught masters degree program and at the same time put my kids into a private school.

The hospitality of the flight crew was amazing. They asked a few questions and when they unearthed that the kids had recently lost their mum they took the kids into the cockpit to meet the pilots while we were in mid-air. They took lots of pictures with the kids and spoiled them thoroughly.

We stayed at the Institute of Theology Training at Cernica and again as word went around that the kids were motherless they were treated like precious jewels.

REFLECTION:

When we boarded our flight back home, we were all sold. We knew this would be a suitable place from which to distract ourselves from pain and make a new beginning. We left after completing formal processes to enable us to return at the start of the academic year in September.

BLESSING:

May God offer you also a new beginning to reignite your life with new inspiration. May God, as an eagle, carry you to new heights today.

29 GIVING UP THE BEST

Vanity of vanities, saith the Preacher, vanity of vanities; all is vanity. What profit hath a man of all his labour which he taketh under the sun? (Ecclesiastes 1:1)

As my job interview progressed, the interviewer asked me the question, "Why would you want to give up your permanent job as IT lecturer at Swindon College for a two year contract job here at Oxford university?"

I answered very confidently and quite seriously though with a little humour in my response and said,"Oxford university is one of the best in the world. Even if you gave me a cleaning job I would accept it as long as I will be able to write on my CV that I worked for Oxford university." The interviewers had laughed at my response, but they went on to appoint me as a Training and Development Support Specialist working for the Oxford University Central Administration, in July 2005.

I went on to become the IT manager and also the Linux Systems Administrator. I loved my work so much that I went to work early and left work late during my peak days on the job. My probation confirmation letter praised my work so much that I was proud of my achievements. I could frame and display the letter that was signed by Maureen York, the best line manager I ever had in all my working life.

Financially speaking, I was well remunerated given that when I finally left the job at the end of 2010 I was earning just a couple of thousands shy of forty thousand pounds per annum. I also enjoyed a very generous number of annual leave days.

It was against this sort of work life and excellent employment conditions that I had to fight my emotional and mental battles. To say it was an easy decision would be a gross understatement.

I reflected upon all the joys of my employment. I thought long and hard about the implications of giving up my work and looking after my children. I evaluated the benefits of my work to humanity versus the potential benefit that humanity could gain if I could get trained as a gospel minister.

I weighed the fact that I was not only no longer deriving any satisfaction or enjoyment from my work against the peace I felt as I read my Bible.

Besides, I was not really working well anymore, if at all, during all the hours I was spending in the office.

I felt that God was calling me to a different role with a higher purpose. I saw the possibility of returning to Africa after the completion of my training. I also thought of returning to work as a minister in the UK after training. I could work as a missionary anywhere in the world. I felt ready and I desired a new beginning, I bravely gave up work to seek solace for my troubled soul. I gave up working for one of the most prestigious and best institutions in the world. I resigned and left the country towards an unfamiliar destination and unknown destiny. A place whose language I did not understand and whose culture I knew nothing of. In spite of inevitable difficulties, this was one of my best decisions for that chapter of my life and the period of my bleeding grief.

My actions were rather radical and brave and probably against the counsel of what many would suggest. But I cannot imagine what better action I could have taken instead.

REFLECTION:

There will be times when you too may have to take tough decisions. Trust in the Lord and lean not on your own understanding. He will keep you in perfect peace because of your trust in Him. Pray and study the Bible and seek God's guidance. Then, after prayer and seeking God, follow what you believe God is guiding you to do.

BLESSING:

May God be with you today and always.

30 THE GREAT TREK TO ROMANIA

Now the Lord had said unto Abram, "Get thee out of thy country, and from thy kindred and from thy father's house, unto a land that I will show thee. (Genesis 12:1)

I had never driven on the right hand side of the road. I had also never driven into any country in which English was not the official spoken language. I wondered about the road signs used in France, Belgium, Netherlands, Germany, Austria, Hungary and Romania because I was going to have to drive my car and bravely take my children with me into all these countries.

It was a bit scary and also exciting. The thought of needing to speak with people at the borders of all the countries was intimidating. I even asked my church pastor at the time, who was from Serbia and regularly drove there from the UK, to give me some advice and guidance to overcome my nerves. The fear of having to talk to police officers in some language that I could not speak was rather frightening too. But the imagination of driving, for the first time ever, onto a car ferry and sailing to France, where I had never been before, was quite fascinating.

The DFDS ferry that I had booked from Dover, Canterbury to Dunkerque, France was scheduled to depart at 4am from Dover. The reservation information stated that we should board at least 1 hour before sailing time. The special priced ticket I had paid for was non-refundable in the event of a missed departure.

Swindon is a good 3 hour journey away from Dover. I had spent the entire day on Sunday packing our luggage and tidying up the house. It was such a lot of hard work putting books into boxes and lifting them into the loft. Basically all the things that could not be fitted into a standard BMW 318i needed putting away. And all that work was mine to do. I was going to sleep afterwards then get up very early to start the long journey.

At almost 4 am, without finishing all of what I had intended to do and without even closing my eyes for one moment to sleep we started driving to Dover. I cannot recall much about that phase of the journey except it was done really fast. At almost 6 am we were already at Dover where, miraculously, we were allowed to sail on the next ferry since we had missed our

4am one. God had smoothed the way for us. The journey to a new life had begun. Yet the pain of grief did not stay behind even as we bid farewell to the UK.

REFLECTION:

In grieving you may feel like getting away and going to some other place. It may not always be possible due to limitations imposed by various circumstances. On the other hand, as was in my case, it may also be feasible to go elsewhere. Running to another place definitely can bring some reprieve, but it cannot wipe off all the pain. Unfortunately the pain of grief will linger on that much longer. Yet anything that can help you feel better, as long as it is noble, respectable and worthwhile is probably worth doing. Even going away for a short while to focus your mind elsewhere for a bit would be beneficial.

BLESSING:

May your mind be at peace today. Even if there remains a lot of pain from grief. May that pain feel lesser and lesser day by day for you as you encounter new situations that make you feel better within yourself. The Bible speaks of a time in the future when God shall wipe away all tears. Have a great day today in spite of any anomalies of life.

31 A NEW BEGINNING

When a stranger sojourns with you in your land, you shall not do him wrong. You shall treat the stranger who sojourns with you as the native among you, and you shall love him as yourself, for you were strangers in the land of Egypt: I am the Lord your God (Leviticus 19: 33-34)

After the adventurous multiple European country crossing journey, we finally reached the warm country of Romania. In spite of having had a satellite navigator, a TomTom that had been sold as one with maps that included Romania the reality was very different. The TomTom could not locate any secondary roads in Romania. Even the city to city roads appeared as lines away from the actual roads. A new multifaceted adventure had just begun.

The children quickly enrolled into the local private primary school named Mihai Ionescu. The paperwork for their enrollment was such a nightmare for me because it was all in Romanian and there was no translation. I also came to realise rather quickly that most of the people who had been said could help me as they knew English hardly could say more than just a few words of English. There were some who were exceptions but those were just a handful.

The Institute allocated us an end apartment, a 3-beds-in-a-room unit, in a block of young female students. This meant that as far as the kids were concerned they got plenty of attention from the young women who they were surrounded by. The attention was so much that one could almost say they seemed to have instantly forgotten about their grief for their mother. At least that seemed to appear to be the case during the day until bedtime when they undoubtedly were quite sorrowful. Both children went to sleep with cuddly toys in their arms soon after our evening prayers. Watching them often brought a tear to my eyes but I managed to keep the tear away from them in those moments.

It was usually soon after they went to sleep that my grief and loneliness seemed to hit me the hardest. I would weep and sob and try to sleep too sometimes but most times I could not sleep. After all I used to put the children to sleep quite early. I sometimes then took a walk towards the campus gate and sometimes outside of the gate too. I recall once when it was raining and my tears were being washed away by the rain as I walked.

The school (and kindergarten) to which the children went was a Romanian only school. Some of the teachers there spoke a little bit of English and tried to communicate better with my kids. I was informed that many of the other children in the school, especially in Vuyo's class quickly bought themselves English books so they could learn the language and be able to speak to him. The Institute I was attending had a van that used to ferry other children from the campus to the same school in the city of Bucharest. So the daily journey to and from school created new friends quickly for my children too, in spite of the language barrier that existed. I recall that after about 2 weeks of daily riding in the van to school as the driver beeped their horn for Vuyo and Vuyiso to come out of the apartment and ride to school, Vuyo shouted out to the driver, "bine" (pronounced beeneh, meaning okay) and it left me laughing. Both kids began speaking the language fairly quickly and seemed to be happy in their new life.

Being the only black children on campus and in their school placed an artificial level of feeling important on both children. Everyone around, both adults and children, seemed to want to spend time with them and take pictures with them and try to speak to them. They wanted to feel the touch of black people's hair and even to shake hands with a black person for the first time in their lives. It was a novel idea that people from a white community could be so fascinated and happy to be with black people. This kind of welcoming and accommodating treatment endured for a very long time after the early days of our arrival.

REFLECTION:

My moving to another country far away after being widowed may be a unique and perhaps even an extreme example. But the experience for my children was priceless. Everyone around knew about their having lost their mother and everyone was very kind to them with very few but insignificant exceptions that are typically so in life anyway. It was this experience of being surrounded by kind and loving people in a strange land that made a contribution to recovering from grief. This aspect may be possible for some situations but probably not for everyone who is grieving. Yet if you have a chance to change your environment, even slightly, I am sure there would be some degree of relief.

BLESSING:

I myself am not able to heal your pain, but God can. I pray that you will experience His healing and love today.

32 TOUGH STUDIES COMMENCE

The eyes of the LORD are upon the righteous, and his ears are open unto their cry. (Psalm 34:15)

The only thing I had found soothing to read prior to leaving my job in Oxford due to distress and emotional lowness was the Holy Bible. The only music I had also found palatable to my ears was soft and spiritual music. The only place I had longed to go to as I left my home of about 8 years was a place where I would study the Bible more and learn more about this God who had allowed my wife to die at a time she was due to celebrate her 32nd birthday.

The thrill and adrenalin of the long journey had come and gone. I had now arrived, after driving through 7 European countries. The kids had started their schooling and they were integrating extremely well into their new life of being treated more favourably because they were new in the country, they were of a black race and they were bereaved. It was now time for me to get immersed in studying the best textbook for all subjects of life.

It turned out that even though I had the Bible as the main textbook for all my courses the courses were nothing but easy. The deadlines for essays to be done in strict academic formats and with huge bibliographies and references as sources to support arguments in the documents were punitive. For I was enrolled onto a masters degree and so I had to endure the demands placed on masters degree students.

The lectures, delivered as modules in English by professors from Andrews university in Michigan - USA, started at 8am daily and ended at 1pm. It was during these lectures that I had many serious confrontations with reality. I was often seen to stand up and walk out to visit the bathroom for many moments of sobbing and reflection.

One of the courses was about family life. It felt as though what the course was teaching was precisely what I and my late wife were trying to do already with our family. The painful thing was that the family that was being described had just fallen apart by the death of the mother figure in the home. Many other courses would strike a similar vein while inducing the same reaction of grief in me.

Another challenge was that most of my colleagues in the course were already working as gospel ministers having done a theology bachelor's degree before. For me this was a conversion masters program. So I experienced a lot of added pressure.

Then there was the most prohibitive aspect to success, my brain. It would be many years before I learned that the trauma of grief had the ability to do some brain injuries that could result in the inability to store lists and historical data and similar things in memory. I now had the most difficulty in retaining almost anything in memory for my examinations.

Sometimes I managed to join revision groups but at other times it was not possible as the groups discussed in Romanian only, which I could not understand. Once in a while, I got to revise for the examinations as a pair with someone from the class. But examinations remained the worst form of assessment for me since I could not cram and recall anymore. I thought at the time that it was due to my age. Much later on I found out it was probably trauma and grief that did havoc to my memory.

REFLECTION:

How I wish I could write down the tried and proven formula to deal with grief! The above is just one example to acknowledge that it is not easy. Yet in spite of all your difficulties, you need to be resilient and keep going. God has promised that He will not leave nor forsake you. Even in your difficulties, He is even closer to you in your days of grief.

BLESSING:

In all the things that you do today, May God bless you and keep you in His care.

33 A MAGAZINE ON THE LONG MOT TRIP

I create the fruit of the lips; Peace, peace to him that is far off, and to him that is near, saith the LORD; and I will heal him. (Isaiah 57:19)

When we finally re-entered the Romanian border near the city of Arad, I felt such a peace as I had only ever felt when I landed in Africa following a period of absence in the UK of two years. It was such a strange feeling and such a queer thought that I could feel so peaceful in Romania of all the places in the world.

I needed to have the annual vehicle road worthiness technical inspection (Ministry of Transport - MOT) test done. But in spite of being resident in a European country, the law stipulated that MOT tests for UK registered cars could only be carried in the UK. So I phoned an MOT station in Swindon and reserved the ferry for crossing from Dunkerque to Dover.

It was a long journey done at the Easter weekend of the year 2011. I got some Romanian friends, a young married couple, Daniel and Raluca to travel with us. The journey seemed full of promise and adventure as we set off. The plan was for Daniel to help me with the driving while Raluca would help me with taking care of the children. The couple would enjoy a holiday traveling with us to the UK by road through all the 7 countries the journey traversed.

Our language communication was not very smooth in that the couple's English level at that time was still fairly basic. It was at some point after we had passed the city of Sibiu in Romania that Daniel told me he urgently needed a magazine. I wondered why my good friend would be so interested in any magazine so suddenly.

After we stopped at the next shops we found along the way I was really curious to see the magazine he was buying. Disappointingly, Daniel did not buy any magazine at all. But hilariously I discovered with the help of the children's translation that in Romanian a shop is called a "magazin".

Our journey was full of fun and play until the vessel pulled in to dock at Dover. It was as though some dark curtains had just been drawn over me. I know that my friends were affected by my sorrowfulness. Returning to the UK felt so painful and got me so distressed all through the rest of the sojourn. Even on the way back to Romania after the visit was still not as good. Depression and sorrow covered me throughout all 6 countries.

But when we finally re-entered the Romanian border near the city of Arad, I felt such a peace as I had only ever felt when I landed in Africa following a period of absence in the UK of two years. It was such a strange feeling and such a queer thought that I could feel so peaceful in Romania of all the places in the world.

REFLECTION:

Travelling and seeing new places and meeting new people could define the very turning point for some of your pain. However, as you return to where you were before, the pain could resume. It is part of the healing process.

BLESSING:

May the Lord walk with you and give you everlasting hope today.

34 TESTIFYING OF GOD'S MERCIES

In everything give thanks: for this is the will of God in Christ Jesus concerning you. (1 Thessalonians 5:18)

As I sat through the lectures day by day during the first weeks of our stay in the Theology Institute I was approached one day by a classmate who was a pastor in a local church. He asked me if I would like to visit his congregation and share my experience with them and talk about my walk with God. At that moment I had just finished writing an assignment in which I had outlined pretty much all my life history. And that narration had brought out right before me, just how God had been with me throughout until then.

I accepted the invitation and subsequently visited a small congregation that met in the city. It was a wonderful experience for me to testify of God's mercies at a time I was still bleeding with grief. I sang a few special songs for the congregation together with my children. At the end of the testimony we left and returned to the campus.

During the week after the visit to the city church group I was approached by another colleague, Tibi, who asked me if I would come to his district also out in the countryside and stay with his family while I visit two of his congregations and also share my story with them. I accepted the invitation and about two weeks or so later, we drove out to Prahova where we had a blessed wintry weekend in the countryside and shared the same testimony with congregations in Urlati and in Ceptura. Again the experience with the congregations was a priceless and a blessed one. And at that time, Tibi had only a small space for his family but he shared it with love with us and we were blessed to stay in his home.

Back on the College campus I was approached by another colleague, Bogdan who also asked to take me and the children to his district in Dor Marunt as well as to his wife's district in Teleorman for an entire weekend on two separate occasions. The love of the congregations was overwhelming and the family of Madalina, Bogdan's wife became as close to us as our own family and remain so till now. The visit in Cervenia church, Alexandria brought us in contact with the Geanta family of musicians whom we enjoyed so much and were blessed to hear playing so skilfully on their instruments.

I was called also to several churches within the city of Bucharest at Balta Alba, Cuza Voda, Popa Tatu and others. I was invited to Craiova as well as to Ploiesti. The most common thing was that I experienced the warmth and comfort being with God's people who listened to me as I spoke and wept with me as I wept. (I always spoke through an interpreter) They did not pass judgment on me or make comments that hurt me. They instead were very supportive and concerned for me. Mostly I felt their desire to want to be as helpful to me and my children as they could be. I also enjoyed listening to many wonderful singing voices in very soothing church choirs in most of the churches.

The multiple visits to these congregations resulted in me meeting many new people who became friends and remain so till this day. Going to a far and unknown country, though a brave thing it had been, resulted in new experiences that I otherwise would never have had.

So within a period of just two years in Romania I had been to almost 150 congregations When I left the country to return to the UK at the presumed end of my studies there were still many outstanding invitations by other churches that I could not attend. I had established an intimate bond with the country of Romania because of the warmth of her people.

REFLECTION:

Some of the experiences we go through in life can bring new opportunities. The visits I made to all the churches I did, did not seem to have much of any impact on my grief at first. But eventually I noticed something was happening to me. The more I talked about my life and my experiences and also about my bereavement and grief the less heavy the pain of grief seemed to be. The story I told about my life was at first making me weep with the church members weeping alongside me. But eventually I was telling the same story without weeping anymore although my audiences were in tears for me. So I learned that talking about my grief helped me get better. But I was not just talking about it, I was glorifying God even in my pain and emphasizing all the good things God had done for me throughout my life in spite of the pain of grief. I therefore can boldly say that if you will praise God in spite of pain, your suffering will become less and less in time.

BLESSING:

May you be brave enough to share God's goodness in spite of your own pain that you may feel the blessings of God even now. May God be with you!

35 WE WILL GIVE YOU LAND TO BUILD AND LIVE AMONG US

Pure religion and undefiled before God and the Father is this, To visit the fatherless and widows in their affliction, and to keep himself unspotted from the world. (James 1:27)

One of my colleagues learned about my life and also about my testimony of praise in spite of grief. This colleague, Daniel Bursuc was a pastor around the Iasi area of Comanesti and so he invited me there for a weekend.

The journey to Comanesti was around 6 hours of driving from Bucharest and we set off fairly early to get there while the sun still shone. It was a scenic journey in spite of the long drive.

On our arrival we were taken to one of the churches for the Friday vesper. The members were very pleasant country folks. I gave a brief evening talk and we parted with that group which we would meet again on Saturday evening at the close of the Sabbath.

The main church that we attended during the Sabbath was in the same building as the pastor's apartment at which we were hosted. Next to the building ran a flowing river which made such a refreshing sound in the quiet of the night when all else was still. It was a really lovely area.

As with all the other congregations we had visited until now, the congregation in Comanesti's main church was really pleasant and warm. We shared a lunch meal together before going out for a walk on some lovely hills close by.

It was then that the pastor informed me about a certain woman that he especially wanted me to talk to. She was suffering from breast cancer. During the walk I had the opportunity to share some words of encouragement with her. I found her very positive, bright and happy in spite of her situation. Her husband seemed much more affected and unhappy.

The evening service was at the other church where we had been to on Friday. The people there had questions for me about my life and plans for the future. After I answered them they made me a surprising offer. They said that they were happy for me to come and live among them and belong with them. As such they could offer me a piece of land to build a house and more land to grow crops and earn my living as they did. All this was being offered to me completely free of charge. Their pastor confirmed that they really meant it and were not bluffing.

I was really moved by the generosity and love of these complete strangers. God puts in place people with unselfish hearts and people who are full of compassion.

The evening ended with the kids enjoying a pillow fight and lots of laughter back at the pastor's apartment. The fun for the kids added onto the fact that my son Vuyo had been allowed to drive the pastor's car around the churchyard. Naturally this meant that Sunday's departure time was a very tearful one. But we had to go back, and anyway, life is bitter and sweet even for children too.

REFLECTION:

God always has something in store for you which you may not see or know about until you get there. Just keep praising Him and moving ahead in faith. It may not be as quickly as you wish or expect. But trust in Him who holds your life in His hands.

BLESSING:

May it be that today your thoughts remain positive. May your day today be a pleasant one.

36 PLEASE WRITE SOMETHING IN ENGLISH IN MY HYMN BOOK

For I know the plans I have for you," declares the LORD, "plans to prosper you and not to harm you, plans to give you hope and a future. (Jeremiah 29:11)

Daniel, the pastor from Comanesti had a twin brother Cornel who was also a pastor in another district around Iasi. He too wanted me to come and spend time in his district and share my story with his congregations. I was delighted to be a part of the people in some very remote parts of the country that formed the district.

There were some famous tourist attractions in the area such as some winery and vineyards by some former monarch of Romania that he called Frumusica. Unfortunately I had lost a bit of time following a delay by the police in the city of Bacau who claimed I had been over speeding as I exited the city. I was certain that on that particular occasion I had not been over speeding but maybe my UK registered car attracted them. The police could not speak much English and I could not speak Romanian either. My children knew not to help the police to put their dad into trouble. In the end I drove away much later and with a speeding fine to be paid some day.

The weekend visit was one of the most hectic ones ever. On Friday night I had to preach in some church. Then on Saturday morning I had to be in two different churches before breaking for lunch. After lunch I had to be at 2 different churches before finally resting for the day. The trouble was that the churches were all not located close to each other.

There were long and windy dirt roads through the country and sometimes these 'roads' traversed through some corn fields where it was obvious they were not even roads at all. But the good pastor knew his way even through the wilderness. He drove so fast, much to the delight of my son who was enjoying the adventure.

We had been delayed at a lunch where a family had prepared a meal for us. Also some visitors who had come from the city of Iasi after hearing of our presence in the area had come to spend time with us at this lunch meal.

The two churches we were meant to visit that afternoon would not give up the wait for our arrival in spite of knowing about the delay. Thankfully the cellular communication networks were functional and so the people were kept informed of our journey's progress.

It was so wonderful to find a small group of people eagerly awaiting our arrival. It was equally satisfying to feel their warmth as humans and their support for the grieving.

But as we had reached this group late, our arrival time for the next and final group was also delayed even further.

When we reached the last group of people they had waited so long, singing and singing even more, apparently. In this group, which was probably the furthest away from the cities, were a good number of people that never in their lives had ever seen any black person except on television. I was so exhausted by this time and so were they but when I spoke, you could hear a pin drop in the audience! The people listened very intently and I could almost feel their eyes all glued onto me. They wept when they felt my pain but I did not weep myself since my healing had progressed.

When I was finally finished speaking, I stood at the door to shake hands with the people as they left the building. Suddenly one lady asked me to write something in English inside her hymn book. I quickly scribbled a verse in the hymn book. When I finished, someone else asked for the same. Before I knew it there was a queue of people waiting for me to write in their hymn books. It was surprising for me but nonetheless pleasant to be made to feel as though I was so important for people to value my writing in their books.

REFLECTION:

Time and time again I have experienced God's overwhelming love via complete strangers. Keep yourself close to God regardless of dire circumstances. Even Paul and Silas sang praises from a prison cell and God did a miracle for them. Keep your heart in tune with God and he will help you in your trouble.

BLESSING:

May you be blessed with eternal hope today by the Lord of the impossible.

37 A CONSTRUCTION WORKER FOR THE LORD

Also I heard the voice of the Lord, saying, Whom shall I send, and who will go for us? Then said I, Here am I; send me. (Isaiah 6:8)

I thank God that I accepted the invitation to go and share my life story with the folks in Craiova. From what appeared as just a poor countryside visit with nothing for me to gain, God wrought miracles.

Another colleague from the theology course, Ciprian Dragut, together with his wife Andreea wanted to also take me to their districts and home churches respectively. They thought I may not accept the invitation since the journey would be long and involve overnight stays in the countryside. But to their pleasant surprise and my greatest delight, I accepted.

We reached Craiova, Dolj in time to go for the Friday vesper. My interpreter Andreea who as an English teacher herself did an excellent job.

At the end of the testimony service on Sabbath afternoon as I shook hands at the door, a certain man came to speak to me via the interpreter. He told me that he had lost his son to death almost a decade before and could not accept it. He said I was the first person to ever reach his heart with my own story of God's goodness mingled with pain. He said finally he could now accept it and thanked me for having come to their village. Apparently he was an elder in the church.

Another man who was introduced to me as a builder and kitchen fitter by trade was Andreea's brother in law, Liviu. Seeing me as just a man of God doing God's work, Liviu was keen to know my future plans when I complete my studies. I was keen to ask him for tips on how I could fix up and update my kitchen back in England. He gave his advice well enough but later sent me a message via his sister in law to say he was willing to travel to the UK and do the kitchen fitting work himself for me. All he expected was that I pay for his flights.

About 6 months or so later I bought him a flight ticket and he went to Swindon, UK to do the work.. The kids and I were there with him as he worked skillfully away. The biggest challenge was that we needed the kids to translate our conversations since he could not speak English and i could not speak Romanian. And the kids wanted to play not translate.

In the end the job was completed and what an amazing job it was. I think the house instantly gained at least £10000-£15000 in value following Liviu's work. The house now had a new and beautiful kitchen. I thank God that I accepted the invitation to go and share my life story with the folks in Craiova. From what appeared as just a poor countryside visit with nothing for me to gain, God wrought miracles.

REFLECTION:

My departure for Romania was to seek solace for my grieving. I knew I would get training in theology. I did not expect to become the living theology whilst still undergoing training. So it does not really matter how big you think your grief is. God can make the unexpected happen for you if you continue to praise Him while you feel low.

BLESSING:

May God do miracles for you and turn any and all of your sorrows into joy today.

38 A VISIT, JUST TO SAY THANK YOU

And he said unto me, My grace is sufficient for thee: for my strength is made perfect in weakness. Most gladly therefore will I rather glory in my infirmities, that the power of Christ may rest upon me. (2 Corinthians 12:9)

I had just completed a church growth course in which my Andrews University professor Dr Joseph Kidder had just impressed upon me the importance of saying thank you. In fact I had learned that it is unbiblical to say thank you privately, just to God, for public blessings that God was blessing you with. After you have been praying for something and even asking others to help you pray for it, when God blesses you with an answer to your prayer then it essential to thank Him publicly for it and give Him glory.

About two or three weeks before I was due to leave Romania and return to settle in the UK my colleague Ciprian and his wife Andreea arranged for me to go to Invingatori church and share my story and glorify God with that audience. I had no idea about the size of the church or the kind of people who go there but as usual, I agreed to go.

It was not during the morning service but in the afternoon when many people do not return for some programs in church. But on this particular afternoon the church was almost fully packed. The building was a very impressively beautiful one and the sound system carried the sound extremely well. So when the church choir sang, it was so beautiful to hear them sing. Also, at the end of my presentation, a trio sang in English the song, "Wonderful Merciful Savior". As they sang that song I broke down and wept much. It was because that song had been one of the songs I used to sing before as a trio together with our friend Catia and my late wife Mandy.

Nonetheless, the service had been another blessing for me and I felt the warm and sincere love flowing from God's people whom I had never even met before. One of them, at the end of the service, invited me to his store in some imported clothes market. He said I should come and choose some clothing for my children as he specialised in imported children's clothes. Another one just asked me for my address because he wanted to send me something in the post. Another invited me to visit their mother's home because their mother was suffering from cancer and they thought I could encourage her and even suggest some treatments based on my experiences. Yet another placed an envelope in my hands and pronounced a blessing on me.

It turned out that the envelope's content was a surprising €100 note. And I did go to the stall of the man who had invited me and from there left with a bagful of a new wardrobe selection for my children including a bow tie and a lovely blue waistcoat that Vuyo liked so much. Using the address that I had given to the man who asked for it at church, the postal services delivered a couple of boxes full of "Inedit" food products. The products included some pates, vegan sausages and vegan mayonnaise etc. Inedit is a renowned brand of health food products in Romania.

The visit to the mother of the couple that had invited me to their home was also a blessing to me. I met the mother who was in a positive spirit. I advised what I could and what I knew and prayed with her. Before I left I was asked if I would accept some honey as a gift. I was told that the family was a bee keeping family and that this was a tithe that the family gave to men of God and they had decided to give it to me. So I left with a huge bottle of more than 5 litres of honey weighing close to 10kg.

I was not looking for any gifts and I had not even been expecting any. But now, with no contacts of some of the people who had given me things I felt the need to go back to the church just to say thank you.

When I arrived that evening I found that there was a baptism service. So I sent a word to the pastor at the time, pastor Emil Eremie, that I wished to say a word of thanks to the church. They kindly made a slot for me for the word of thanks, which I gave as I also said farewell to the congregation from deep down my heart within 3 minutes. I was due to leave the city that same week. At the end of my little thank you speech I was invited to stay at the end of the baptism service and join in the meal in the basement.

It was a lovely meal that they had prepared to celebrate the baptism of new church members. During that time it seemed they quickly convened a meeting and brought me another farewell gift to help me with fuel as I travel. They gave me an envelope with 1000 lei inside (1000 Romanian lei was equivalent to £200 at that time). My visit to say thank you left me carrying away a wad of cash. I know that God was in it all.

REFLECTION:

Many times we cannot imagine what will happen tomorrow. But when we are thankful for yesterday and even for today and when we give honour and glory to God for His love and mercy, he will provide more that what is sufficient for our needs. Even as you grieve, remember that God never leaves you alone. He never left me alone.

BLESSING:

May God give you strength to keep you moving on. May He show you ways in which to express more and more gratitude everyday and enable you to see the roses among the thorns. Have a blessed day.

39 A YEAR IN AN APARTMENT, FREE OF CHARGE

Every man according as he purposeth in his heart, so let him give; not grudgingly, or of necessity: for God loveth a cheerful giver. (2 Corinthians 9:7)

During my first year of living on the campus of the Theology Institute at Cernica, Romania something interesting happened. I learned about a meeting of the Adventist Service Industry (ASI) members and leaders. Someone told me it was "just a bunch of rich people" having their meeting on campus. I decided that I would keep myself well out of their way and stay in my room and study my Bible, listen to my music and also to some sermons. It seemed like a completely reasonable plan.

The day progressed fairly well and I did manage to keep out of the way of the rich ASI members. That is until they found my UK registered car in the car park. I am not really sure if it was the car or the kids they found first but the kids ran to our room to tell me that some people who were speaking in English wanted to see me. Reluctantly I left the room to go and meet whoever was looking for me.

It turned out to be a very pleasant Romanian couple, who had lived in England before and spoke to me in good English, who wanted to see me. I thought they would just greet me and then leave me alone but they did not. They wanted to know more about my life and why I was in Romania.

Telling them a bit about me did not send them away either. The man, Dragos, wanted to see my room on campus and what facilities I had in it for the kids. He said that he had a son who was a little bit older than my son but who could play with my son and possibly speak to him in English too. I actually met the son, Philip, who was already playing with my kids. I strongly suspect this said playing had been responsible for blowing my cover, besides the foreign car that had been discovered.

When Dragos came to the room he immediately said, "Oh, by the way, I have a fridge which I could bring to you on Monday in which you can keep perishable food for your children." "I will also bring some toys that they can play with and other stuff for kids that I can find."

It all sounded unreal, but it was true as Dragos was true to his word. He drove in to the campus and brought a lot of toy cars and dolls and teddies along with the refrigerator as promised. We kept contact and we were invited to go for lunch at his home one Sabbath and then took a walk in one of the loveliest parks in Bucharest (I will always miss the beauty of the parks of Bucharest).

Our stay in Romania seemed to have reached its end when we left for the UK at the end of just over a year being in the country. I had not been very happy to depart from the country and neither had the children been happy. But the time had come to leave and so we left. Kids wept about it and I choked my tears quietly as we drove back to the UK. After a few weeks back in the UK I learned from the Theology Institute that I was required to do some additional courses in the next academic year to complete my courses.

I was chatting online with Dragos about the second year of study requirements and planning to go for a couple of weeks at a time along the year when Dragos told me that he and his wife had decided to let me stay in their apartment in the city. I just needed to check if the school still had a place for the children so they could continue their studies for another year. When the school confirmed that there was indeed still a place for the children to come back, Dragos told me that I did not need to pay any rent to live in his apartment for the whole academic year. I would only need to pay for my own utilities.

We went back to Bucharest and stayed at a lovely 2 bedroomed apartment at Gara de Nord for an entire academic year. All the while I never had to pay any rent, just for the utilities. At the start, I was very certain that I wanted nothing to do with any rich people and I hid myself away from where I knew them to be meeting. Miraculously I was found out and not only was I compelled to meet them but they more than befriended me to the extent that I felt embarrassed of seeming like I wanted to take advantage of their kindness.

REFLECTION:

Sometimes God will use people to cut through our prejudices and show us some genuinely kind people. When you are grieving you may, like me, be particularly suspicious of those who genuinely want to help you. Leave everything to God as He is the one who judges motives, our own and those of others. God can help you through other human beings and whether they are poor or rich should not cause you to fail to function at a human level.

BLESSING:

May God bless you and give you strength and confidence to accept any help you may be offered. May you be strong in the Lord.

40 WHAT WILL I DO WITH THIS?

Give, and it shall be given unto you; good measure, pressed down, and shaken together, and running over, shall men give into your bosom. For with the same measure that ye mete withal it shall be measured to you again. (Luke 6:38)

As Dragos had brought me a refrigerator and toys for the children, he had also asked me if there was anything that I needed help with. He understood just how difficult things could be for someone living in a foreign land.

It turned out that I actually did need some help with a couple of things. Firstly I was struggling to find and get to places. In addition to frequently starting off from the car park on the wrong side of the road (all my life I had driven only on the left side of the road), I could not find many places I needed to go to. Incidentally, because of my being accustomed to driving on the left it was quite common in my first months of living in Romania to find myself facing oncoming buses and cars, as I tried to turn left into the wrong lanes.

So I asked Dragos if he could get my TomTom satnav loaded with a Romanian map that would enable me to move around with more than just the major national roads. I needed local street navigation not just city to city directions. I also asked if he knew any reliable mechanic or garage that could give my car a full service as soon as possible.

He said he would check with his mechanic and come back to me soon. Within two days he came to collect my car from the campus and left his old runaround dacia. He returned later in the day to give me my serviced car back. I asked how much I needed to pay and he told me it was 500 lei (roughly £100 equivalent). I needed to get the money from the ATM but Dragos was in a hurry to go. So we agreed to meet later in the week when he was in the area.

On Friday afternoon, just after I had arranged to have some colleagues go to a supermarket with me, Dragos rang to say he had the satnav ready for me with Romanian maps on it. We agreed to meet at the Auchan hypermarket that was closest to us.

Dragos showed up in a fancy lotus sports car which he said belonged to one of his friends. He asked if I wanted to go for a little drive. I did want to feel the sports car. Getting into it was like climbing down into some very low cave. And driving in it was like being in an aircraft just before takeoff.

He gave me the satnav back and I asked for the cost of the map. He said it was free.

I then gave him the 500lei for the car service. He seemed to have forgotten about it already as he took it. Giving it back to me, he then said, "What will I do with this? Maybe it will be useful for you but I don't need it. Buy something for the children with it."

I thanked him and I am sure he long forgot about it. But I will always remember it not only because it made a huge difference to my finances but because it was a rather pleasant surprise that he had just effectively serviced my car at his own expense.

REFLECTION:

The people that God will send to your aid in your time of trouble may not even be the ones you expect. The kind of help you will experience may also not be what you may imagine. But God will certainly send you help. Be sure to be attentive and be still and know that He is God.

BLESSING:

May the Lord of peace give you peace today.

41 A TV INTERVIEW

Then shalt thou delight thyself in the LORD; and I will cause thee to ride upon the high places of the earth, and feed thee with the heritage of Jacob thy father: for the mouth of the LORD hath spoken it. (Isaiah 58:14)

As the word spread around about me and the kids being in Romania and telling our story, the Speranta (Hope) TV presenter, Dorian Gravila heard about it and invited us over. It would be a Friday afternoon recording for a program called "Album de Familie" (Family Album). The episode of our interview was titled, "Si Barbati Plang" which means "Even Men Weep".

We needed to arrive at the studio quite early and hence we would have had to miss our lunch meal from the campus cafeteria. But Dorian's wife had thought about this already and sent us some packed lunch which we found at the studio.

We also had to travel about 10 miles from the campus to the studio. Yet again Dorian himself had made a special budget to pay for our fuel, out of his own pocket. In fact I later learned that he was not even a salaried employee of the TV station but a volunteer.

We were shown into the sound engineering room where I gave the technicians the family photos, that had been requested beforehand, to display during the interview. I also gave them a sound clip to play at specified moments during the interview as had been instructed by the show host.

It was my first time ever to appear as a guest on a TV show. I sat next to my children and listened intently as the interview began. The host would ask me questions in Romanian which the late Emanuel Cristicel interpreted into English before I could respond in answer. It was quite stressful for me because I could not even give the full answers that I wanted to give before the next question was asked. So I felt the disadvantage of not knowing the local language.

The children, on the other hand, were also interviewed but only in Romanian. We had only been in the country for just 6 months and their comprehension and speech were still elementary. Yet I was well impressed that they actually held a dialogue.

What also stressed me during the interview was that my 3 year old daughter, Vuyiso fell asleep and snored away softly for much of the length of the interview. Her snoring made a whizzing sound that was picked up by the microphone and broadcast into the program. Also, my 6 year old son, Vuyo, because he needed the toilet, had to get up and walk away from the studio then come back while recording was in progress.

The same points of my stress turned out to be what Dorian later said was actually good and authentic. He said that that was exactly what could be expected in a typical family situation. Children do sleep and snore on their parents' lap and children do get up and go to the toilet as needed.

All in all I was thankful for the experience of being a guest on a TV show. It was something I had never even imagined could happen for me.

REFLECTION:

While it is not everyone who is bereaved who will end up as a guest on a TV show, God has His ways of working for each one of us. In my case I was given a countrywide audience to reaffirm my faith in God in spite of my grief. I ended up being recognised in so many places I had never been before and by people who felt as though they knew me well and treated me as such. Being in a foreign country whose language I did not understand and being treated as a respected individual was very helpful in soothing my grief. I do know that God works in mysterious ways and He will work through your situation too in a way that is very unique to you.

BLESSING:

May God supply all your needs according to His riches in glory in a way that only He can do. And may you grow to trust Him in spite of your difficulties.

42 A FRIEND INDEED

He that walketh with wise men shall be wise: but a companion of fools shall be destroyed. (Proverbs 13:20)

A colleague in the theology course, Bogdan Platica, approached me one day. He told me that his wife had made some pumpkin pies (called placinta in Romanian) and he had brought some for my children and wondered if I would accept them and allow my children to eat them. I asked what the ingredients were and thankfully accepted them.

We then talked about the possibility of visits to his districts and getting him and his wife to interact more with me and my children. Among other upcoming events in the future that we could possibly attend was a children's Christmas program day in Branceni, Teleorman.

Bogdan made arrangements with his wife's cousin's family to host us for the weekend of the program and we became special guests in a household as well as in the church. They even modified their program planning to give me a speaking slot in the afternoon. They wanted to hear my testimony and how I ended up there.

While we remained there I was impressed by a choir of children. This choir had very sweet orchestral violin music being played by children. The conductor of the orchestra was an old man, whom later I found out was called Cezaar Geanta.

I asked Bogdan about how I could get this old man to teach my children so that they could play violin too. He told me to wait a little while he went to speak to him about it. After some minutes he came back to say the man and his wife wanted to speak to the children. Cezaar Geanta, asked the children if they liked violin and if they would like to learn to play it. He also gave them a violin to try playing a little on the spot. After all the analysis the Geantas told me that they were happy to teach the children.

I wondered how the tuition could be done as we lived about 2 hours away by car. But God had a solution already. The wife of the violin orchestra conductor, Viorica Geanta, already had a schedule that took her weekly to Mihai Ionescu, my children's school in the city of Bucharest.

There was even more surprising news. The tuition was going to be done all free of charge. I just needed to commit to bring the children to any concerts in future. I did not even need to buy any instruments as the kind Geantas themselves would provide.

This was how my children first got to even hold a violin in their hands. More tuition transpired much later by other kind experts but their first teacher was Viorica Geanta. The friend who facilitated it all was Bogdan Platica, my classmate.

REFLECTION:

Life kept going on in spite of my continued grieving. Thoughtful people like Bogdan just used their initiatives to console me in spite of how I was at that time. God will place people in your way too. Accept their comfort and allow them to bring you relief. It may be very little by little but one day you will look back and realise how useful all the milestones were.

BLESSING:

May you have a peaceful and blessed day today. May God's presence abide with you.

43 A VERY "UNTIDY" FRIEND

Bear ye one another's burdens, and so fulfil the law of Christ. (Galatians 6:2)

There are many friends who have come and gone from my life along my years of living. Some moved away to far away places or I moved away myself far from the friends. But in my sojourn in Romania I met with several extraordinary people who made a real lasting impact on me. One particular friend I met was Bogdan Platica. He and his wife Madalina stood by me and supported me in so many ways that I probably did not even recognize till much later. At the time they were there for me I think I was too consumed by my state of grief to fully appreciate their selfless sacrifices. There are too many times that they did things that not too many other people could have done.

There was a point in time when I needed to continue attending College daily but the children had a break from school. I was living in the city at an apartment and I had no childminder available to look after the children. Madalina got her cousin, Veronica to come and live in the city and then took my children to stay with them for an entire week to enable me to continue with my course for the week. They incurred food costs, and refused any money from me. Their cousin also traveled from Teleorman just for my children but at no cost to me.

As if that was not enough, anyone who went to pastor Bogdan's Militari apartment, in Bucharest could be excused for dismissing him and his wife as disorderly, untidy or disorganised. But what they may never have known was that the untidiness was not of their own doing. The untidiness was a direct result of their sacrifice for a friend, me. Their home was not even untidy but full of extra clatter by me.

As I left Bucharest to return to England I had too many possessions that were impossible to take in the car with me. I only had a small BMW 318se to carry children's bicycles and toys and clothes.

Also, I had bedding and books as well as clothing and all cookware and cutlery to move away with.

It was virtually impossible to take everything away. But i could not imagine just throwing away my effects just like that. So Bogdan and Madalina stepped in and saved the day. The result of their sacrifice for me was that the tidiness of their house immediately fell into disrepute. So that anyone visiting them would have assumed they were the clumsiest couple ever.

Not only did I just leave my baggage in their home but I also asked them to store a very noisy computer server of mine in their bedroom. To make things clearer, the computer needed to remain plugged in to the mains (noisy as it was) day and night and everyday of every week throughout the year. Also, the computer would be using electricity which they were paying for, not me. I was at the start of running a voice communication system which made international phone calls cheaper. And that computer system was an integral part of my system.

One Christmas season the Platicas decided that we could not be left without family and all by ourselves. So they arranged for us to go and have a day of fun on the snow at the Azuga ski resort area. Of course the fun was appreciated more by the kids than by me who grew up where not a single flake of snow ever flowed even once in my life. But the kids were so delighted while I was just happy for them and appreciated the efforts by my friends and their company. I was still not in a state to be overjoyed by almost anything at that point in my grief. Even though I am sure my friend recognised the state of brokenness I was in, they still did good things for me and for the sake of my children. I am sure they could see that I was not as appreciative as I could have been had I been in a normal state.

A lot more things were done by the Platicas than I can even list. But the fact that they did so much for me makes me grateful to God for putting people like them in my way to minister to my needs and to those of my children.

REFLECTION:

With hardly anything on my part, God kept providing the support I needed through His people who were strangers to me at first. Trust him to do the same for you as you also deal with grief.

BLESSING:

May God be your friend today as you go about your errands. May your day be full of joy.

44 CHEATING IN EXAMINATIONS

He that covereth his sins shall not prosper: but whoso confesseth and forsaketh them shall have mercy. (Proverbs 28:13)

In 1985 I was doing form 1 at Fletcher High school in Gweru, Zimbabwe. I was in the class with the best performing children having obtained excellent grade 7 results. On one of the first examinations I took we had to sit in the hall as an entire group of all 6 form one classes. I think there were other forms too but I do not recall well now.

What I do recall is that I had some class notes that I had been using for revision. I did not refer to the notes even once or even touch them as i took the exam. But yet the notes were on my examination desk and not even concealed. Maybe in my childish mind I had thought if it shows you are not hiding things then it is also evident that you are not cheating.

I emphasize that I did not intend to use the notes in the examination. This is why I will never forget how shocked I was when one invigilator who was also my history teacher, Miss Dolphin, came and took my notes and my answer sheet and wrote in block capital letters on my answer sheet with a red pen, "CAUGHT CHEATING!"

Almost 30 years later, I was in Romania, battling with my memory as I took masters degree examinations for my theology modules. I was doing theology because I felt that God had called me to serve him as a pastor. I was doing theology also because I wanted to know more about this God who had allowed my 32 year old wife to die and leave me alone with 2 small children. I wanted to understand God, and the word theology actually means the study about God. I was also doing theology as it gave me a chance to restart life and as I could study while at the same time my children were with me and doing their own schooling too. With my main textbook being the Bible and my classmates being either practising pastors or pastors in training, I figured that I was in the best company. What could go wrong when you study a book of which God Himself is the author?

I was sitting some particular module examination at the theology institute. I had no class notes on my desk as I did in 1985. I was really struggling to remember the things that I had learned for the examination. Then, in the silence of the examination room, I heard some whispering. I turned to see who was whispering and what I saw shocked me.

Some of my colleagues were not only whispering to each other but were passing notes between themselves. If this had been the first and only time I was to witness this then I could say maybe I did not see things well enough. I did not do so well in that examination and I think my course grade was only helped by coursework. The cheating colleagues, on the other hand, passed well.

On a different day and while sitting a different exam I witnessed something even more convincing. The invigilator left the room for a moment and some of my colleagues not only spoke louder to each other but showed each other their papers. I advised the MA programs office about this behaviour and they improved their examination room controls.

I know for a fact that some, if not all of my colleagues who were cheating never became pastors after the course. It was a real shock for me to see cheating by theology students. This is not to say I was better in any way than my colleagues or my integrity is any more superior. But I never cheated in my exams in either childhood or adulthood. When I got good or bad grades, I got them all with honour.

REFLECTION:

The answer to my pain was not just in theological studies. I only got partial relief from pain from the course. I was even disappointed by the behaviour of some of my colleagues. How could a pastoral student be a cheat? The answer is to never look at any human being because they will fail you. Even pastors can let you down. Only God should remain your focus as only he can help you.

BLESSING:

May God lift you up today as you humble yourself before him.

45 RACIAL PRIVILEGE

And we know that all things work together for good to them that love God, to them who are the called according to his purpose. (Romans 8:28)

When black or white people speak of racial privileges they almost invariably refer to white supremacy domination. Black people are normally given the inferior status while their white counterparts enjoy the status of exaltation. I have experienced the exact opposite along my travels.

Being asked to sign autographs at some remote Romanian church was just but a tip of the iceberg. The country of Romania had so many people who helped me regain faith in humanity. There were people who influenced my understanding and acceptance of the fact that people do not all hold the same and usually negative views of others just because they are of a certain skin colour. Actually I found out that some people in Romania in fact revered black people in ways I have seen a lot of black people elevating white folks.

Several times I got to meet people who thought I could help them somehow to leave their country and find a job and a better life in England. However I think this had nothing to do with the colour of my skin at all but who knows?

One Romanian man I met once told me that he liked black people because they do not tell lies.

A few other people remarked about black people's physical strength and how safe they thought I should feel among Romanians. My dentist also confirmed that I had much stronger and bigger teeth than he was used to.

I learned that generally, blacks who have moved to Romania as students were seen as some of the smartest people ever to come to the country. These perceived geniuses were known to come to study medicine and other well respected professions. I learned that even when it came to choosing a doctor in Romania, Romanians preferred black doctors to fellow Romanian doctors.

What fascinated me was how my ethnic minority kids seemed to glean a majority of friends. And the things that kids can do could make you wonder how on earth they came up with the ideas.

I learned that at school as my son Vuyo arrived in the morning his friends or classmates used to form a daily parade for him. They stood in two rows and flanked him on both sides so that he could only walk between them while they saluted him as armed forces saluted a head of state.

Racial privilege is not just a construct of some people's minds. It really exists and yet can become dangerous when one becomes used to it and expects the preferential treatment that it affords them. What is true also is that, though some may deny it, it is not only a privilege for white people but also for blacks in some countries such as Romania though even there only a few will readily admit and acknowledge it.

REFLECTION:

Bereavement landed me in a country that brought me and my children some weird and wonderful experiences. It is funny how unexpected things kept showing up. All these things seemed to be bundled up for a purpose. All things work together for good to those that love the Lord and who are called according to his purpose.

BLESSING:

May God surround you with His love today and may all things work together for you today.

46 LISTENING TO ROMANIAN WITHOUT INTERPRETATION

If any man speak in an unknown tongue, let it be by two, or at the most by three, and that by course; and let one interpret. But if there be no interpreter, let him keep silence in the church; and let him speak to himself, and to God. (1 Corinthians 14:27-28)

Not forsaking the assembling of ourselves together, as the manner of some is; but exhorting one another: and so much the more, as ye see the day approaching. (Hebrews 10:25)

One of the most frustrating things that I experienced as a result of moving to Romania and staying there was my zero understanding of Romanian. The language structure of Romanian is so far removed from the English, Ndebele, Shona and Setswana languages which I was fluent in at the time I moved. I had imagined that I would learn Romanian fairly quickly as I could already speak a number of other languages. But I had a big surprise awaiting me. Yet there was no turning back since I was in the country already. Nonetheless many Romanians told me not to bother trying to learn Romanian for two reasons.

Firstly they said that Romanian is a very difficult language and would be too difficult for me to learn. Secondly they said that because Romanian is not used elsewhere in the world except in Romania it would be useless for me to learn it and just a waste of my time. But I realised that because of the problems the country was facing, many people I communicated with were seeking a way to move away from Romania in search of greener pastures. As such they could not really understand how anyone would want to move from a first world country like England to Romania. Why would anyone bother to learn Romanian when there was, in their view, no hope for Romania?

As I attended church services, the people always recognised my presence and my lack of understanding of Romanian. They therefore always asked someone to sit with me who could interpret for me. Sometimes this felt okay and fairly useful but most of the time it was not good at all. It was not good because I did not understand much of the whispered interpretation and also none of what they were trying to interpret.

In the end I was just frustrated and stressed by noise next to me by an interpreter as well as noise from the speaker at the podium. I asked the people not to interpret for me anymore. Yet I still never missed attending the services in spite of not understanding anything. The only time that interpreting was truly beneficial was when the interpreter stood next to the speaker at the podium and spoke only when the main speaker was quiet.

I tried suggesting that a group be set up to offer dual language church services at which both English and Romanian would be used via interpretation. I argued that this could help both foreigners trying to learn Romanian as well as locals trying to learn English. I even volunteered to be the facilitator for such a group but my idea was not taken on board.

Instead I was directed to join an international group that met in the city on some afternoons. I did try it but was frustrated by the fact that often times the group comprised of just me, Raymond, who was a university student and the pastor plus my children. The children ended up just running around and bored and unengaged and subsequently I gave up the attendance of this group.

The best solution for me would have been interpretation from the podium as the speaker paused and the interpreter moved along. That kind of interpretation had helped me learn at least one language before and I think could also have helped me learn Romanian.

As I could not get my choice of interpretation, in the end I just sat and listened without understanding. Yet I was still blessed to be in the presence of worshippers. I never missed attending services every Sabbath. But my Sabbaths became increasingly more of me being at the pulpit than me listening because many churches invited me to speak. So I often got to hear what I was saying in English being repeated in Romanian. And both I and my Romanian audiences were blessed in the end.

REFLECTION:

The difficulties that we can come across in grief are endless. But instead of focusing on the present prevailing pain and difficulty it is important to look beyond it. It is helpful to spend time in worship and take a weekly break from all your wants and cares and spend time with your creator. Even as I dwelt among people of a strange tongue to me, I still experienced worship among them.

BLESSING:

May your mind be filled with hope today. Amen.

47 DENIAL OR FAITH BEYOND DEATH

The last enemy that shall be destroyed is death. (1 Corinthians 15:26)

In counselling and psychology they state that in grieving, many people go through distinct stages. One of those stages is what they call denial. There are those who would want to define the experience I am about to relate as the said denial stage but I categorically refuse to define it as such.

Just a few days after Mandy died I had a few thoughts in my mind. I remembered about Jairus's daughter. I also remembered about Moses. I remembered even about Dorcas and also Lazarus. All these had died and then were brought back to life in different miraculous resurrections.

I was struck by an idea. I wanted to go to the mortuary and ask them to allow me to pray once again for my wife. I still believed that God could raise the dead even in our present day, not only in Bible times.

For how I felt, I would reject the term denial. Yes I had accepted that she had died. But I did not want her to die. So if I refused to find death as acceptable would that make me a denier?

It had so happened that for the previous months we had been as individuals and also as a family, so dedicated in prayer. We had set a fixed prayer time and a prayer format. Some changes had now become necessary due to the loss of the mother of the household.

On a daily basis and for 11 months we had sung the song "Jesus loves me this I know". We had prayed so much for Mandy's recovery but it had not happened. Now Vuyiso's prayer became adapted for the prevailing circumstances. Initially she being only two, had to learn to stop praying for mummy to get well as she had always been praying. Then gradually she moved to some very solemn lines that went," Thank you for mummy because she died. And we are going to find another mummy who is just like her." I would not ever dare say she was in denial neither.

Next, after her new prayer she then set out to carry out her quest in faith; that of finding another mother. I lost count of the number of women that she asked the question, "Can you be my mummy?" It did not even matter to her if the women were already married or not. She had no idea that her mother would of necessity have to be my wife.

Faith was high but yet it was apparently not in line with the way God chose to deal with the situation. In this sense I agree that accepting that this is how God would let things be was incomprehensible.

REFLECTION:

What I do comprehend very well is that death is an enemy of God. Death is not only just an enemy. It is even the very last enemy which the Bible tells us is going to be destroyed.

BLESSING:

May the reassurance that death is an enemy renew your courage and trust in God and give you peace today.

48 1ST DECEMBER TV CREW

Let nothing be done through strife or vainglory; but in lowliness of mind let each esteem other better than themselves.

Look not every man on his own things, but every man also on the things of others. (Philippians 2:2-3)

My good friend Bogdan Platica and his wife Madalina decided once again to give us a taste of the local attractions. They saw that we would otherwise never know about certain things and events in their country. The kids would have stayed home and would have been bored just with me on the 1st of December 2011.

We took the "Metro" underground train and rode through several stations, changing trains once or twice along the way. It was unbelievably busy that Sunday morning as many people were travelling by train. All wagons had standing passengers as the trains kept ferrying people on.

There were a lot of other people who did not even board the trains but who journeyed on foot. The pavements of the city were busy as crowds made their way. They were all making their way to the national war memorial monument, "arcul de triumf" in the city of Bucharest.

Around the monument was a heavy military presence. The streets in the area had been closed to traffic and so the streets were packed full of pedestrians. There were crowds lining the streets as far as the eye could see. People stood in strategic positions and lined themselves along the park near the monument. Small children were made to sit on the shoulders of their parents or other relatives.

Through some loud sound amplification systems one could hear what I learned were the songs about the pain of war. I remember hearing a song whose lyrics kept repeating,"doare". I understood the word meant "painful".

The military tanks came rolling through. Drummers and brass musicians played their music. The national guard stood at attention as the national president inspected them. The national anthem was sung while canons were being fired. Planes in impressive formations flew above and past the crowd. It was indeed a spectacular national parade.

Then as we were moving to the monument to explore a little and see the permitted sections of the monument, some smart TV crew spotted me among the crowds with my dark skin. Training their cameras on me they came to ask me why I was in this crowd and where I had come from.

Very quickly the reporters discovered that I could not even speak Romanian. So they switched to English and asked me a few questions. I don't recall much about this impromptu interview except that it was later broadcast to the nation of Romania on TV.

REFLECTION:

A friend who knew of the 1 December events took the trouble to indulge me and my children in what turned out to be an interesting event. I would never have known about it otherwise. The friend did not ask me to tell him if there was anything he could do for me. He was proactive and innovative. I think a grieving person should be pampered by friends and family. He or she may not even show much appreciation at the time or at all ever because of grief. But the help and kindness they get will go a long way to help them cope with the situation. We need to help them even though it seems hopeless to do so.

BLESSING:

May God bless you today. May your day be filled with His love.

49 A TOILET EXPERIENCE

**Man that is born of a woman is of few days, and full of trouble.
(Job 14:1)**

Among my good friends from Romania was one very kind man called
Tiberiu Koos (Tibi). From my early days in the Theology course Tibi came
to speak to me and made me feel respected. He made me feel as someone
who also belonged among the people there and not just a foreigner and
a stranger. He told me that some years back he had been to Africa on a
mission trip. Tibi later took me around to visit many places in the country
with my children. It was through contacts from Tibi that I ended up in the
church about which I relate the events on this story.

One of several occasions that he arranged for me to visit one congregation, I was invited to share my testimony as I had been invited to do
so in other places. This particular church in a village called Tatarani was
one just outside of the city of Ploiesti, Prahova. According to my archived
emails it was on 2nd July 2011 when I went to the church at the address
Calea Barcanesti nr. 757. I had not eaten any breakfast that morning before
I left the College campus in Bucharest. Everything seemed okay and normal
except that I had had an insect bite during the night as I slept. I had no idea
what the insect was and what its bite could cause, if anything.

The testimony was at some time after 11am and the congregation was
sitting and listening attentively to me speaking. On this particular occasion
Tibi himself was my interpreter as I addressed the people. The kids and I
had sung a song together which was a song of thankfulness for everything.
I had also sung a song, a solo, about taking up the cross and following Jesus
and I had expressed that I was accepting the challenge to follow Christ.
Not too long after I started speaking I experienced something I have ever
only experienced only in that church in Tatarani. First, I felt a very strong
pain in the stomach and asked the members to be praying for me. I also
felt dizzy while I spoke and I had to tell the congregation that I had not
eaten that morning. Someone brought out a jar of clear acacia honey with
a spoon for me to eat a little and hopefully get some energy. But I had to sit
down and try to continue speaking from a chair. Then suddenly I could not
continue talking because I needed to go to the toilet at once! I did not even

know where the toilets were (I was one for never needing to use any toilets till I return home). I was shown where the toilets were and when I got inside the toilet I felt so lost. I did not know how to use the toilet because in all my life and through all of my travels I had never seen any toilet like that before!

I got out of the toilet and looked for Tibi and timidly told him that I did not know how to use the toilet. Tibi was surprised by this because he thought being African I would have been familiar with the kind of toilet that was in Tatarani. Eventually I understood how I was to use it. It was one toilet commonly referred to as an Indian toilet or a squat toilet. I was well familiar with pit latrines and even bucket system toilets or squat toilets that had a larger hole on them not a little circle that was not much bigger in circumference than a standard tea mug. It had some fancy white floor area that seemed to me like only for standing on while passing water. I even took a photograph of the toilet as I had been so fascinated by it. Later I found out that this kind of toilet was even found as a pay-to-use toilet at the main train station in the capital city alongside other more common toilets. It was a toilet type included even in fancy modern buildings among the other toilets we usually use in the West and even in Africa.

After finally using the toilet, with suffering a bout of diarrhoea, I returned and completed my now abridged version of a testimony. I still have no idea where the stomach bug had come from. Yet I always remember the bug that stung me in the night and make a mental association with the stomach bug (I intend to make no pun of these similar words). Thankfully the illness did not persist beyond the loo visit.

REFLECTION:

My life took me through all kinds of experiences. Some things, such as my unexpected practical lesson about different toilet kinds, humorous as they may be show how God has a good sense of humour too. He enabled me to be among people who gave me some honey to supply my energy needs on the spot. He made me remember that I was not invincible even as he let me meet different situations on my journey to recovery. This was just one challenging incident among many smoother ones. Not all was cosy and rosy on my travels. It may be that not all is rosy and cosy for you neither.

BLESSING:

I pray that one day you will look back at the way things happened for you and be thankful for how things went. May you live with a positive mind and hope that one day things will become better for you.

50 A FIGHT WITH FURNITURE

The LORD is my strength and song, and he is become my salvation: he is my God, and I will prepare him an habitation; my father's God, and I will exalt him. (Exodus 15:2)

My social media archives take the credit for preserving the details of this story which took place on 10 November 2010. The setting of the event was the cafeteria of the Theology Institute at Strada Decebal, Cernica, Ilfov, Romania.

We had just sat down for our supper. At our table were just the three of us, my 6 year old son Vuyo, my 3 year old daughter Vuyiso and myself. I thought everything was okay until I felt some tension and distress as I saw that there were actually 4 chairs in total at the table and that somehow highlighted that we were not 4 anymore.

I quietly stood up and took away the chair and put in at another table. But Vuyo quickly asked, 'What did you do that for?'. I responded, 'I just don't want that chair there'. Smartly, he quickly said, 'Mummy should have been sitting on it isn't it daddy?'.

It became even harder for me to hide my tears now as I admitted that this was actually the reason why I had taken the chair away. But yet I think both kids did not see the tears on this occasion.

I was thankful to God just for the fact that I had managed to hide my tears because there otherwise would have been 3 weeping people at dinner. I was now really concerned about how much I kept on crying. It was even more distressful that when the kids saw me crying, they too would cry with me. So I was fighting hard to not cry anymore or at least not in front of them. 11 months after my wife died I was still bleeding with grief and even innocent furniture set me off into weeping. I tried hard to convince myself that I was now okay. But reality could not be fooled. Some may feel grief and deal with it in better ways than I did but I happen to be a very emotional person.

REFLECTION:

They say grief is as unique as people themselves are. Yet I hope that learning of my experiences can help you relate and hence feel better somewhat.

BLESSING:

May you, if and when you have your own empty chair experience be comforted to know it is normal. May God give you enough strength for today.

51 A GRIEVING CHILD

He healeth the broken in heart, and bindeth up their wounds. (Psalm 147:3)

Thou tellest my wanderings: put thou my tears into thy bottle: are they not in thy book? (Psalm 56: 8)

He was born in 2004 and was the first and most treasured baby of the family. He received all the attention a child could get and maybe a bit too much as the first child.

His development was well documented by his mother. Records of his first words were written in a diary. So were records about the appearance of his first teeth and first steps and so on.

On his birthdays some of his friends would come over to spend time with him. With other parents, discussions seemed to always be comparative about what their kids could now do against what Vuyo was able to do.

His initial reading abilities always caused our friends to marvel and suspect that he had memorised things and pretended to read and so was not actually reading in real time. As such, it always brought joy and pride to us as parents that our son was really gifted. Even when he went to start school, he was already way ahead of other children.

He had spent most of his time at home with his mother. Even as he had started going to school he was always eager to return home mostly to be with his mother. Although he was fond of playing with me when I was home, I was usually too busy or too tired to play as much with him as he would have liked to. So his mother was really the one to take the prize for giving him all the attention he needed. He was well loved and he knew that well.

On July 21st 2010, just 6 months after his mother's death, the usually brave young man was overcome with pain. It was in the evening, at bedtime that the 6 year old Vuyo, out of nowhere wept more painfully than usual. 'I want mummy,' he cried repeatedly. I tried to reason with him but he would not stop. He would not be consoled even by his little sister. In the end the same little sister also ended up joining the weeping. There was no more mummy to love them anymore! So, much to my distress, the two children cried themselves to sleep that night. Though deeply hurt, daddy managed to stay calm and strong for once.

REFLECTION:

Even for the children, the pain of death is real. We must never overlook their grief as it is as real as that of adults. I find encouragement in the knowledge that God sees our tears: Psalm 56:8 says He puts the tears in a bottle! I also believe the Bible when it says that God shall wipe away all tears.

BLESSING:

I pray that you too are a candidate for heaven. As I eagerly await the resurrection day, I hope that same hope of the resurrection gives you courage, peace and hope.

52 A BITTER-SWEET CHRISTMAS CAROL TIME

But even the very hairs of your head are numbered. Fear not therefore: ye are of more value than many sparrows. (Luke 12:7)

During my sojourn in Romania, my children attended a private Christian school. They fully integrated with other children and participated in all activities with my encouragement and support. Towards the end of 2011 in December there was an evening of Christmas carols at the Muntenia Conference in Bucharest. As all parents were invited and as my children were also participants I also made an appearance to witness the event and support it.

Vuyo happened to have a solo within one of the choir songs, "O Come All Ye Faithful". I so much looked forward to hearing him sing his solo and what was more thrilling was the fact that the Romanian kids were also singing in English.

At last the long awaited carol involving Vuyo's solo came. The choir started off by singing the first verse in harmony. Then started my son, loud, clear and refined on his solo. I was so thrilled to hear him singing. But right in the height of that thrill, and only a few seconds into his singing my brain injected a bitter thought. I had just remembered his mother and I was thinking of how she was not there to see all this performance and to hear her son singing. I could not hold back my tears!

At the back of the room, leading to the auditorium was a flight of stairs which appeared isolated and private enough for my emergency. I retreated to the stairs and sobbed so uncontrollably while I was facing the wall. That was so much for the hearing and support of my son's singing.

Eventually the crying stopped and the carols ended. Yet I do not remember much else about that night. Indeed the crying for my loss slowly but surely subsided over the years and I can confirm that I am now able to live without the deep pain that I experienced back then.

REFLECTION:

I thank God for the healing process. I know He can heal you too just as he healed me in many ways. Even your hair is numbered by the one who provides food for many sparrows. Today may be hard but in time even your pain will become less and less.

BLESSING:

May you have a blessed and wonderful day today that is filled with healing.

53 A CHILD WITH HOPE

And Jesus called a little child unto him, and set him in the midst of them, And said, Verily I say unto you, Except ye be converted, and become as little children, ye shall not enter into the kingdom of heaven. Whosoever therefore shall humble himself as this little child, the same is greatest in the kingdom of heaven. (Matthew 18:2-4)

In the month of May, in 2007, she was born and crowned the princess of the family at birth. She was born with eyes that were open as she began looking around the theatre, being the delivery room in which she took her first breath outside of the womb of her mother just a few minutes before midnight at the Great Western hospital (the same hospital that her mother died in later). I remember that May night all too well as I was in the delivery room too at her birth.

The girl was really the completion of her mother's dreams. Mandy had waited long for her to be born and I am sure if it had been up to her the first child should have been a girl then a boy after. She used to say that she could not wait to play with her girl as she would play with a doll. Before Vuyiso was born, her mum also said that she would enjoy doing and undoing many hairstyles on her, just like on a doll.

So when she was finally born, Mandy declared that she was now complete and with Vuyiso's arrival the Khanye family quartet was now complete. You could see proof of the joy from how many photographs she took of her baby. Even photographs with her brother, who bonded very well with his sibling were rather on the plenty side. Her very name Vuyiso means someone who makes you happy.

A lot of dolls quickly filled up the house and I thought the dolls quickly outnumbered the car toys in the house. But maybe I was biased. The day after her mother died I was sitting in the living room and talking to some friends who had come to visit me. A bubbly and innocent two year-old Vuyiso had been in another part of the house. Suddenly she showed up, clearly not understanding what had just happened in her jovial spirit.

As soon as I set my eyes on her I burst into tears. Not only did she, in my eyes, resemble her mother but just looking at her and thinking that she now had no mother was so painful I had to cry. And so I did cry, which was even more confusing to her because when she saw me she smiled. I did smile back but very briefly and then my smile instantly turned into tears.

Eventually Vuyiso learned about the resurrection. But yet she had a greater sense of urgency about it. Even as she added years to her life she still knew what she was waiting for. Yet she did not know why it had to be so long.

At the age of 5, on September 26, 2012, I suddenly heard a question being asked by Vuyiso. 'Daddy, why can't Jesus resurrect mummy now?' Then expressing her disappointment after clearly having been too patient for way too long the princess added, 'It's too long and I want the resurrection to happen now!'

How I wish I could tell her exactly how long it will be until the resurrection day comes! If only she knew how I too longed for that same day of resurrection. I could only try to keep her hoping. I gave her a hug and told her that it was indeed too long. I also wanted Jesus to resurrect mummy soon. But we just had to wait and nobody knows when Jesus will come. We all hope it will be soon.

REFLECTION:

The pain of watching my kids without a mother has always brought tears to my eyes. Somehow I have always felt more pain from looking at them than just from thinking of the situation. But over time I have learned that their pain is probably not as great as mine. In time, even my own pain gets lesser and lesser as the years go by.

BLESSING:

May God be your pain relief. May He diminish your pain and help you to live a versatile and joyous life in spite of tribulations.

54 MINGLING WITH THE SINGLES

Finally, brethren, whatsoever things are true, whatsoever things are honest, whatsoever things are just, whatsoever things are pure, whatsoever things are lovely, whatsoever things are of good report; if there be any virtue, and if there be any praise, think on these things. (Philippians 4:8)

I never had imagined that one day I would feel uncomfortable with being referred to by some commonly used and acceptable identity phrases like single parents. I never even imagined that I would become single again after I had been married and had children. So the term 'single parent' as it is commonly used was never a term that was worth me thinking any deeply about, until I became widowed yet being also a parent.

I first became alert to my new status as I completed application forms which I think were for passports. The section for marital status had 3 fields, single, married, divorced but not widowed. That omission made me feel excluded. From that moment onwards I became alert and sensitive about the status given to people.

I knew that I did not like to be referred to as a single parent at all. For me that term did not clarify exactly why I was single yet also a parent. I did not in any way look down on anyone who was single because of any other reason than widowhood. I just did not think widowed people should be grouped as single parents like everybody else. In the single parents group belonged widowed people, parents with kids born out of wedlock and divorced parents. It had been a noble thing to get married and I had been respected for it by those with higher standards of family values. Because of death I now felt my earned honour being snatched away from me.

At the end of 2011 I wrote down on December 28th, some of the other issues I had been forced to confront. I concluded that life can be funny and interesting at the same time. That my friends were still married and busy with their homes while I was no longer married. So I had to mingle with the unmarried. The unmarried mostly had no kids and households to look after; while I had two lovely angels and responsibility!

I had started to learn to be independent but at times it was so hard and painful. Yet I saw a brighter future and I was determined to journey onwards! So, I told my Facebook readers in conclusion, that everything would be fine in the end. That therefore if it was not yet fine, then it was not yet the end!

REFLECTION:

As the issue of singleness after being married before weighed down so heavily on me I thought it possible that other people may also find it unfair. There are too many unfair things in this life and many of them are beyond our control. There is however no reason to allow our minds to dwell on issues that do not help us in our well being. There is absolutely no need to fret and worry over things of no benefit. Focus on the good and those will help facilitate your healing process.

BLESSING:

Today may your mind stay tuned only to good things. May all bad news and unhelpful stories evade you today so your day may be delightful.

55 AN 'ANVELOPE' FOR WINTER

Look not every man on his own things, but every man also on the things of others. (Phillipians 2:4)

The fun that came as part of my stay in Romania sometimes came from some words that sounded familiar but yet whose meaning was so different. I already told the story of a magazine that was not what I expected but a shop.

The winter season had arrived and new legislation had recently been passed in parliament by the Romanian law making authorities. It was not as if I was an avid reader of Romanian law or a keen follower of Romanian news. I had friends, many friends who took upon themselves the trouble of informing me that they had just changed or were just about to change the tyres on their cars to winter tyres. They told me that winter tyres would make it easier to drive on snow. To make a stronger impact, they explained that in Romania snow could be as high as 2 metres.

So I got told all about tyres. The M+S inscription on tyres they said stood for mud and snow and so the tyres of that type were all season and usable in both winter and summer. This inscription, they said. would ensure that the police would leave me alone. But they added that all season tyres were not good enough for snow driving.

Next I got told about a snowflake symbol also inscribed on tyres. Tyres marked with a snowflake were the best as they were winter tyres. These tyres would also not attract any fines (amenda) from the police. The new legislation was that it was now compulsory in Romania for all cars to have either winter tyres or all season tyres from October till March (or thereabouts).

Now I was convinced that I needed to go tyre shopping. Someone in the class sought to help me. They all knew that I would not be able to go alone to search for tyres without speaking any Romanian. So they announced that they were looking for someone to go with me to buy some 'anvelope'. I immediately objected and protested that I did not want any envelopes but tyres.

But it was another vocabulary moment for me. I found out that a tyre in Romanian is called an "anvelope" which sounds almost identical in pronunciation with envelope.

REFLECTION:

It was not all doom and gloom on a daily basis in my world. Life did go on and jokes and ambiguous words learned and clarified. I still had my moments of mostly private pain and grief but much of the time I spent trying to focus on life rather than on death. I am confident that in time the same will be for you even without any envelope issues in your way.

BLESSING:

Today may you be blessed and distracted from pain because of enjoying the beauty that surrounds you. Have a great day today.

56 I CAN RAISE THEM FOR YOU

Be not forgetful to entertain strangers: for thereby some have entertained angels unawares. (Hebrews 13:2)

My theology class group was a mixture of people of different levels of involvement in the ministry of the gospel. Some were novices in life itself, having just completed high school and doing the course just because it was a course. I know this to be true because once a professor asked about it and got responses to that effect.

Others of my colleagues were involved in other careers already and following other disciplines but looking to change. They looked to change because they felt a higher calling and wanted to work for God.

My other colleagues were already serving pastors with their own districts consisting of at least 2 or more congregations. They had already completed their bachelor's degree and were now furthering into a masters degree. Yet others were serving as pastoral interns under the guidance of senior pastors.

During the school year, in the middle of a term there is often a week of recess on which children stay home which is referred to as half term break. The half term breaks often occurred at times that did not coincide with my College half term breaks at all ever. And on the children's half term I still needed to attend classes. So during my classes that commenced at the same time as half term for my children's school I was often found sitting in my College class with my children. At times they would get a little restless from the length of time they needed to remain in the class but mostly they were just fine and patient and calm.

It was after one of the half term breaks that one classmate approached me. He said that he had already spoken to his wife about it and was now coming to me because they wanted to try to help me look after the children. His offer was to take my children away to their home in a town called Aiud, somewhere in Transylvania in the Alba county of Romania where he was serving as a pastor. Their plan was to raise them for me so that I would not have the burden of looking after them. He said though they were not rich, they would provide them with all the food and clothing as needed and share their home with them as if it were their own home. I would not need to contribute anything at all.

I was deeply moved by the kind gesture but I could not let my children go away from me. So I thanked the kind brother for his gesture and I kept the kids with me on campus. The brother and his wife really wanted to welcome my angels into their home.

REFLECTION:

Even in my sorrow and grief, people kept on making considerations to help me with my affairs of life. I believe it was God who moved them to be compassionate on me. I was a stranger living in a far country and yet was afforded so much attention and care together with my children. God always cares for His children and in many different ways too. At times we are too engrossed in our own sorrows to recognise God is working to relieve our predicaments.

BLESSING:

May you have a peaceful and calm day today. Be still and know that He is God.

57 MAKE A GIFT FOR YOUR MUM

Therefore all things whatsoever ye would that men should do to you, do ye even so to them: for this is the law and the prophets. (Matthew 7:12)

Days of honouring or celebrating a cause are very good at helping people to look forward to something in their lives. Take for instance the Christmas period. During the Christmas season many people can be seen with a genuine smile on their faces which otherwise is absent for most of the year. Also, the amount of money spent on Christmas presents, dinners and family unions is phenomenal. All this by people who mostly want nothing to do with Christ!

Other days that have a prominent presence in the calendar include easter and then days that do not have holidays associated with them like Remembrance Day and Halloween as well as Valentine's day.

Invariably businesses do profit from the existence of all these days. People do not seem to mind spending their money around or for those days too. In fact, many people plan ahead about their expenditures on the days before they come. Sometimes the planning is done a whole year before the days come.

One of such special days in the UK is called mothering Sunday or mother's day. It usually falls on or around the 30th of March. In March, I think it was in 2010, I visited my younger sister in the city of Portsmouth. This would have been just 3 months after I lost my wife to cancer.

On Saturday, the Sabbath day, we went to the Portsmouth Seventh-day Adventist church to worship. I attended the children's class during the time that the church members usually splits into small groups for Bible discussions.

There was a very lively group of children with an enthusiastic teacher. She asked all the children to say what they wanted to thank their mothers for. The next task was that each child was going to be to make a gift out of some craft material for their mother. As soon as she said each child was to say what they wanted to thank their mothers for, I saw the reaction of uneasiness in my children and that look at me that seemed to be trying to tell me, 'Say something daddy.' So, choking away my tears, I explained to the lovely lady that their mother died.

The teacher had not done anything wrong at all. She had not even been insensitive. In fact she quickly suggested the gift could be for an aunt or someone in the family. It is not easy to think of every possible situation that can hurt someone else. It is equally not easy to imagine what of the things considered normal can trigger a painful reaction.

REFLECTION:

Being aware of all the various triggers of pain in grief can help prepare to avoid hurting others. But not everyone who has not personally experienced grief can be alert about grief pain triggers. Even with those who are aware it can just slip up on them and cause unintended pain. As a bereaved person you should expect anything to trigger your pain. This includes things that have never caused pain to anyone else. We all grieve differently and not all variations can be documented.

BLESSING:

May God be your shield from all pain today. May anything turned against you today not hurt you at all. Have a wonderful day today.

58 THEY NEVER COOKED ON SABBATH

And he said unto them, This is that which the LORD hath said, To morrow is the rest of the holy sabbath unto the LORD: bake that which ye will bake to day, and seethe that ye will seethe; and that which remaineth over lay up for you to be kept until the morning. (Exodus 16:23)

To the law and to the testimony: if they speak not according to this word, it is because there is no light in them. (Isaiah 8:20)

I grew up in a Sabbath keeping family. That means when the sun set on Friday evening we were having our Sabbath welcoming prayers and joyfully singing praises to God. All household duties were done before sunset on Friday because on Sabbath we were not to be busy doing things like sweeping, mopping, cooking, washing, polishing shoes, ironing clothes and even repairing torn clothes or replacing buttons on the clothes. The Sabbath being made for mankind meant that mankind would benefit from resting from all daily chores and enjoy fellowship with the creator who himself gave an example of ceasing his creating activities and spent time with his created beings Adam and Eve. The Sabbath was God's memorial of creation which we are given a chance every week to prepare well for.

When the Israelites were out in the wilderness where there was no food, God provided manna for them. He deliberately omitted the provision of manna on Sabbath. Surely that was not so much work for God to just let fresh new manna fall down from heaven on Sabbath morning. But there was no manna to pick on Sabbath because the Israelites had been instructed to pick a double portion of it on Friday so that on Sabbath they would spend time in fellowship with God their maker.

I was first shocked to find cooking taking place at a Seventh-day Adventist institution that I attended in Zimbabwe. There I was told that it was impossible to cater for all the hundreds of students who lived there unless food was actually cooked on Sabbath. It was a hard thing for me to understand that the very institution where pastors were trained at was violating the law of God and giving excuses for it. Later I understood that the church has been infiltrated by the enemy in the form of humans, some of whom belong to the Jesuit order. These Jesuits are possibly within our ranks now from the pastoral offices, the lowest offices of administration to the very highest administration in our church headquarters. I have personally witnessed unquestionable evidence of this and I know of at least one individual who joined the church under false pretenses for the purpose of this said infiltration. Sadly many members are so gullible and are fooled by some logical arguments that come from some of these well spoken wolves in sheep's clothing. Even I myself know that I am not smart enough to detect the deception so smoothly done in a manner akin to that of the serpent to Eve.

When I went to visit the Institute of Theology Training at Cernica in Romania I was pleasantly well surprised. The cafeteria closed after lunch on Friday with students being given packed meals to last them through the Sabbath hours. The staff at the cafeteria also got to keep the Sabbath holy and fellowship with other members. The next meal served in the cafeteria was breakfast on Sunday morning.

When I participated in Sabbath meals served at the various churches or even homes that I visited in Romania the food served there was never cooked on Sabbath. It was warmed when needed but never prepared from scratch on Sabbath.

My arrival into the United Kingdom gave me a serious shock and challenge to my faith. I found that not only did the Sabbath keeping brethren cook on Sabbath but they even had kitchen facilities built into the church premises for the purpose. Worse still, I even discovered that some go shopping and buy food on the Sabbath! When I commented about it I got castigated for it and in the end I took my family home for lunch every Sabbath to eat our delicious meals that we had made ready before sunset on Friday. It was even a bigger blessing for us because we always took a different guest or a family of guests to share our meals with us and enjoyed the fellowship at home.

Exodus 16:23 expounds on the commandment of Exodus 20:8 in which God commands us to remember the Sabbath day to keep it holy. We can be left in no doubt about just how to keep the Sabbath holy after reading Exodus 16:23. Jesus says, "If you love me, keep my commandments" (John 14:15) and keeping the commandments will not make us love Him. We should keep them because we love Him. And yet if we do not keep them it implies that we do not love Him. Perhaps the forgetting of how to keep the Sabbath holy is the reason why the commandment starts with "remember".

Even those whose denomination name prides itself as the keepers of the Sabbath seem to have forgotten how to keep the Sabbath holy.

REFLECTION:

Being in a place where I felt that the Sabbath was being observed and kept according to the commandments of God was a breath of fresh air to my soul and helped me deal with my grief. I would like to think that it did a lot of therapy to my mind and gave me peace to know that I was among God's people who diligently kept His laws. (Of course there are some who have never known or understood about the Sabbath and God, who is a fairer judge than man, will save them according to the light they have received.)

For me, the Sabbath gave me an oasis of peace that helped with my healing process. If you have not experienced the blessings of the Sabbath I urge you to seek knowledge and ask God to give you more light on the subject.

BLESSING:

May peace be with you and may you determine in your heart that you will obey God rather than man who changed the keeping of Sabbath to suggest that any other day was okay. God says not one jot of the law shall pass away even though earth and heaven may do. The Sabbath is a major part of the law which is elaborated well enough in the Bible for you to understand. May you be blessed abundantly and enjoy fellowship with God today and always.

59 MY WIFE CAN LOOK AFTER THE KIDS

As we have therefore opportunity, let us do good unto all men, especially unto them who are of the household of faith. (Galatians 6:10)

While classmates and schoolmates can be seen to take notice of their colleague and have a concern for his welfare, college administrators and professors may not be thought to do so too. The last thing I could have expected was any college staff to notice the plight of a simple student and his children on campus.

The student population at the institute of theology training was not that big. There could have been several hundreds of students but I think a thousand could be the absolute maximum that we were at the time I attended.

The institute offered degrees and diplomas in education, social work as well as theology. There were undergraduate and graduate programs taught by a mix of academics. The language for tuition delivery at the institute was predominantly Romanian except perhaps for the English courses and the masters degree for which I was enrolled.

I had been to the kindergarten school that was housed in a wooden house located at the bottom of the hill near the entrance of the institute. The purpose for my visit was simply to search for a vacancy for my daughter to attend the kindergarten.

A few days or even weeks later I was approached by one professor. How he had got the information about my enquiry at the kindergarten I do not know, but he was interested in helping me find a solution for my children.

When I attended the institute, Professor Florin Laiu was a theology professor. He could speak English but he was not one of the professors on the program I was doing. My professors usually either came straight from Andrews University in the USA or were adjunct professors of Andrews University and other places like Bogenhofen College in Austria.

So professor Laiu, even though he was not teaching me, apparently was also watching me and the kids with compassion. He offered for his wife to provide me with childcare and I think they also offered kindergarten care for my daughter. Nonetheless it was a gesture that I noted and was thankful for even though in the end I sent both children to the Adventist school, Mihai Ionescu, which was in the city of Bucharest. There the siblings were admitted into kindergarten and school respectively.

REFLECTION:

The kindness I was shown, without doing anything to deserve it, shows me that God still works via His people. From so many different people and about pretty much the same aspect of taking care of my kids came the offer to help me. The people involved had no knowledge about each other's offer to me. That to me is too much of a coincidence and for that reason I believe the same hand of the Lord that moved the hearts of different people to help me can't do the same for you.

BLESSING:

May God open the windows of heaven and pour out many blessings on you today!

60 MY MUM CAN HELP YOU WITH THE KIDS

"Fear thou not; for I am with thee: be not dismayed; for I am thy God: I will strengthen thee; yea, I will help thee; yea, I will uphold thee with the right hand of my righteousness." (Isaiah 41:10)

It is easy to imagine that only those who were my classmates looked compassionately at me as they knew about my circumstances. But that assumption would be so wrong. A lot of people who really had nothing to do with me were somehow touched by something.

It may be that I looked exceedingly sorrowful or like someone whose life looked hopeless. I really do not know how I was then except that I was in pain and I was truly mourning. Nonetheless I was trying as best as I could to be brave and strong and move ahead. In my mind I knew very well that there was no use of dwelling, through all my days, in misery about a painful loss that could not be reversed.

My children on the other hand appeared to have been tougher than me. They were playing and having fun to the limit, with their many friends. They seemed to be speaking fluent Romanian with their friends. And as they spoke well enough in Romanian, adults, not just children, tended to speak to them too.

Some of the young adults who spoke to them were students on the campus. Many of the young ladies who were students at the college were friends with my children. Among these young ladies was someone who came from Tiganesti, Teleorman called Florina Movileanu.

Florina had heard the story of the children and that they had lost their mother. She loved taking care of children and playing with them and I think had she not been a student she may have sought some way to look after them. This I say because one day, out of nowhere Florina wanted to speak to me.

All that Florina wanted to say to me was that she had talked to her mother on my behalf and on behalf of the children. Her mother apparently also loved children and had a lot of experience with looking after children. As it was not possible for Florina herself to look after them, Florina's mother had agreed to take my children to her home in Teleorman and look after them there for me.

Of course I was not about to part with my little ones but the gesture touched me. And I will always thankfully remember Florina for her kindness and selfless effort to try to help me.

REFLECTION:

Somehow the people around me were moved to want to help me. They were desirous to support and be of use to the children. I am of the strong opinion that the kindness they showed was God given. As such I do believe that God will send you the most suitable people at the right time to help you get through your situation.

BLESSING:

May you today not only know but feel the love of God. Have a wonderful day.

61 BECOMING A VITAMIN C PROPONENT

Give, and it shall be given unto you; good measure, pressed down, and shaken together, and running over, shall men give into your bosom. For with the same measure that ye mete withal it shall be measured to you again. (Luke 6:38)

When confronted with a choice between conventional and natural medical intervention to the cancer diagnosis, my late wife Mandy decided to choose natural medicine. She read books, web sites and watched videos and documentaries that covered a lot of natural treatments that included herbs, oils, foods and water therapies. Naturally I was there reading alongside and also learning the many different methods of treatment that existed for the reversal and treatment of cancer and for the boosting of the immune system.

After she died, anyone could be forgiven for thinking that I would have given up any faith in the natural treatments that I had learned about. It would appear logical that since the treatments did not preserve her life then they do not work and so they should be done away with. By contrast, I learned so many things that I was convinced that if only I had known them all before, the cancer would have been reversed in its early stages or even prevented from developing.

Of course some things I learned about natural remedies did not only have cancer as their target illness but other illnesses. I learned about the power of vitamin C overdose. Firstly, I learned that cancer cells cannot survive in an alkaline environment and hence for any cancer to survive the blood be very acidic. When Vitamin C is allowed to flood the bloodstream then cancer cells die. Unfortunately the process of overdosing vitamin C orally causes diarrhoea. The only way to effectively administer vitamin C therapy is intravenously. The administration of intravenous vitamin C becomes a clinical procedure which is not easy for everyone to perform. Also the rate of flow needs expertise from people who have a deeper understanding of electrolytes and the functions of the human anatomy. A clinic in London called the Dove Clinic does the vitamin C treatments as do other private medical practices that are scarce in the UK but easier to find in places such as Mexico. There is an institute known as the Linus Pauling

Institute that has done some scientific studies about vitamin C from whose web site a lot of information can be obtained.

For me, in my simple way and layman's understanding, I began to use vitamin C that I bought from Holland and Barrett, the natural products chain store in the UK. I began to keep a supply of vitamin C for my family's use in times of attacks by the common cold. I saw miraculous recovery after miraculous recovery from using vitamin C with my family. They too now know what to use when they catch a cold.

REFLECTION:

The loss of a loved one through illness (and even through any other way) is always devastating. Yet the ones who remain, in the case of death by illness, may pick some very useful information that can potentially help them and others in their lives in future. I would therefore encourage people to share what they know about the illness and help others. Sharing not only benefits the recipient but also the one who is sharing the information.

BLESSING:

It is always a joyful thing to give and is more blessed than to receive. May your day be filled with blessings today.

62 PLEASE TURN OFF THE LIGHT

"Peace I leave with you, my peace I give unto you: not as the world giveth, give I unto you. Let not your heart be troubled, neither let it be afraid." (John 14:27)

Back in 2010 when I went to Romania for the initial fact-finding visit I asked the people at the College to help me find a reliable childminder who could speak English. My Spanish childminder, about whom I discuss in a different story, was about to leave as her 3 months were about to end. She needed to go back to university. So I had Nicoleta Moisoiu come to Swindon to take care of the children so I could continue working in Oxford.

The children loved her and she was very good with taking care of them. She also helped to keep the house tidy as well as keep the children busy with fun activities when they were not at school. She would take them to the park to play as well as do some crafts and play games at home. She would get them to do colouring in colouring books and she herself was very good at colouring and would colour the books with the children. She kept written records of what she was doing on a daily basis as well as what the children were achieving or finding difficult to do. Having her in the house was very useful in that the grief of the children, and also my own grief to some degree, was cushioned greatly.

I began to notice however, that in the evenings, after the children had gone to sleep and after she too had supposedly also gone to bed, she never seemed to turn off the light in her room. If that was not part of my electricity bill to pay, in addition to her wages, then perhaps that would not have mattered much. But as it appeared to be ongoing night by night I decided to intervene. I asked her one night why she was not turning off the light in her room and she responded by saying that she was awake and still reading. So I left her alone and went to sleep.

At some point, on a different morning I woke up around 4am and I found her light was on and later I asked her why it was not switched off. She again told me that she was reading. On a completely different night I woke up around 2am and still her light was on. When challenged, she still insisted that she was reading. So I asked Nicoleta to explain to me why she was reading all night and how it seemed that she was not sleeping at night. As much as I was happy with her help in the house I really could not afford to have high electricity bills because of her. Nicoleta told me that she usually slept for only about 2 hours every night. She could not sleep at all otherwise and so she indeed would be reading all the time and every night.

Now that I had heard the full story of why the light was not being switched off, it was time to seek a solution. I had spent many months not too long before in trying to help my late wife find a solution to breast cancer. So I figured insomnia would probably now be just a walk in the park with the kind of resources at my disposal. I asked Nicoleta if she was willing to try any of the natural solutions I would find for her and she agreed.

One of the most unimpressive remedies I had come across before, was castor oil. When I first heard of its use I even detested the very idea of trying it. But at this juncture I had been converted and I was convinced that it works. So I let Nicoleta know about this remedy and got her to apply it over her eyebrows as she went to sleep. The result was that from the very next day I had a problem in that Nicoleta was not waking up on time anymore and in fact she was so late I had to wake her before I went to work. She began to sleep so long that she would even be late taking the children to school! But as long as she applied castor oil on her eyes, she was able to sleep at night.

REFLECTION:

Bereavement has many unknowns and many unknowables that cannot be prepared for in advance. One thing that I learned is to take each day as it comes. Things will be different, yes, but to keep focused on never giving up on life is key. Otherwise in bereavement it is easy (and often does happen) to fall into depression. The mind can go into a negative spiral which leads only downward, when not checked. It is okay to grieve but the grieving person does need to think of living into the future not remain in the dungeons of pain. From the pain of sickness and loss came knowledge about natural remedies and one thing that happened for me is that I was delighted to help others discover how they could use natural remedies for their problems. Helping others helped me to a degree, to remain sane as I was busy helping not only just mourning.

BLESSING:

May today be a day of hope for you. May you find peace in God and determine in your heart that life is still worth living.

63 A BOOK DELIVERED TOO LATE

Therefore, my beloved brethren, be ye stedfast, unmoveable, always abounding in the work of the Lord, forasmuch as ye know that your labour is not in vain in the Lord. (1 Corinthians 15:28)

I learned that apart from insomnia, there are many other conditions that castor oil can remedy, including re-balancing of electrolytes to correct hormonal imbalances and menopausal problems. It can remedy anxieties and depression, gallbladder stones, infections and is useful in, dare I say even cancer! But I am not a clinician so I only share my experiences and what I found from research. You should do your own diligent research and not just accept my claims as facts. My first knowledge about castor oil came about as I was trying to help my wife fight against cancer.

I had been spending literally days and nights researching about anything and everything natural that I could find to combat breast cancer. Mandy's condition had gotten worse and the tests she had recently done had shown signs of metastasis (spreading to other parts of the body) to the liver. My brain was the busiest that it had ever been all my life. I had to find a solution for her and I was confident that there was something out there somewhere in the natural world that works.

I sent out emails to all the lifestyle centres I had ever heard about. I searched even for those I had never heard of before and contacted them too. Among them all I received a few replies from some kind and empathetic people who were willing to try to assist me. Among them was a man called Mamon Wilson of Centurion Ministries in the USA whom I learned had reversed one in every two terminal conditions that doctors had given up on. Effectively he had saved people's lives who had been sent home to die as there was no hope for them anymore.

Mamon took the trouble to prepare a new treatment plan for Mandy. He customised all sorts of herbs and supplements that I had never heard of before in my life. I acquired pretty much everything that was in the list even though I had to order some things from overseas. But I was not just buying and using things without seeking an understanding of how they worked. I searched hard and wide for information about each item on the list.

One of the items on the treatment plan was called castor oil. That to me was one of the most unthinkable ideas that an oil applied to the breast and the abdomen could help in any way to deal with cancer and effectively (being my first time to ever hear of castor oil). So I searched the web for anything I could find and I came across a very old out of print book titled "The Oil that Heals" by Edgar Cayce. I ordered it immediately and moved on to researching the other things that were on the treatment plan.

As the illness grew even worse, one of the things we wanted to do was reduce the number of items being used to treat Mandy. This was because she seemingly was not coping well anymore with all the things that were being done to her as treatment. Castor oil treatment was never something convincing to me or even Mandy herself and her sister who was also around. So we reduced its intense usage.

It was at the end of January of 2010 when I returned from Mandy's funeral in Botswana with the kids. Just a few days after our arrival the book I had ordered finally arrived. Sitting on my bed in Swindon, I wept bitterly as I read the book and learned so many things that the oil had been successfully tested on by a physician. I wished I had known details about how castor oil worked before.

REFLECTION:

What I wept and regretted about was that I had lacked knowledge. There will be some regret about one thing or another in all of us in bereavement. It is important however to let it pass and learn from the experience. Life goes on but yet can be unpleasant if we glue our minds onto the regrettable past.

BLESSING:

Let nothing hold you back today from moving onwards and focusing on the future. May God help you stay positive today and always.

64 ANOINTING THE TUMMY WITH OIL

The following is just an account of what happened and should not be taken as medical advice or guidance for anyone. If you do as I did you then it is at your own risk and I will not be held responsible or liable for your actions.

If any of you lack wisdom, let him ask of God, that giveth to all men liberally, and upbraideth not; and it shall be given him. But let him ask in faith, nothing wavering. For he that wavereth is like a wave of the sea driven with the wind and tossed. (James 1:5,6)

On the second week of January in 2014 a Facebook friend in the USA posted a status message stating a request for prayers as she was unwell. I did pray for her but I also inquired about what her specific problem was as I felt that I could possibly make some useful suggestions.

It turned out that among other things, she was suffering from lack of sleep. She told me that she could only sleep for a maximum of 3 hours at night. So I told her what I knew about castor oil and sleep!

The use of what is referred to as 'castor oil packs' is well known among users of natural remedies for their potency. There is a myriad of sources of how to prepare and use the packs ranging from websites, internet forums and YouTube videos. Briefly though, all that the use of packs entails is placing a flannel cloth soaked in castor oil (but not dripping, for the sake of preventing a mess) over the abdomen area. The cloth should preferably be wide enough to cover the left and right sides of the abdomen but even if it is not, at least to cover the liver which is to the right hand-side.

The cloth is secured into place by a bandage around the entire waist/lower back. This can then be covered with cling film (from the roll of kitchen plastic cling film) to prevent oil soiling the sheets. In fact old sheets and towels are recommended for this treatment as castor oil stains are usually irremovable.

The final step is to place a heating pad or hot water bottle over the castor oil pack to increase the temperature of the oil on the abdomen. It should be left in place for between 2 and 3 hours but my experiences with several different people is that even leaving it overnight is just fine.

So I told my friend about the oil. How to anoint the eyes and I also detailed how it had apparently relieved my mother's arthritis pain on her knees. I was delighted to know that she was going to try the oil that very evening.

Naturally I was eager to hear about the result and if the suggestion was helpful at all for her. On 9th January 2014 at 03:36hrs in her very own words my friend sent me a message that said, "Last night I slept like a baby for 6 hrs! That was great! I apply it to the bottom of my feet as well. Going to do a wrap for my daughters knees for her arthritis."

REFLECTION:

The procedure described above of applying castor oil packs over the liver is recommended for a long list of conditions. It is not invasive and has no known contraindications. It could potentially help in dealing with stress and anxiety that are characteristic of bereavement. The procedure could be tried by anyone, even those who feel well. The sum effect of its use is a feeling of calmness and relaxation. To the naysayers I would ask, "What harm is it to apply a massage oil on your skin?" Is there any risk in trying it then sharing your results with others as one who knows the results first hand and not as a third party? You decide. If you are concerned then perhaps check with your doctor but chances are your doctor did not study about castor oil in medical school. I am just sharing my experiences and lessons learned in order to help someone else.

BLESSING:

May God give you the wisdom to distinguish between nonsense and sense and may your day be full of delight today.

65 OILY EYES

The following is a description of attempts with mixed results of both apparent success and apparent failure. I share just to show lessons learned from my experience. Your discretion is called upon to decide how useful or not, this information is. For the record, I advise you to always seek the guidance of a competent optometrist. I take no responsibility for anybody's actions that resemble anything described in my writing.

Because thou sayest, I am rich, and increased with goods, and have need of nothing; and knowest not that thou art wretched, and miserable, and poor, and blind, and naked: I counsel thee to buy of me gold tried in the fire, that thou mayest be rich; and white raiment, that thou mayest be clothed, and that the shame of thy nakedness do not appear; and anoint thine eyes with eyesalve, that thou mayest see. (Revelation 3:17, 18)

Early in the year 2011, while attending college in Romania I learned from one of my classmates that she had been experiencing some chronic problems with her eyes. This was when I had recently read a book about castor oil by Edgar Cayce called 'The Oil that Heals'. I suggested she tries the oil, just a few drops at a time, for her eyes too and she said she would. A few days later she told me that the oil had been so helpful and she just could not believe it after trying so many other eye remedies before. I simply noted this remark and kept it in mind for when I would need it myself or suggest it to another person who could use it.

Sometime later I felt that my overuse of the computer was taking a toll on my sight. So I decided to have a go at the oil on my own eyes and indeed I found an amazing relief resulting from putting some little drops of castor oil into the eyes. My worst challenge, however, was how to place the drops into the eyes. Ideally I needed a tiny dispenser for the oil or at least someone else to administer the required drops of oil. Since I had neither, I used my finger to anoint my eyes and allow some of the oil get inside the eyes. This not only had the effect of relaxing my eyes but also that of making me sleepy.

About two or so years later, upon hearing of my conviction about castor oil, my mother-in-law asked if she could use it on her eyes too. I asked what her eye problem was and she said there were some black spots that were beginning to appear and that she was now seeing some fogginess. For her the problem was also that she did not have anyone who could put the oil into her eyes as she mainly lived alone. So occasionally, whenever she got someone visiting her who could help her put the oil she asked them. Apparently with this irregular use of random oil application, in roughly 2 weeks both the fog and the black spots disappeared.

I understand also, from a lifestyle centre owner in the USA that the oil could also dissolve cataracts in the eyes and potentially restore sight to the blind! I thought this was a bit of a stretch but I have not had anyone trying it who had gone blind. For that the dosage is 2 drops in each eye every evening before bed for just 1 week.

My very own mother has had surgery done in one eye to remove cataracts. She has successfully tried castor oil for many things that I told her to except for her eye problems. Either she may have severe and irreparable damage in her eyes as she is almost aged 80, or the remedy has been over-praised on this aspect. I would really like to hear back from anyone who has tried using castor oil particularly for cataracts and confirms results from their own personal experience.

So there has been both apparent success and failure to achieve results. All I have done is report honestly about both.

REFLECTION:

Today's account of events is simply just one of many that occurred along my own road to recovery from grief. It may be miles away from the experience of any other person's but yet it was my experience. So I say just keep your head up and determinedly live your life, learn new things that are helpful for you and others as well as that can give you some distraction from focusing on your loss.

BLESSING:

May God lift all your burdens and sorrows today and replace them with joy and peace.

66 ALLERGY COMPLETELY DEFEATED

The following is a description of actual and real things that happened in my own mother's life. I share the information here to show lessons learned from experience and not to give a prescription for anyone. Your discretion is called upon to decide how useful or not, this information is. I take absolutely no responsibility for anybody's actions that resemble anything described in my writing.

Bless the LORD, O my soul: and all that is within me, bless his holy name. Bless the LORD, O my soul, and forget not all his benefits: Who forgiveth all thine iniquities; who healeth all thy diseases; Who redeemeth thy life from destruction; who crowneth thee with lovingkindness and tender mercies; Who satisfieth thy mouth with good things; so that thy youth is renewed like the eagle's. (Psalms 103:1-5)

There are certain problems in life that have to do with health that in the distant past I would have never imagined I could even think to make any difference about. I would normally have just sat back and let the doctors do and say as they think and as they know how. This is in spite of the fact that sometimes even they admit that they don't have any idea what to do for some things. And they usually say things like, "Let's try this for 10 days and then see how it goes then review." The problems whose solutions are unknown are a source of great distress and deep anxiety for many. The distress is deeper when such problems affect our immediate family members, our loved ones.

Back in Zimbabwe, Africa, my mother was experiencing severe acute allergy problems with a swelling face after eating so many different kinds of food. She could no longer enjoy eating corn or watermelon, a delicacy that only myself and her used to enjoy in our family while everyone else was not interested in it. She now literally had a long list of foods that she was allergic to. For the allergy, there was no solution in sight.

Food had become so dangerous to her that she had been rushed to the hospital many times after allergic reactions that occurred just after eating something. Some food reactions took literally seconds to deform her face with swelling. The worst ones were when her tongue got so swollen that it was literally almost choking her. Only emergency injections and medication brought the swelling down.

She had been to doctors and had had tests done and food allergy tests with needles poking and different foods being added to the list of danger for her. This was obviously not ideal and I had to research more about what she could do. Meanwhile, based on my experience obtained from my dying wife's natural treatments and based on my new understanding of the body, Besides recommending a plant based diet, I told my mother that she needed to cleanse and purify her blood. I told her one simple method was to simply juice beetroots and carrots and drink them together every morning before breakfast. I said these things and never took them that seriously myself as a definitive solution. I was still looking for answers to the problem. But my mother took it very seriously and did as I said.

So one morning a month or so later, as I was telling her about a way that could be used to boost immunity for someone else (was talking of vitamin C), she suddenly said, "Oh, you told me something amazing that time you said I should drink carrot juice and beetroot juice mixed together." She said that since the time she started drinking it she had not had any swelling at all ever and could now eat the same foods that used to cause swelling and yet she remained just fine. What was even more exciting was that she said that she had been sharing this information with other people that suffered from allergy and they too got HEALED! In fact she said that some of them jokingly said to her, "You are the one that had bewitched me in the first place and now you have restored my health!" There could be no better news for a son to hear than the fact that he helped his own mother to get healed! I praise God for His healing power and His imparted wisdom.

REFLECTION:

Look back at your own situation and search deep and hard for something useful. My bereavement was severe and my loss indescribable. But my knowledge of solutions to some ailments which I picked up in my tribulation is priceless as you may agree if you are benefiting from what I have written. It may not always be obvious that what you know is unknown and useful to others. Still, take it from me, sharing is one of the most satisfying things you could ever experience. So as and when you feel ready and able, I encourage you to share your unique and helpful knowledge and experience with others.

BLESSING:

May radiance and peace from our Almighty God above fill your soul today.

67 OILY TEETH AND GUMS

The following is an account of reality. None of it should be taken as a prescription to anyone. I will not be held responsible for any attempts by anyone to replicate my experience. For any issues with your oral hygiene please consult your stomatologist.

Thy teeth are like a flock of sheep that are even shorn, which came up from the washing; whereof every one bear twins, and none is barren among them. (Song of Solomon 4: 2.)

One day I was talking to my mother on the phone when I asked her if she had discovered any useful and innovative ways to use castor oil from the book (The Oil that Heals) or by her own experimentation. She told me about how my nephew was suffering from a toothache one weekend and how she had applied castor oil directly onto the decayed tooth. She said the pain went away and never came back. She said she would have still wanted to take him to the dentist but not for pain but just a filling to restore the tooth. But the lad had refused.

About two or so Sundays later, my daughter woke up with a toothache and she could not even eat any food. Being a Sunday. I had a very hard time getting her through the day with no access to dentists. Then I remembered my mum's use of castor oil and decided to try it. I applied it onto her tooth overnight with a piece of cotton wool and the next morning I was literally shaken as I observed that she now had a big swollen cheek.

I hid my terror and shock and acted as calmly as I could. I gave her some super-high dosage of vitamin C and placed a small castor oil drenched piece of gauze in her mouth between her tooth and her cheek. I also put an oil-soaked piece of flannel on the outside of the cheek and secured it into place. The good thing was that, in spite of the swelling she said that she could now eat without any pain on the tooth but only from the gum when pressed.

There was only a very slight improvement by the next morning with regards to swelling after a repetition of the treatment of the previous night. I decided that it still would be best to bring down the infection first before going to visit the dentist for either a filling or an extraction as the dentists would then decide best what to do.

Meanwhile, I had a root canal treatment that had left me with an incurable infection just beneath my nose and above the upper lip. Antibiotics had been used but they had failed to resolve the pain. So I lived with this chronic pain for about 5 years. Fortunately, I only felt the pain when I applied pressure on the affected area. In the region of the pain I also had what felt like a little bump way above the gums. On the gum area just above the culprit tooth had been a kind of pimple that occasionally grew big and when I applied pressure on it it popped and released a little bit of blood and some pus.

On the first night that I tried using castor oil on my daughter's tooth I also placed a gauze with castor oil inside my own mouth above the problematic tooth. The greatest surprise for me, the next morning, was that I could now press the painful region and feel a significantly lower pain than I had felt in years! I was well impressed and I really had not expected to find my daughter's mouth so scarily swollen.

I examined my daughter's gum and thought I had found out what the problem was. I saw what I thought was a big new tooth growing next to the old decayed tooth. I arranged an appointment with a dentist for an extraction of what I believed to be an abnormal tooth growth. Before the day was over my daughter came to show me that she had pressed her cheek and some whitish-red liquid had come out. It was at this point I realised the similarity between the infection of my own chronic tooth infection and that of my daughter's.

After repeating the castor oil application and administering vitamin C and later turmeric powder (which I found out about when I wanted to cure the gum infection), the swelling went away completely.

The solution to the problem seems to have been consistent repeated application of castor oil until there was no longer an infection. When I stalled the oil application, the little bump filled up and looked white like a new tooth was about to grow. But the most amazing result was the successful treatment of a chronic infection of half a decade that had failed to respond to antibiotics on me.

REFLECTION:

Adversity and complications in life introduced me to the appreciation and usage of natural medicine. I never relented even through bleeding edge grief. In fact, I learned even more, thanks to grief. God allowed the trial to bring me some blessing with it. But I must admit that I only recognise the blessings in their full colours of the rainbow after the storm.

BLESSING:

May you have a clear vision that enables you to trace the rainbow through the storm.

68 A DESPERATE BASKETBALLER COOK

The following is an account of reality as it transpired. None of it should be taken as a prescription to anyone. I will not be held responsible for any attempts by anyone to replicate my experience.

Heal the sick, cleanse the lepers, raise the dead, cast out devils: freely ye have received, freely give. (Matthew 10:8)

One day while I was visiting with my sister in Portsmouth, I went downstairs to the kitchen to get myself something to eat. There I found 3 tall Nigerian young men cooking dinner (they were my brother in law's friends and visitors).

One of the three sat on a high kitchen bar chair clinging tightly to his left little finger and making groaning sounds with his mouth to express pain. He also was equipped with vicks vapour rub, which has some strong eucalyptus smell, that he had apparently been given to use by my sister. Curiously, I asked him what was wrong, what had happened to him.

He showed me a little finger that was bent and swollen. He explained that he had had a nasty accident while playing basketball. The pain was almost visible just by looking at the swollen finger.

I asked him if he would like me to give him something else that would kill his pain immediately.

'Yes please', he replied desperately! 'Ok then, give me a minute', I assured him as I popped back upstairs to get him my trusted remedy that I knew would not disappoint me or him.

I came back with castor oil and poured some into a thin little bottle for him to dip his little finger in. The man sat with the finger in the oil for about 20 minutes before brandishing it for all to see that the swelling was gone! He could now bend and straighten his finger again which he could not do twenty minutes before. The pain was completely gone, he said, from the part of the finger that was deep inside the oil. He just still felt some pain on the part of the finger that had not been immersed in the oil.

REFLECTION:

I saw one happy and relieved man who said that he was delighted that he no longer had pain! The treatment cost him nothing! I explained to him many other things that castor oil can do. I also told him that this specific kind of application was not documented anywhere and it came as an innovation and experiment only by me, based on experiencing the pain of loss and studying the purported usefulness of castor oil which I was very sceptical about at first. Had I not been afflicted by the pain of grief I perhaps would not have gained as much knowledge and experience of using simple and yet potent remedies.

BLESSING:

Jesus said freely you have received, freely give. May you be filled with joy today and may you share your joy with those around you and help eliminate pain and suffering. May God be with you always.

69 BASHING MY THUMBS

The following is an account of reality as it transpired. None of it should be taken as a prescription to anyone. I will not be held responsible for any attempts by anyone to replicate my experience.

Who hath believed our report? and to whom is the arm of the Lord revealed? (Isaiah 53:1)

As life carried on, I had made several attempts to move back to the UK but Romania kept me back. It was that difficult to define where I lived. I wanted to return to the UK but I just could not because I was more peaceful in Romania and it appeared as though I could have a future in that country. So, I was in Swindon, England to arrange for tenancy of the house as some tenants had left. I had a viewing that was scheduled at a very short notice and so I was not quite ready but yet I still agreed for the prospects to come.

I desperately needed to wipe and polish the dining room table and to do so very very fast. So I got to work at once, armed with a can of polish and a lint-free cloth. Unfortunately, in the ensuing moments of rushed work I hit my thumb so hard against the top edge of a wooden dining chair. It hurt so bad that I let out a loud groan and also observed a black blood clot forming quickly beneath the thumb nail. I decided to try something I think I had read on some online forum not too long before. I poured some cold-pressed castor oil into a bottle cap. I stuck my sore thumb into the oil and groaned on quietly.

After about 5 minutes with my thumb still in oil I began to feel a bit of relief from the annoying pain. It was after another 10 minutes that I decided that I cannot feel any pain at all anymore. I put away the oil so I could carry on with my hurried tidying-up work. I expected the pain to return after a few minutes but to my pleasant surprise, that was the last time I felt the pain and it never came back!

A week later, while back in Valea lui Mihai, Romania I set out to repair the hand-rail at the bottom of the staircase. All was going well until, with a lot of pressure/force in my hand, I missed the screw I was driving with a screwdriver and banged my other thumb into the wood! This time the pain was much more intense than the previous time. I immediately ran for the castor oil bottle and put it into a bottle cap again to work another miracle cure in 15 minutes. I went and sat at the kitchen table with one hand on my cheek and the other inside castor oil!

After about 20 minutes the pain was only a little bit better. I even had my eyes closed and my head bowed as one who was praying. I remained at the table waiting patiently for the pain to go away but it was only after sitting there with oil on the thumb for a total of 45 minutes that I felt the pain had finally gone. Again, I expected that it may still come back but it never did, ever! The blood clot was still there but without even the slightest pain. So the length of time needed to heal with the oil depends directly on the intensity of the problem the oil is meant to heal.

REFLECTION:

These two thumbs experiences enhanced my already growing belief that whatever else I learn could be healed with castor oil I ought to at least give it a try for myself or tell someone else who may need to. Isaiah 53 points out how the death of Christ resulted in many believing in the gospel message. Grief in itself was horrible and a very unsuitable state from which I could learn new and useful things. But sometimes even on the darkest nights, if we search hard and long in the sky, we may find some twinkling stars.

BLESSING:

May God bless you and keep you today and may He show you stars shining where they may not even be expected. May joy and peace fill your heart today.

70 A DONATION TOWARDS TRAINING AND WELFARE

Let nothing be done through strife or vainglory; but in lowliness of mind let each esteem other better than themselves. (Philippians 2:3)

In this day and age, where humanists and where behavioral psychologists tell us to take care of 'number one', yourself, God still says the same as He always did, put others first. I think we need to choose between what the Bible teaches and what psychology teaches as they have discordant philosophies to offer.

Unfortunately there is not even a point of intersection when it comes to deciding between who to place first. The results of egocentrism versus altruism are bare for all to see and select their own choice. For most people, due to selfish human nature and self centeredness, biblical guidance takes second place if any place at all.

When I quit my job to go for pastoral ministry training, I also lost my means of living. I took a leap of faith and left the issue of funding in the capable hands of God. I expected to be able to at least be able to finance my own start but I did not know how I would finance myself until the end. Selling the house was out of q   uestion as the mortgage was higher than the value of the house.

At a farewell luncheon hosted by my friends at Swindon SDA church hall, a fundraising activity took place. With nothing to gain for themselves, people pledged their support and offered to give some donations. That made me emotional to accept my helplessness and take gifts from others. I had never imagined myself reaching such a point in life. All my financial strategic planning had always been about me dying first and what my wife would do in that event, not the other way round of her dying first.

Out of all the kind donors whom I was very grateful for, only one family offered to give a regular amount for a period of time. These kind donors were Maxwell and Florence Muchura. Not only did they make the promise to deposit £50 every month into my account but they faithfully kept their promise. They did not even have any months of needing to suspend payments due to some unexpected situations (I am certain they had plenty of those situations). They continued to fund us until my studies were said to be completed and we came back to the UK. What a huge difference it made to receive £50 whilst living in Eastern Europe. It was actually enough money to pay for the monthly cost of the children's commute to school.

As I understand it, the family still have debts to catch up with and even had to remortgage their house. But this did not stop them from giving so generously and so faithfully over such a long time. A special blessing upon them is my prayer, and that where they depleted for our cause, God may replenish with multiplicity.

REFLECTION:

Before I was widowed, people often offered donations to support us. At first I used to turn them all down and tell them I was not in need. That was until one day my mother counselled me and told me to accept God's help and blessings through His people. She pointed out that even rich people accepted donations. I began to accept donations from then, even though at first I was very uncomfortable with it. There is nothing unethical about accepting donations in bereavement. Costs can be overwhelming and some donations can go a long way to alleviate the burdens and not leave one to grieve for both financial distress and loss of life.

BLESSING:

May God give you a bounty of blessings today. May you never be in want and may you prosper in all that you do today.

71 A DONATION, BUT TELL NOBODY

Be careful for nothing; but in every thing by prayer and supplication with thanksgiving let your requests be made known unto God. And the peace of God, which passeth all understanding, shall keep your hearts and minds through Christ Jesus. (Philippians 4: 6)

A few days after I talked to my mother, and told her that we had been getting and refusing a lot of offers of money from friends who wanted to support and help us, we got one big surprise.

Linda Johnson had fairly recently returned from the USA where she had been rebaptized and rejoined the church after having left it in her younger years. Mandy and Linda soon became mother and daughter when Linda discovered that Mandy's mother had died and when Mandy discovered that Linda had always wished to have a daughter but had never had one.

They grew so close in time that they were always talking pretty much like a mother and a daughter would. They had even started to compose and sing songs together. They referred to one another as mum and daughter. Linda actually used to explain to people that Mandy was her daughter that she had wished for but had never had.

It was a Sabbath afternoon just after the services were finished that Linda asked to speak to us in one of the rooms at the back of the church. She sat us down and asked about how the plans were going for Mandy's treatment. She said that she knew we were spending lots of money.

Linda then said that she had been planning to go on holiday in Egypt and had just received a bonus at work. She said she would rather give up that holiday and give that money to the people that she loved and who needed it most. She then handed us a cheque of £2000 and asked us not to tell anybody about it. We were overwhelmed and surprised by her kind gesture. We thanked her and prayed together before leaving the room.

For clarity purposes and because in writing it will not be clear unless stated, I must add that Linda is as British as can be. She is also of a white race. Linda truly loved Mandy as though she were her own child. I was not only just a witness to this but I also enjoyed being her son also, being her daughter's husband.

When you have problems and yet you can turn to your mother and tell her all about them, it gives your mind some peace. God was the provider of the peace that we found in the midst of the storm through the motherhood of Linda. May God continue to sustain her and bless her even in her retirement years.

REFLECTION:

There were not many people who were present when Mandy died in hospital. Linda, her adoptive mother was there. She in fact was the one who took care of the little ones during Mandy's final hours of life. God put a grandmother in place for the children at the right time. He was to continue putting the right people at the right time even from then onwards. He will faithfully put the right people at the right time for your situation too.

BLESSING:

May this day be to you a special day on which you will be tranquil and rest your mind in Christ alone.

72 TAKE THIS AND GO, I WILL STAY

Casting all your care upon him; for he careth for you. (1 Peter 5:7)

Our families were friends with each other. There were other families with which our families became friends but with the Selepes our friendship was on a whole other level. I refer to Molapo and Mahali Selepe together with their children Rea and Halle.

We had this unique family friendship relationship that was okay with an unannounced 10pm visit by a whole family. Or a visit that had been planned to end on a Sabbath afternoon could be spontaneously extended to the next day.

Our children from both families were a year older than each other for the boys and exactly the same age for the girls. They got along so well that a visit to each other's homes was looked forward to by both parents and children alike. There was no need to persuade kids to go for a visit. What needed a lot of persuasion was the end of the visits because the kids did not want to part.

The biggest challenge we had was that the distance between our homes was hours of driving apart from each other. The Selepe family resided in Brecon in Wales, while we, on the other hand were in Swindon. So any visit ideally needed good planning or risked a huge disappointment after a lengthy journey.

We enjoyed a lot more of the surprise visits due to being situated close to the M4 motorway between Cardiff and London, which often was the route most people living in Wales were likely to travel with some degree of frequency. Such flying visits became even more frequent when our household was faced with the affliction from breast cancer.

A few days after Mandy's death, I was preparing for the long journey to the funeral in Africa. The Selepes were amongst those who also came to mourn for Mandy and to comfort us, the remaining little family. The traveling arrangements were not easy or straightforward as there were complications associated with the autopsy and coroner involvement. It was during this time that I learned that Mahali had actually been planning to also travel to the burial of her friend.

"Instead of me spending the funds on the flights", Mahali said, as she handed me £650 cash, "please use this money to assist with the funeral costs and I will no longer travel". As emotional a person as I am, such an act of compassion and selflessness naturally sent me to tears immediately as I hugged and thanked her.

The costs I was facing were phenomenal. I had no idea how I was going to meet them all. And God inspired the Selepes with a vision that saw a good fraction of my expenses reduced. With as financially savvy and genius a plan as I could ever hope to conjure up, I would never have come up with that amount of money at that point and that quickly. I did nothing to merit such help. It was a kind gift for which all I could do is sobbingly just say thank you.

REFLECTION:

God knows all our needs and He has promised to supply them too. Cast all your cares upon Him and let Him take care of you.

BLESSING:

Whatever you do and wherever you may roam today, may God remain with you and keep you courageous.

73 WILL YOU ACCEPT FOR ME TO BUY YOU A TICKET?

Giving thanks unto the Father, which hath made us meet to be partakers of the inheritance of the saints in light. (Colossians 1:12).

There are times in life at which we may never imagine who has our welfare and our interests at heart. We become friends with people who God puts into our lives with no ulterior motives but the desire to fellowship together and minister together and to each other in God's vineyard. This has been my experience throughout my life as I have, out of necessity lived in different places of the world.

In the year 2015 I happened to be living in Irvine, Scotland and fairly close to Glasgow. There I was a part of a community of believers who worshipped at a small church on the High Street in Irvine. Together we enjoyed many different activities ranging from choir singing to lunches together. We greeted each other with a hug and were always happy to meet again every week.

One day we heard from a family through our website. This caucasian white family wrote from Canada and were intending to relocate to Ayr, Scotland where they used to live many years before. Something had transpired while in Canada and the lady of the household had learned about the Sabbath and decided to accept it as biblical truth. She had then left her old faith to become a Seventh-day Adventist. So as the returning family established where they would stay, Isabel, the mother in that family established contact with the church so that she and her teenage daughter Bethany would be attending with us.

Isabel always wore a broad smile and always gave everyone a warm bear hug. She was also very keen and enthusiastic to share her faith. She was really so much on fire that it put the rest of the old members to shame that they were not as dedicated to share as Isabel was. When we did our Christmas carol singing on the street in Irvine and inside Tesco supermarket, it was Isabel who distributed the most literature to passers by. She was really and genuinely keen to let others know about Jesus.

One Sunday afternoon, on 29th November 2015, the same day my father died, I was busy trying to find a way to enable me to travel to

Zimbabwe for the funeral. I had been phoning around and trying to borrow some money from friends so that I could buy a plane ticket and go. I think I had just finished giving my account details to someone who was kind and willing to lend me a thousand pounds.

The phone rang and Isabel was my caller. She conveyed her condolences to me for my loss. Then she said that she was aware that at that moment I did not have much money. She asked me if I would accept for her to buy me a ticket so that I would be able to go and bury my father. She asked for the costs and flight details and I told her how I could make the costs less by taking several indirect routes. She got me to take the more direct flights and paid the entire costs. I no longer needed to borrow money as all my costs had been paid by Isabel Wake.

REFLECTION:

Unfortunately Isabel died about two years later. I was devastated by the news and I offered my condolences to her husband Rob and her daughter Bethany.

The kind people we meet are God's agents in this world. We never know when and how they show up or even when and how they eventually exit from our lives.

BLESSING:

May your day today be filled with love and the peace of God that surpasses all understanding. May healing be upon your soul.

74 TERRIFIED BY BAPTISTRIES

Go ye therefore, and teach all nations, baptizing them in the name of the Father, and of the Son, and of the Holy Ghost: Teaching them to observe all things whatsoever I have commanded you: and, lo, I am with you always, even unto the end of the world. Amen. (Mark 18:19-20)

The Ethiopian eunuch in the Bible's book of Acts is said to have been baptized by Philip who had caught a ride in the Ethiopian's chariot. And as they went on their way, they came unto a certain water: and the eunuch said, See, here is water; what doth hinder me to be baptized? And Philip said, If thou believest with all thine heart, thou mayest. And he answered and said, I believe that Jesus Christ is the Son of God. And he commanded the chariot to stand still: and they went down both into the water, both Philip and the eunuch; and he baptized him. And when they were come up out of the water, the Spirit of the Lord caught away Philip, that the eunuch saw him no more: and he went on his way rejoicing. (Acts 8:36-39)

Seventh-day Adventists believe in baptism by immersion. The word baptize actually has its root in a Greek word baptizo which means immersion. So when the word baptism or to baptize is used in the Bible, it means to immerse under water. Sprinkling of water on someone's head or forehead therefore does not meet the definition of the word baptism itself nor does it give any representation of the symbolic meaning of baptism. Infant baptism also falls short in that the Bible says to teach the people before baptizing those who accept and believe. An infant cannot decide to be baptized and cannot accept the Bible teaching of Jesus as a saviour. So that places such a method in the category of unscriptural traditions. All other forms of baptism that are not immersion are not in accordance with the Bible's teaching.

When her mother was buried I was holding my then 2 year old daughter, Vuyiso, in my arms as I stood right next to the grave. She knew that her mother was in the coffin because she had not only seen her inside the coffin but I had told her what was going on. I did not want to have to answer the question later about where mummy was without her seeing her go down. I did not realise that this was going to cause a new kind of problem. She saw the baptistry as a grave, which symbolically speaking it really is a watery grave. When we go through baptism we symbolically die to sin and resurrect to a new and cleansed life.

One day there was going to be a baptism in a church in the city of Craiova, Romania. We were planning to go there to witness the solemn occasion of baptism with my friends and hosts. But before we could leave home my daughter pleaded that she be not taken to see the baptism. She was very terrified and had even started crying as she asked me not to take her there. In the end I arranged for her to be with a friend who was going to remain at home while I went to attend the baptism service (which turned out to be such a wonderful event).

What solution could I have given for the fear of a grave? I myself actually have always had a real fear of graves for all my life. Even now whenever I see a graveyard my heart goes, "boom!" It does not matter what country I am in or what time of day it is. Graves always make me shudder. But the fear of a baptistry is something unique to my daughter whose associative mind got a bit too creative I think.

REFLECTION:

There are so many variables when it comes to bereavement that it is impossible to predict what reaction anything can cause. I never could have foreseen the smartness of the mind of a two year old in associating a grave with a baptistry like a mature old theologian does. We really can never be too meticulous with grief.

BLESSING:

When you go about today minding your own business, may you feel the presence of God in your life. May tranquility be part of your comportment throughout this day.

75 PASSING AWAY TO WHERE?

Now if Christ be preached that he rose from the dead, how say some among you that there is no resurrection of the dead? But if there be no resurrection of the dead, then is Christ not risen: And if Christ be not risen, then is our preaching vain, and your faith is also vain. (1 Corinthians 15:12-14)

There is a very commonly used phrase which purportedly means, in a polite way it is said, to die. When Jesus spoke of the death of Lazarus in a polite way he said Lazarus sleeps. So from whom do we get the example of our politeness from and with what connotation? As soon as I discovered the true and original meaning of the term commonly now used to imply someone died, I decided to stop using it myself. In all my talks and in all my writings I am very careful to avoid saying that someone "passed away".

Why the big fuss? You may wonder as you think of me making a big deal out of nothing. Perhaps if you took the time to discover how the term first came about you too may decide to carefully use your words. We all probably know that a lot of people use dirty words for every other good word that passes out of their mouth. But yet we do make a big deal about what words we ourselves choose to use.

Some people, for instance, shout the name of Jesus Christ as and when they want to exclaim about something. It does not bother them that they do not even believe in God. But they shout out his name ever so often that it makes those of us who do worship Jesus as our God very uncomfortable. The Bible, in the book of Exodus in chapter 20 very explicitly states it as a commandment, "Thou shalt not use the name of the Lord thy God in vain". Yet people use it as a swear word. People who want absolutely nothing to do with Christ!

So it really matters what words we use because words can build or destroy and words can bless or curse and they can hurt or please. We should therefore pay attention to what we say when a life is lost. The words we use to refer to the loss need not give an impression that we believe in or belong to some occult or some anti-Christ movement.

The term "passed away" originally referred to a belief that someone does not truly die. This very aspect should get us thinking of the serpent in Genesis telling Eve that she will not surely die. In other words God had lied to Adam and Eve, but Satan (in the form of the serpent) was now telling Eve the truth that she will not surely die.

In explaining the "passing" it is said that a dead person remains conscious and aware of their surroundings and conversations throughout the time all the funeral rituals are taking place. They are said to be listening and understanding everything that is going on until the funeral is over. Only at that point do they then "pass away" to their next destination which is either heaven or hell.

There are many who understand that this is not a Biblical teaching. Yet being unaware of the connotation of the phrases they use, they inadvertently promote the teaching that the soul is immortal and that nobody really dies but they "pass away" to their next phase of either eternal hell or eternal paradise. With this belief there remains no need of a resurrection day or a second coming of Jesus. This belief also means no future judgement day is going to come as each is judged as they "pass away".

Since I gained an understanding of the meaning of the "passing away" phrase I decided that it is not for me. The absence of this phrase from my writings is deliberate because I do not want to promote an unbiblical philosophy that even contradicts the Bible. Some may argue that language evolves, but I say even as it has evolved to use the name of Jesus as an acceptable swear word or even swearing itself as acceptable by some, I still choose not to be a party to it.

REFLECTION:

Think as you ponder over the state of your deceased loved one. Would you want to believe they are burning eternally in hell right now? Or would you rather think of them being in heaven with God and watching all you are going through yet unable to do anything about it? Either of these two choices is not what the Bible teaches. Go back and study it and receive comfort from knowing that the Bible says the dead know nothing and even their memory is lost. Hell is not a place but an event to come a thousand years after Jesus' second coming. So nobody can go there now and indeed nobody is in hell as it does not exist yet. The righteous dead are not in heaven now either. They await the resurrection day that will come as Jesus comes again.

BLESSING:

Today may your mind be at peace knowing that nobody is in hell. May God keep you safe and calm in His hand.

76 A PAINFUL FIND

He healeth the broken in heart, and bindeth up their wounds. (Psalm 147:3)

So long ago, I cannot even remember what the item was but I witnessed a vehicle that had overturned being looted by members of the public. The vehicle happened to be a truck and it happened to have been carrying goods which were destined for some retail outlet. The people helping themselves seemed all fascinated by what they were doing and happy to have found some free goods which they could pick and go. It was as though they had discovered some relics which they could instantly claim possession of that could easily and readily converted into monetary wealth.

I don't know how good the looters really felt as they picked up spilled merchandise and quickly ran off back to their cars and left the scene. Somehow the way they were trying to get away quickly gives the picture of a robber. All if not most bank robberies are characterized by the robbers getting away from the scene fast with their loot. They run away as fast as they possibly can so as not to get caught. They know that they are breaking the law.

The law that bank robbers break is the law of the land, the governmental law. Yet this law is universal because in all the countries of the world to rob a bank would definitely result in being arrested. But this law does not originate from man. It originates directly from God the creator who from the very beginning created mankind with the law on their heart. There was no written law at the start but yet God had instructed Adam and Eve about what they should never touch.

As soon as they both ate of the forbidden fruit they were overcome by guilt and shame. They ran and tried to hide away from God. The same way the looters and robbers try to get away as quickly as possible to hide!

"Thou shalt not steal" is a commandment that everyone is familiar with. Even those who have never read the Bible know just how detestable stealing is. For anyone who has ever stolen anything anytime (including a cookie in the jar at home in childhood or in adulthood) the feeling of guilt is well known. What eventually makes the conscience die and allow anyone to ignore the still voice cautioning them against stealing is the repetition of the action without apparently being discovered. Starting from little pilferages here and there grooms one into a full blown and brave robber.

When one finds some long lost item, it can be a very delightful experience. People actually set out on treasure hunting or excavating missions. They travel the world to areas from which they hope to find things that nobody has found before. Things that have perhaps even been buried in the ground for centuries. But as they find the treasure, it does not belong to them because often the local government has the ownership rights of the treasure and not the treasure hunters or excavators.

I was going through the wardrobe and removing the clothes that belonged to my late wife Mandy. Then I decided to check if the pockets of the clothes were empty. Some and most pockets actually were empty. But a few pockets, especially those of jackets, were not empty. In some pockets there were receipts from shopping. There was one navy blue jacket which had a £5 note in its pocket. I remember firstly reacting happy for the find. But instantly my happiness turned into sorrow because the money was not mine, and I could not give it to its owner now. I felt guilty for taking that money since I could not communicate with its owner. I also felt sorrowful because I would much rather have had no money to find but have the owner of the money being still alive.

REFLECTION:

Recovering money and clothes of the deceased can be a bitter and traumatic experience. One can feel the pain of loss and the guilt of "stealing" from the dead. This is a phase of grieving that is necessary as a part of the long recovery journey. By and by the pain of loss should begin to heal, albeit painstakingly slowly.

BLESSING:

May God, the one who declares that he is the one who heals you, help you to feel better today than ever before.

77 "GOD MADE JUICE"

Following is a narration of aspects of health and nutrition which does not constitute advice. I write what I have learned and experienced due to exposure to illness. Please consult your doctor and nutritionist for any specialist advice you may need.

Get wisdom, get understanding: forget it not; neither decline from the words of my mouth. Forsake her not, and she shall preserve thee: love her, and she shall keep thee. Wisdom is the principal thing; therefore get wisdom: and with all thy getting get understanding. Exalt her, and she shall promote thee: she shall bring thee to honour, when thou dost embrace her. She shall give to thine head an ornament of grace: a crown of glory shall she deliver to thee. (Proverbs 4:4-9)

I have always liked to drink tasty sweet drinks. Of all the flavoured sugared fizzy drinks I used to drink, I enjoyed drinking Fanta grape the most. I remember back in the days when I also used to drink "liqui fruit" brand juices from South Africa and Namibia. I would fill up a glass with juice, then I would take a few generous gulps before raising the glass with pleasure and saying, "God made juice!"

All I was satisfied with at the time was that the juices that I drank had their package boxes marked on them with "100% juice". I was not paying any attention to processes of sterilisation which they employ to destroy any organisms that they squeeze in during the making of the juice. I was not even attentive to the fact that some packs of juice were marked "from concentrate". I did not notice a lot of differences between any of the drinks except their flavours. That was all that affected me, how they tasted. Yet I did like to buy what I considered to be the best of the drinks. To me the "100%" juices meant that I was getting the best there was. I argued that since I did not spend any money on alcohol, as some people do, I had no excuse for giving myself inferior quality drinks. The best was what I deserved as a non-alcohol consumer.

Another gimmick that hooked me onto the labels of juices that I drank was the "no sugar added" inscription. I had not even ceased using sugar in my diet but yet that "no sugar" phrase had a unique appeal to me. In a sense it made me feel satisfied in myself that what I was drinking was healthy. Who would have imagined that I was actually jumping from the frying pan and into the fire? Truly, ignorance is bliss and knowledge is power. What you do with either is a personal choice but when most normal people gain knowledge they usually implement changes that are related to the knowledge they receive.

As I learned about some of the causes of serious illnesses such as cancer, alzheimer's, dementia and stroke, I learned for the first time about artificial sweeteners that are used instead of sugar. I learned of one substance called aspartame which the American Cancer Society says is 200 times sweeter than sugar. This very cheap and controversial substance is most commonly found as the sweetener of choice in all the "no sugar added" drinks. Innocently health conscious people consume what they believe is the best for their bodies and yet inadvertently feed themselves with substances that are far worse. In the same group of dangerous artificial sweeteners are saccharin, acesulfame and neotame or sucralose.

I learned about squeezing fruit to produce my own juices which had not been heated. Heating I learned actually destroys many enzymes and nutritional value that the body needs. What remains in sterilised drinks becomes some unhelpful sweetness with a flavour but void of the nutrition one would get otherwise if they did not heat the juice.

When I bought a juicer I found and read a leaflet that explained some things that were shocking to me. The leaflet explained things about monosodium glutamate (MSG) which is used in many take-away fast foods to enhance flavour (apparently without the MSG food would not taste as delicious). It explained about aspartame and also about how these tasty substances were excitotoxins that wreak havoc in the brain. The saddest thing that I learned was that these poisons are so slow and yet so sure in their work that it takes decades for symptoms of diseases such as parkinsons to show up. By that time however the brain has already suffered irreparable damage and hence the doctors normally say these are diseases that come with aging and nothing can be done about them. It takes decades of abusing the body with some of these dangerous substances before the pronouncement of a prognosis that could have been avoided.

REFLECTION:

I became a label reader and a food and drink selector and chooser. I do not wish to see anyone suffering because of lack of knowledge and so I suggest that everyone should do their own research about what they put into their mouth. Our taste can be modified in the same way that it first got introduced to the foods it likes. Study widely and wisely because you can be sure that there is a lot of conflicting data out there. Decide for yourself what you want to believe and do not just take my word for it. But for me, who lost a wife to cancer, a thorough understanding of as much as I can learn about foods is critical. Do not wait to learn about things when your loved one is on their deathbed.

BLESSING:

May God bless you with wisdom, knowledge and understanding so you can choose and do what is right for you and your loved ones. Have a pleasant day.

78 MY DENTAL ESCAPADES

The following personal experience account may contain controversial ideas to some. Yet it is no more than my personal experience and not advice for anyone to follow.

And Jesus answering said unto them, They that are whole need not a physician; but they that are sick. (Luke 5:31)

"Heal me, O LORD, and I shall be healed; save me, and I shall be saved: for thou art my praise." (Jeremiah 17:14)

When I lived in Botswana I had a rare opportunity of randomly meeting a dentist who also turned out to be a Sabbath keeping Christian. He was a very kind man who at times would make provision to open up his surgery on a Sunday for me at a time me and him agreed. Sometimes he came as the visiting preacher to my local church in Broadhurst. Before the sermon time he would sit and join the Bible class discussion. Once I remember while he sat next to me he nudged me and whispered, "How is the tooth?" He had worked on my tooth just the day before, humming hymns as he worked. That was back in the late 90's.

When I moved to England, I met some new friends at the local Swindon Adventist church. One of these new friends, who happened to be from Finland, was a dentist. With my legacy of dental problems, I quickly registered myself as her patient. I was always comfortable and relaxed as I sat on the dentist's chair knowing that the person working on my teeth was a friend and so would never do anything less than her best for me.

All through the many years of my dental visits I never knew of any reason to worry about any dental practices. I never questioned the dangers paused by the use of radiation in obtaining radiographs. I never imagined that there were dangers associated with the use of mercury for dental fillings. And I had many fillings done with mercury being stuffed into my teeth. I never even knew that there were concerns about the use of fluoride and that it had quite a reputation as a toxic substance that could cause all kinds of health issues including cancer.

The last dentist to have worked in my mouth was a Romanian who had also become my friend in Romania. He sounded like someone who had caught on to the information about the dangers associated with fluoride. He had lots of alternative solutions to the normal dentistry chemicals. He even removed all the mercury that was in my old fillings and replaced them with substances that he said were not damaging to me.

Cancer was the reason why I first made a discovery of the dangers associated with dental practices. Of particular concern became the fluoride toothpaste and fluoride in tap water and some bottled water. YouTube documentaries played a big part in convincing me to avoid fluoride. One clip in particular, that I found on YouTube titled "The Fluoride Deception", had a lot to say that caused me to begin to avoid fluoride.

REFLECTION:

Someone once remarked, when they learned of all the things we were doing, that we were doing all the right things. They advised us to keep on doing what we already were doing. But cancer is so complex. There are too many variables that make cancer very difficult to conquer. All the changes are probably best done before the disease comes. Yet even then those changes may not even prevent the onset of cancer. Yet I would much rather do some preventative and remedial changes than throw my hands in the air and leave all to fate.

BLESSING:

May God be gracious to you and give you peace and a stress free day today.

79 DANGEROUS AIR FRESHENERS AND PERFUMES

And the LORD said unto Moses, Take unto thee sweet spices, stacte, and onycha, and galbanum; these sweet spices with pure frankincense: of each shall there be a like weight: And thou shalt make it a perfume, a confection after the art of the apothecary, tempered together, pure and holy: And thou shalt beat some of it very small, and put of it before the testimony in the tabernacle of the congregation, where I will meet with thee: it shall be unto you most holy. And as for the perfume which thou shalt make, ye shall not make to yourselves according to the composition thereof: it shall be unto thee holy for the LORD. (Exodus 30:34-37)

I don't know if it is due to my added years or transformed sensitivity due to altered preferences. I just know that I now cannot stand the smell of many kinds of perfumes and air fresheners. My sensitivity in this aspect is so bad that often I begin sneezing when I am in an environment that is filled with perfume smells. The same sensitivity occurs also when I am in the presence of someone who has been smoking or if I am exposed to the clothing of smokers (for example if a smoker leaves their jumper or coat in my car or if I enter into a car that has been smoked in).

Whatever the cause of my reaction, I am highly sensitive to strong smells. I do not let my 12 year old daughter sit in the front seat next to me when I drive if she has just sprayed some perfume on herself. I particularly cannot stand anyone spraying themselves with perfume inside the same room that I am in and worse still, inside the same car.

I also suffer great difficulty in breathing whenever I am in a room that has been sprayed with very strong air fresheners. Sometimes I experience the same trouble when I am in a space that has diffusers of some strong air fresheners.

I was not always this way though. I used to like perfumes of all kinds and air fresheners of all sorts in their full strength and power. I cannot put my finger on exactly when I became so sensitive because I was not aware of the change in sensitivity. What I was aware of was a deliberate change in preference that I made the moment I learned of the toxicity of the chemicals used to make the air smell nicer and camouflage body odours.

My transformation began the moment I learned that many of the chemicals used in perfumes and are fresheners were not only just toxic, but were downright carcinogenic. I was shocked to learn this and I also did not like the news since I liked the pleasant smells. But since I encountered the same claim from many sources and since I had a cancer patient next to me, whom I was trying to help recover, I had to make radical adjustments.

We stopped buying and using perfumes as we also bought into the idea that air fresheners were really used to conceal bad smells. Bad smells should really be dealt with by cleaning the environment not by masking them with perfumes. Even the harsh strong smelling cleaning products we learned were dangerous for our skin. The skin absorbs these chemicals from the clothing. The smells, we learned are also dangerous for our nostrils which breathe them in, particularly from the house cleaning products.

We discovered that there are some good and therapeutic essential oils and dispensers that could be used if needed. These we thought to use only after ensuring cleanliness has been achieved first. And the primary reason for using them should be their health enhancing power rather than hiding the smells from dirtiness.

REFLECTION:

Although I lost a wife to cancer, I learned some useful things against cancer. There are those who may debate the validity and accuracy of the things I learned but I do not claim to be an authority in the area. My experiences are my own and it is those experiences that I share. As I share what I know, I feel some pressure being offloaded from me. I would therefore urge others who have experienced grief and trauma to also share any lessons learned. You may never know who it helps. It certainty can help you feel better.

BLESSING:

May you enjoy a breath of fresh clean and unpolluted air today. May the smell of nature give you joy today.

80 HEALING AS WE WATCHED

The following is not a prescription to be followed but simply an experience shared to bring an awareness to something I learned. You are strongly advised to do your own research about the remedy referred to.

Blessed is the man that trusteth in the Lord, and whose hope the Lord is. For he shall be as a tree planted by the waters, and that spreadeth out her roots by the river, and shall not see when heat cometh, but her leaf shall be green; and shall not be careful in the year of drought, neither shall cease from yielding fruit. (Jeremiah 17:7-8)

My mind has searched hard for lessons learned from the experience of watching my spouse afflicted with cancer. I believe the good Lord must have helped me recall something really miraculous and potent. The particular remedy did not prove itself on a tumour but on a totally unexpected situation altogether. Also, the way we got to discover the power of the remedy was simply just extraordinary.

Early one summer Sunday morning we were all dressed for our usual car boot sale trip in Blundsdon. We usually took the trips fairly early in the morning because if we reached the venue late the best items were already sold out. So we were always in a bit of a hurry to get away from home. It was in the moment of hurrying away from home that something went amiss. The 5 year-old Vuyo in his Sunday summer sandals suddenly ploughed into a hard object on the ground. He let out a loud shrill with pain. A quick examination revealed a tearing of the skin on the toe and heavy bleeding.

At the time, Mandy was taking goldenseal root powder as part of her treatment regimen. The powder we had learned was obtained from some roots of trees that grow in some Mexican mountains. At that moment we had quite a generous supply of the golden seal root powder in the house. So we put some goldenseal powder on the wound before proceeding to Blundsdon. The crying had already stopped even before applying the powder. Perhaps the hope for healing upon seeing action being taken was greater than the pain.

We went through the whole day without paying much attention to the injury. At the end of the day when a good friend, Ricky Porter, dropped by for a visit and wanted us to show him what had happened to Vuyo. Earlier on he had heard that Vuyo had been injured. It was at this point of trying to show Ricky the wound that we had such a pleasant surprise. The wound had already sealed up! The next day Vuyo was able to wear socks and put some shoes on. The toe did not hurt anymore.

REFLECTION:

When I recall the potency of that bitter yellowish herb called golden-seal I just wish I still had a good supply of it. The only reason I can think of why I do not have it is failing to find it locally. The only time we had a supply of it was back in 2009. It had come as part of a consignment from the USA that had set us back around £600-700 altogether. There was no price that was too much to pay! Yet even that was all in God's capable hands to supply.

BLESSING:

May the good Lord supply all your needs abundantly today according to his riches in glory.

81 GARLIC ON YOUR FEET

The following may not make good sense for some. I share it just to show what I went through and what influenced some of my choices and behaviours. I am not guiding your choices or prescribing anything to you here.

I will praise thee; for I am fearfully and wonderfully made: marvellous are thy works; and that my soul knoweth right well. (Psalm 139:14)

One of the lessons that were tough to accept for me was that everything you put on the skin potentially can get into the bloodstream and travel around the body! How senseless I imagined this was but eventually, having no evidence to the contrary to counter the claim, I accepted that the claim did make sense after all. The proof of the claim is all too easy for anyone to try and so agree with or disprove it as absolute nonsense. I will now give you the method of proving the theory and leave it up to you to decide what to do with it.

The idea is to peel a clove of raw garlic. Crush it so that it produces some juicy liquid. Ensuring none of the garlic goes anywhere near your mouth, you should now take the crushed garlic and liquid onto the soles of your feet and rub it on thoroughly for about a minute. Wait a few minutes, maybe 10 to 15 minutes at the most. You should now feel some taste of garlic in your mouth, in your saliva!

How on earth could this happen? You never put any garlic in your mouth. In fact you carefully avoided bringing any garlic even near your mouth. If you have proved that the test of garlic does reach your mouth with just rubbing it onto your feet then you can believe that other things you use on your skin also have the same potential. This is nothing deep but just some simple logic which everyone is free to take or leave.

I personally was not only convinced that things I put on my skin, anywhere on my body could really have access to my bloodstream. In fact I now found it easier to appreciate how castor oil can heal some conditions by a topical application only. Also I began to appreciate how the use of various creams and oils, including carrier oils, becomes effective.

This understanding brought a new dilemma for me as I supported my cancer suffering wife. It suddenly seemed as if all that we had been using on our skin now needed to be thrown into the bin. We had deodorants that we liked and we also had roll ons and antiperspirants. Some of these contained lead, mercury, ascernic, talc and other ingredients which we could not even understand. We began to understand that these beauty products that we were using were not only being placed onto the skin but were most likely seeping into the blood and causing incurable diseases, such as cancer. I remember how one antiperspirant that I liked very much caused swelling in the lymph nodes in my armpits.

With the revelation that all we put onto the skin can get into our blood, came the time to ask, "So what shall we use then instead?" The answer to that question came as something of a novelty. The answer was to always put onto your skin something that would be good enough to be used also as food should it become necessary (but realistically speaking not all usable things are food). So the new task became that of finding creams and lotions and even soaps that were all made of things that could be consumed orally. We found out that not only do they exist but that they are many.

Even the medicines that we could use needed to be composed of things that were not poisonous if consumed. I must admit that this was one of the toughest ideas at first. But eventually when we discovered that in the natural remedies world it is quite common to use one kind of herb or oil for many different uses, it made some sense. Many things can be remedied just by food and water. We even learned the famous Hippocrates quote, "Let food be your medicine and your medicine be food". Since the year 2009 food has largely been the medicine used in my household. We have not even had to visit any medical professionals because we have been well all these years, including the children.

REFLECTION:

Some of the health education we got was completely unexpected and even shocking. Sadly it did not come to us many years before. And in any case that is not to say the knowledge about toxic creams and lotions could have averted the development of cancer. It may have been too late for my wife but I hope it may be useful for someone else now. It very well may be too late for your loved one too as you read this but it could be useful for somebody you know, to study these things further and make the best choices for their own health.

BLESSING:

May what you eat today enhance your health and be your medicine against diseases. Have a lovely day.

82 NO COFFEE FOR ME

"According to my earnest expectation and my hope, that in nothing I shall be ashamed, but that with all boldness, as always, so now also Christ shall be magnified in my body, whether it be by life, or by death." (Philippians 1:20)

All of my life I have always known that coffee and all caffeinated drinks were to be avoided as a plague. I was taught that they were addictive stimulants that my body did not need. Also, at my baptism I made a vow to avoid narcotics, drugs, caffeine and coffee that are all harmful to the body. I knew therefore that I ought not to allow myself to go onto a path that would lead me to dependency and also harm my body. Thus I avoided coffee consumption at all costs not only for just myself but for my household. I did not even keep coffee for my visitors since I do not believe it is ethical for me to give someone something I consider harmful.

One of the lifestyle centres I got in touch with was run by a very kind gentleman, Danny. He took the trouble not only to reply to my enquiries and appeals for help but he made many suggestions and gave advice as he replied to each email that I sent him.

Danny told me all about the need to assist the liver in the detoxification of the body. He introduced me to the Gerson therapy that incorporates the cleansing of the colon. Apparently our colons can remain carrying some waste matter for decades before cancerous tumours are formed in the body by the same stuck faecal matter. Danny explained how one of his patients who had not eaten any meat for at least 15 years had a black piece of meat in his stool which was analysed in the laboratory to determine what it was.

The story was shared with me to convince me of how critical it was to encourage my ailing wife to do a coffee retention detoxification enema. I was not convinced easily about it but after some technical information about how the coffee would induce the liver to secrete more bile and how the coffee would be drawing out toxins as the blood traversed the entire body at least 3 times within 12 minutes I wanted more clarity. I finally got convinced that coffee used for an enema was processed completely differently than ingested coffee. I was now ready to learn about another completely new multi-purpose therapy.

We did not get any laboratory stool tests on the strange black items we saw in Mandy's enema treatment. But it may well be that the strange looking black items were flesh consumed years before as was with the man at the lifestyle centre. Whatever they were, the very first enema treatments brought a really remarkable improvement. The very same afternoon that the first treatment commenced, Mandy took a walk to the shops with me after having been confined to only being upstairs for at least a week.

REFLECTION:

The coffee enema is a detoxification method that is loathed by some and also loved by some. As one of the many things resulting from my experience, I include it here to bring an awareness of its existence rather than as an endorsement of it. It is, as it were, a possible rainbow in some storm that has a potential to bring relief. Still I strongly urge anyone considering it to do some research for themselves. God can work miracles through even something like this.

BLESSING:

May God fill you with knowledge and wisdom. May the same wisdom bring you joy and happiness today and always. May God bless and strengthen you and help you to remain steadfast in Him.

83 A BOUQUET DELIVERED

And why take ye thought for raiment? Consider the lilies of the field, how they grow; they toil not, neither do they spin: And yet I say unto you, That even Solomon in all his glory was not arrayed like one of these. Wherefore, if God so clothe the grass of the field, which today is, and tomorrow is cast into the oven, shall he not much more clothe you, O ye of little faith? (Matthew 6:28-30)

As some of my readers are not Seventh-day Adventists I need to give a quick primer on the structure of my church. The Seventh-day Adventist church is an international organisation which has a structure. The church has a headquarters offices known as the general conference. Reporting to the general conference are the "division" offices under which are the "union" offices. Below the union offices are the "conferences, missions and fields". All of the administrative offices are presided over by a pastor who has the designated office of a president.

Around the third week of December in 2009 I had just become a widower for less than a week. Well-wishers were knocking on my door and post and parcels were constantly being delivered. I really could not even stand the sound of the doorbell chiming to tell me there was yet another person on my doorstep. I was just too distraught to have a mind of receiving more and more visitors. At the same time, I appreciated the fact that people cared enough to want to mourn with me as I mourned. People were sending many well thought out messages of condolences as cards.

One morning at my home on Thorne road in Swindon, I heard the doorbell chime as was now the trend in those days. I did not know what to expect and when I reached the door I found someone with a bouquet of flowers. The tag on the bouquet was from pastor Sam Davis, president of the South England Conference (SEC) of Seventh-day Adventists. I was touched and thankful. I never expected that the president would send me anything at all. I did not even imagine he recognised me or even that he had any knowledge about my loss. Along with the bouquet was a lovely card with a beautiful message of condolences by pastor Sam Davis himself.

My grief, like that of Job, was very great but yet I was thankful for the kind gesture. I have since received many flowers but I do not remember ever having been given any flowers before that.

REFLECTION:

I may not be able to do the same thing for others myself as was done for me but I know what impact it had on me. So I would do it too as and when I have the chance. I will certainly always lift up in prayer all those who are mourning that I know about. Where possible I will also let them know that I am praying for them in their moments of sorrow.

BLESSING:

May your day be filled with discoveries of how marvellous God is. May your heart be full of joy today.

84 POUR YOUR HEALING OIL

But unto you that fear my name shall the Sun of righteousness arise with healing in his wings; and ye shall go forth, and grow up as calves of the stall. (Malachi 4:2)

This is one of those experiences that one would love to forget about but which are so significant that they will never be completely forgotten from memory.

Although the ultimate end did not become our desired result, let nobody ever imagine that the enema procedures were carried out haphazardly. On the contrary, the process occupied a very solemn moment that even the 5 year and 2 year old offspring got to know just as mummy's treatment. They were never in the room themselves during the several times a day that the procedures were carried òut but yet they were aware that something was happening.

We always began with a prayer for the process. Then setting up the equipment in a position where the flow of the fluid would be optimal. Then the patient would lie on her rug over the carpet in position before she opened the tap to start the fluid run.

Meanwhile the other equipment that became an integral part of the process was a laptop with music playing. The background music was not just a random sound but a very carefully selected set of music.

One specific song had some of these lyrics that seemed so fittingly put together for those moments:

"Pour your healing oil through me. Like a river of love, pour your healing from above

Take the days gone by, heal my memories inside." I prayerfully sang along as the treatment was in session.

For my ailing wife and patient, the sum result of doing the enema processes was that she seemed to feel relieved and rejuvenated. There seemed to be some added strength that she gained from the procedure. Indeed the moment she started doing the enemas, combined with some few other protocols and dietary changes that she was following caused an improvement that was tangible. I remember sending a message to our relatives who were in Africa that she was now getting better and that daily she was becoming better than she had ever been. Every new day brought some new improvement that was cumulative.

At our invitation and with a feeling of inadequacy on our own, we had a visitor coming to live with us. She was really kind hearted and had the best intentions with her ideas for causing changes to what we were doing on our own. Nonetheless the positive changes that we had seen for some days turned back into negative changes again. The negativity of the trend was not to be turned around this time and in what was a huge blow to us, in the end, we lost the life of the mother of two. I became a widower with two young children to take care of and to raise without their mother.

REFLECTION:

As we did all the various treatments we were so much looking forward to giving testimonies of a complete recovery and a miraculous healing. We assumed, or presumed that God will give us an earthly healing of the body. But God knew best. Painful as it is and as it will always be. Jesus did not heal everyone who was sick and who prayed with faith when He was on earth. He still does not heal everyone even now.

BLESSING:

May God bless you in all you do and may He make you know and accept that His way is always the best under all circumstances.

85 A GOOD THING

Whoso findeth a wife findeth a good thing, and obtaineth favour of the Lord. (Proverbs 18:22)

David says that weeping may endure for a night but joy cometh in the morning (Psalm 30:5). I had been waiting for daybreak for so long. I had been waiting for the morning to come. I had been waiting for the joy that comes in the morning to manifest itself. I was determined not to weep myself into the grave. There was plenty of life still left in me and plenty to share with another.

Was I ready to get married again or was it best to wait. How long would I need to wait? Who was to tell me how long it takes? Was I happy to be in the company of women? Or was I better off alone to my sorrowful thoughts of mourning? Would it really be "a good thing" for me, for my children to meet someone new? Or would it be a betrayal of their mother and of my own feelings towards her? Such were the questions racing through my head on a daily basis. But yet God was still in control of everything even though I was being torn apart with indecision. It was He who said finding a wife was finding a "good thing".

Indeed it was such a necessary and ideal thing for me to find someone I could love. I had a truly humongous supply of love for someone. I had even more than just my own love to give. I had the love of my little ones who were orphaned by losing their mother. They were just waiting to love a new mother figure in their life.

I had some ideal requirements in my mind about all the characteristics of the woman that would be worthy of becoming my new wife. Firstly and most importantly, for the sake of my children, it would have to be someone who loved them. Someone who was going to love them as though they were her very own. They also needed to be someone from my continent, someone from Africa. And they needed to be someone of my own race, a black African. I also imagined that an ideal wife would be someone close to my own age as we would likely share the same or close to the same perspectives of life. Lastly but critically important, she would have to be of the same religious persuasion as myself because two cannot walk together unless they agree.

With those ideals in mind, I now had a plan. My future would be a happy one and all sorrows would be forgotten as I would live happily ever after. I left England and found an oasis of peace and calm in Eastern Europe. I enjoyed some tranquil moments in Romania as I watched my children being overwhelmed by the love and kindness of Romanians. Suddenly Romanian women became very attractive as they were not only beautiful but were so kind and loving to the children and also to me. I knew I was now facing a new challenge. I needed to find myself a good "thing".

REFLECTION:

It felt really awkward to look forward to finding someone new. I was not happy to think that I could not be with my late wife anymore. But that was the reality and no matter how much I would have wanted her to be with me, she was now gone and not with me anymore. My marriage to her had ended as we buried her and my vows had been 'till death do us part'. Thinking of the resurrection morning with a wife who died and a new wife next to me I found solace in knowing that Jesus said there will be no marriage in heaven. We will all be as the angels of God in heaven (Matthew 22:30). So I mentally moved, or tried to move on.

BLESSING:

May the grace of God be with you today and may He cover you with His love.

86 TOO MANY TOO GOOD

Then the king's young men who attended him said, "Let beautiful young virgins be sought out for the king. And let the king appoint officers in all the provinces of his kingdom to gather all the beautiful young virgins to the harem in Susa the citadel, under custody of Hegai, the king's eunuch, who is in charge of the women. Let their cosmetics be given them. And let the young woman who pleases the king be queen instead of Vashti." (Esther 2:2-4)

When I was much younger I could never understand how everyone seemed to be able to attract the people that they liked to themselves. It appeared as though everyone could choose their friends except me. I just had to be so happy when some people had accepted me into being their friends. So eventually I got to be able to make friends with just those people who were pleasant to me and seemed open for my friendship. I slowly but surely developed my social skills. Yet it was always difficult for me to understand how there were still people who did not avail themselves to be my friends even when I was trying to show myself being friendly to them.

As I matured I became aware that it was impossible to be liked by everyone. In fact, I saw that there could even be people that would dislike me for no apparent reason at all. It was senseless and futile to try to change myself in any way in order to be liked by anyone else. Trying to be someone who I was not was one of the most pitiful things I could ever do to myself.

The principles of making friends never really changed much until I was in a vulnerable position of being a widower. I say vulnerable because at that point in my life I could now attract pity and compassion and yet misinterpret it for charity and affection. In some cases and I am certain in most cases people did genuinely care about me and my children. They genuinely did cherish and love us and wanted to take care of us and our needs as the Bible teaches.

The complication was brought about by the fact that at the same time that I needed attention and care, some attractions were deeper than just those of caring for a brother and his children. Some of the young and lovely women who were so good and kind to me were also vying for my attention.

In some cases it was way too obvious that the girls hoped I would make them my special choice and push the others away. Some would actually even tell me about what was being said about me behind my back. It was not bad things but good. And yet all too overwhelming. In other cases I completely missed the signals and I am sure I disappointed some people

Amidst all this turmoil of heart feelings there were also two children involved. They were being entertained, loved and spoiled. At the same time my 3 year old girl stuck to her prayer for a new mummy every evening. She also followed up by occasionally asking the women who she found pleasant the question, "Can you be my mummy?" Daddy just had to do something.

REFLECTION:

The time God would allow things to happen was always known by God. I reasoned and argued with myself about why some people should have or should not have been in my company. But God never left me alone in my right and wrong decisions and actions. I needed a childlike faith that God was in control and that He would direct my paths if I asked Him and let Him. Otherwise, even though I felt better, my inclination was to keep to the fact that I still needed to mourn.

BLESSING:

May you hear the voice of God leading you and directing you today. May it bring you everlasting peace.

87 A FAIR DAMSEL

Except the Lord build the house, they labour in vain that build it: except the Lord keep the city, the watchman waketh but in vain. It is vain for you to rise up early, to sit up late, to eat the bread of sorrows: for so he giveth his beloved sleep. (Psalm 127:1-2)

As already highlighted, in all my mourning and weeping I remained determined to pick myself up and go on with life. I had a massive exposure to many lovely young women who were very attractive. The fact that I was living in Romania made my eyes look upon the Romanian girls who were always spending their time with my children. I quickly learned that Romanians are people who love children very much. I also paid attention to who of these people my children seemed to get along best with. I also prayed for someone who would be my companion and accept my late wife's children as her own. Some influential older people who saw how torn apart I was from my loss reasoned that as it had been three years since my loss I was free to marry again especially as that would make me happy again and provide stability for the children.

Of course the choosing of a new bride was not going to be an easy task especially as I was surrounded by a number of amazing loving and lovable young women. I would have certainly enjoyed sharing many details of my interactions with the young ladies. But doing so, though it could also be potentially entertaining to the reader, would most likely bring pain to some of the parties involved in the story. So, while sparing the juicy details of the narrative of the development, sufficeth it to say I finally found myself a new fiance, Erika. She was born of Hungarian parents living in Bihor, Romania.

Erika was not only the most ideal person for me but also for the children. She loved them dearly and played with them and gave them so much attention that, as she reminds me, I became jealous of it all. She could speak English fairly well and so could communicate with me, a very important thing since my Romanian was still close to zero at the time. The kids on the other hand spoke to her in Romanian. They played games and did some activities that kids enjoyed doing. Maybe, just maybe, I felt a bit left out of the fun since they were all playing and having fun in a language I did not understand. But I was satisfied that the people that I loved were happy. I had met a fair damsel to reinject life into our home!

As we were making preparations to get married. There were so many complications that we faced which are worth addressing as a completely different subject by themselves because even in those complications, God came through for us.

REFLECTION:

Sometimes decision making can be difficult and lead one into analysis paralysis. Having been a widower for 3 years, I stepped out in faith and God gave me a second chance to get married again. I found myself a new companion to walk the road of life with. I thank God because even in my time of sorrow, God never left me alone to my own destruction.

BLESSING:

May the merciful Father give you hope and faith in your daily walk with him.

88 PROVE THAT YOU ARE NOT MARRIED

Intreat me not to leave thee, or to return from following after thee: for whither thou goest, I will go; and where thou lodgest, I will lodge: thy people shall be my people, and thy God my God. (Ruth 1:16)

Romania, with all its wonderful and lovely people is a country that loves papers. Romanian officials, as far as I got to know them, always demanded all sorts of documents in almost all circumstances. Sometimes their demands for documents were rather over the top. They demanded documents even for situations and aspects for which no documents were even in existence.

We were arranging for a pastor to officiate at our wedding which we were starting to make arrangements for. The marriage registration office had told us what kind of documents were needed from us to be able to get married in Romania. When we got to the office in person, the officials suddenly seemed all unsure of what was actually required. In fact one could be excused for thinking that each official seemed to be making up a list of their own requirements.

Among many other things, they demanded that I should not only provide my birth certificate but that it should be sealed and apostelised with a Hague convention seal and then translated by an authorised translator into Romanian. Zimbabwe, my country of birth, has nothing to do with the Hague convention!

They also asked for proof of my marital status and I provided the death certificate of my late wife.

After repeatedly going to the office and being advised of yet another document required, we were told to obtain documents from Zimbabwe about my marital status since i was born there. So the death certificate, which was issued in England, needed not only translation and apostelisation but an additional document from Zimbabwe to prove my marital status. At that point we reached the decision to investigate the requirements for getting married in the UK where I was a citizen and resident. The requirements for getting married in the UK turned out to be standard and simple. The list of the requirements was not variable and dependant on who the official giving the list was.

Flying out from Cluj Napoca airport, we arrived into London in December 2012 and filed banns of marriage straight away. We had moved many steps closer to getting married in the new year just by shifting our venue from Romania to the UK.

REFLECTION:

Nothing seems to ever be smooth or straightforward following bereavement. Not even moving beyond grief into a new beginning. But as one pays attention to solutions that emerge in the midst of all the complications a divine presence can be perceived. That is why I can say that amidst all my encounters with obstacles, He never left me alone.

BLESSING:

May you experience a divine presence in your life today and always.

89 A MARRIAGE FEAST

And the third day there was a marriage in Cana of Galilee; and the mother of Jesus was there: And both Jesus was called, and his disciples, to the marriage. And when they wanted wine, the mother of Jesus saith unto him, They have no wine. Jesus saith unto her, Woman, what have I to do with thee? mine hour is not yet come. (John 2:1-4)

After a lot of complications and challenges the long awaited day finally dawned on the snowy 20th day of January 2013. The life of being a widower had now come to its end. Morning had broken just like the first morning and blackbird had spoken just like the first bird.

It was never projected to be an extravagant wedding event. The semi-nomadic groom having been out of work for three years and surviving on just a little bit of rent income and the mercy of a few donors. The bride was a school teacher in one of the less privileged countries of Europe. Yet the wedding was going ahead. The planning was complete and the wedding day would soon come.

Far from parents who firstly would not have had the financial muscle to deal with the costs of the wedding, and were too far anyway and needing visas to come to the wedding, there were a few major players who stepped in and ensured that the wedding went ahead. My cousin, Peace, and her husband Vincent and all her younger sisters and brother were a big part of the success of our wedding. Together with my younger sister Sihlobesihle they rounded up all our other cousins, all their friends and church members close to them and formed one huge family. The weather threatened to disrupt the event but yet the church building was so full as was the hall area which was our reception room for the wedding feast. This was in spite of the fact that quite a number of people who had promised to come did not show up in the end. We had guests who had flown in all the way from Romania and we also had guests from within the UK. It was such a delightful day of happiness.

The opening song, (and oh what singing there was that day) for our service was titled, "Love at Home". Our officiating minister, Rudika Puskas preached a sermonette based on Jesus's miracle of turning water into wine. To this day we do not forget the sermon as it was so appropriate. He advised us that one day, when we feel that we have also run out of wine we, as Jesus's mother did, should turn to Jesus and ask Him to provide us with wine.

All of the delicious vegetarian and vegan food served at the wedding was not financed by me or my wife. My cousins and my sister and the aforesaid huge family financed it all. We had a professional photographer who Ricky Porter organised for us at a discounted price at the last minute. We had the professional musicians, the Geanta family, whom we flew in from Romania and they did not charge us any fees for their wonderful music of violin, cello and flute. The huge family members also sang and later even danced to some pure African compositions. It certainly was a wedding to be remembered.

The wedding did not set us back any funds as to leave us with any new debts in our new beginning. Yes, after a lot of complications and challenges the long awaited day finally dawned on the snowy 20th day of January 2013. The life of being a widower had now come to its end. Morning had broken just like the first morning and blackbird had spoken just like the first bird.

REFLECTION:

In spite of His response to her, Jesus did miraculously provide even better wine as His mother asked Him to. He is the one that does provide the wine. The good Lord who cares about every creature in the wilderness does not leave His children, who are created in His image alone, ever. He guided me through my most sorrowful times to a new life. He made it possible for me to marry again without being dug in further into debt. He is always there and He indeed never left me alone.

BLESSING:

May God give you a foretaste of heaven as He fills your life with delight even in the most tumultuous life we live in.

90 NEWLY WEDS NAVIGATE EASTWARDS

Be anxious for nothing, but in everything by prayer and supplication, with thanksgiving, let your requests be made known to God; and the peace of God, which surpasses all understanding, will guard your hearts and minds through Christ Jesus. (Philippians 4:6-7)

Soon after our wedding we were all set and just about ready to return to Romania where my wife was still employed as a teacher. I say just about ready because it suddenly turned out that our 2006 Vauxhall Vectra caused some friends to advise me not to even try driving away without getting it attended to by professional mechanics. So our imminent departure had to be instantly placed on hold. It was meant to be a simple and quick repair that would not delay us much.

Unfortunately the simple repair became a complicated one which spanned several days and also several hundreds of pounds. So about roughly 3 days and £600 later we were finally cleared to go.

Leaving behind a vacant house, we set off from Swindon towards the port of Dover in Kent very early on 24th January. It did not take us long to discover that the cigarette lighter socket was not working anymore (it was working well before taking the car to be fixed). Having a functional cigarette lighter socket was critical as a source of power for the satellite navigator but unfortunately for us it was dead after the expensive car repairs. So I had to use my knowledge of the route to get us to the car ferry. We would then resolve the problem ahead by just installing a new fuse, we thought.

In Dunquerque, France I attempted my first fuse check. Without finding any apparent fault quickly enough we decided to keep going further since we still knew some of the roads. The next fuse check happened in the Netherlands where I even bought a pack of new fuses and wiggled the old ones out and replaced them with the new. Still there was no power from the cigarette lighter socket to use the satellite navigation system on. We carried on driving without any navigation.

After passing through Germany, we knew it would be late at night before we could reach Bogenhofen, Austria, where we had reserved ourselves some accommodation in the castle. We stopped and bought ourselves a book of the maps of Austria. Using that map book, with my wife as the navigator and me as the driver, we finally reached Bogenhofen late at night and tired as dogs. *

We enjoyed attending a German speaking Sabbath service in the chapel at Bogenhofen though we did not understand German. I even met one of my theology professors after the service. We enjoyed wonderful meals at the canteen and took one of the coldest ever walks in a snow covered field before going to rest in the castle. When night time came it was time to resume our navigation from Austria into Hungary. With kids fast asleep we circumvented our way through some narrow country roads throughout the night into Hungary and across the country into Romania via Letavertes on the other side of Debrecen, Hungary. I remember saying to my wife, as we drove through some beautiful snow filled landscapes, that it would.be a lovely and enjoyable scenery if we were not lost and were sure of our directions! We had gone Southward instead of going towards Vienna.

REFLECTION:

We safely reached Romania in the early hours of Sunday morning. We had an entire day to rest as well as the Sunday night before my wife had to resume her teaching duties. All the worry about being late and being lost without any satellite navigation system or map now appeared senseless. God had taken care of all our navigation. Yes we had stopped and prayed in distress as we had to make our way across Hungary from some minor roads through which we had entered from Austria. All I can say is I am never alone because God has never left me alone!

BLESSING:

Today may God navigate your life for you. In whatever you need to do, may you feel His power guiding you at the very point when you know you are unable. Have a lovely day today.

91 A VILLA FOR NEWLY WEDS

Then went king David in, and sat before the Lord, and he said, Who am I, O Lord God? and what is my house, that thou hast brought me hitherto? And this was yet a small thing in thy sight, O Lord God; but thou hast spoken also of thy servant's house for a great while to come. And is this the manner of man, O Lord God? (2 Samuel 7:18-19)

In the county of Bihor, Romania between the city of Oradea and Satu Mare or more precisely between Sacueni and Carei is a tiny country frontier town called Valea Lui Mihai (which means valley of Michael). The town is just 8km from the border with Hungary and roughly 35km from Debrecen, the second largest city of Hungary.

The distance from Valea Lui Mihai to Debrecen is closer than from from Valea Lui Mihai to Oradea within Romania. So flying from London to the border town of Valea Lui Mihai is often most economical via Debrecen airport which is less than an hour's drive. It is also fairly common to find one way flights of £8 per person on the Wizzair airline - a fare cheaper than the cost to travel by road to the airports in either country. It was in Valea Lui Mihai that my new wife was employed as a Biology teacher at a secondary school. Her parental home, where we first all moved to is in Sacueni. We needed our own place to live and I quickly learned that properties to rent in Romania are generally not found by searching from estate agents. Instead when one needs a place to rent they just need to tell a few people around and very quickly word of mouth goes around and returns also fairly quickly with offers of "rooms" to rent.

In the agricultural village town of Valea Lui Mihai are some big and small properties to suit different family sizes and also different income sizes. When word got out that we were looking for a place to live we also quickly got a few offers of properties. They were properties of varying sizes and varying prices too. But almost all of them were owned by absentee landlords who had left the country for greener pastures as economic migrants. The property that we finally settled for (whose owners had moved to Belgium for better work opportunities) was said to be a villa situated on a piece of land size of about ½ an acre. With a garage for the car at the back of the house and a paved driveway the 4 bedroomed house was a bargain price at €100 per month plus utilities. The only drawback for me about the property, apart from higher heating bills of close to €100 monthly was the graveyard view from the kitchen window.

Incidentally, it was such a good place to learn that a huge house requires huge fuels to keep it warm. It also requires more time and cleaning supplies to maintain it clean. Also the huge yard demands more time to keep it neat and tidy. I had to get a lawn mower to deal with the foliage. Yet it also makes it easy to entertain guests. In it we had a few guests coming to visit a few times as we also hosted at least one birthday celebration.

REFLECTION:

Not only was the graveyard a clear view from the backyard but many of the burials and funerals taking place in the cemetery were within view too. Also, some graveyard rituals involving the lighting of some special grave lights on some nights were performed according to the culture of the people in that area. This was not an ideal situation for someone trying to forget about death. Nonetheless with each reminder about death my mind was always reminded about the resurrection.

BLESSING:

May your day be bright and joyful and without any worries about anything including any challenges you may be facing - may they not worry you.

92 WHERE HELLO MEANS GOODBYE

Not to many people of a strange speech and of an hard language, whose words thou canst not understand. Surely, had I sent thee to them, they would have hearkened unto thee. (Ezekiel 3:6)

When I first arrived in Romania I knew that I would experience some challenges with the Romanian language. I did not expect the linguistic challenge to multiply. I never even imagined that one day I would be trying to communicate with people whose language is officially recognised as among the world's most difficult languages. This was of course until I had the occasion to call Valea Lui Mihai my home.

As I understand it from my wife, the area of Romania known as Transylvania in the past was part of Hungary. This explains why Transylvania has many Hungarians living there. Also, all the villages and towns in Transylvania have two names which are on road signs too. The names are really the same meaning but in both Romanian and Hungarian. The Hungarian name for Valea Lui Mihai is Érmihályfalva and is found also on road signs.

The people themselves, as with those in the rest of Romania, are really pleasant and welcoming and friendly. My wife tells a very touching story of how her grandfather who went to World War 2 refused to shoot at Romanians during the war. Apparently he said that he had grown up with and lived with Romanians and they were truly his brothers. So he would not shoot them but instead he shot into the air. The commander told him that if he did not shoot them then the commander himself would shoot my wife's grandfather. Just afterwards the commander himself was apparently shot dead. As he took over, the next in command who had witnessed it all, then told the grandfather to shoot wherever he liked. In that incident I can clearly see God's hand of intervention.

I was now in a place of bilingualism with two of the most complicated languages I had ever encountered in my life. I was only just beginning to make sense of some words in Romanian when I thrust myself upon a predominantly Hungarian community. It was so difficult to even make sense of the language especially when, at the end of a trip to the shop as I was leaving them, they said in clear and plain English, "Hello" while waving goodbye.

REFLECTION:

Grief landed me among people who to me were people of a strange tongue. As God told Ezekiel that people would listen to someone of a strange tongue, so they did listen to me via interpreters. But my unique colour and tongue got people to pay more attention to me. God indeed works in mysterious ways. He never left me alone!

BLESSING:

May you taste of the goodness of God in your life today.

93 A TRAMPOLINING DOG

For without are dogs, and sorcerers, and whoremongers, and murderers, and idolaters, and whosoever loveth and maketh a lie. (Revelation 22:15)

Romania has a very significant number of stray dogs in general. I witnessed this in the capital Bucharest, Oradea, Ploiesti, Valea Lui Mihai as well as along the highways, particularly at laybys along the road. Most of the dogs are quite harmless and are just seeking food from travellers. Some travellers do give some of their food to the dogs and the hounds wag their tails with gratitude. Some dogs however are not necessarily friendly and harmless but are quite aggressive and dangerous,

As we dwelled in Valea Lui Mihai there were a few dogs that we noticed seemed to have no owners. Yet interestingly the dogs seemed to understand who was friendly to them. My son Vuyo rather quickly became a friend of most if not all the dogs in town. He could almost never walk or cycle to anywhere without any dog or dogs by his side.

It appeared as though the neighbour's dog found out somehow about how both our children liked dogs. This dog seemed to now feel entitled to even go to school with them in the morning and come back home with them too. The dog owner, a little Hungarian boy whom the children used to play with, did not seem to have the same attention of his own dog.

The dog became so eager for the attention of the children that several times it followed them right inside the house, our house. At that point I learned how to tell a dog to leave in Hungarian. We now told the children not to allow the dog into the yard. But it was too late. The dog even jumped over the fence to get in if it did not find openings to squeeze itself in.

Once we found out by a loud happy repeating rhythmic bark and kids shouts of joy that our kids and those of the neighbours were all jumping on the trampoline. I got them to take the dog out and send it home but soon it came back. The same day was when a long tearing of a hole appeared on the trampoline's protective net. The happy bouncing dog had bounced itself into the net and ripped it torn. That was how the children learned a bit of why they should not have been bringing the neighbour's dog to our house.

REFLECTION:

Kids just wanted to have fun. They even wanted a dog of their own to keep. I objected because I know how much responsibility owning a pet demands. Also because in the past when my pets died the effect on me was as devastating as though a human had died.

BLESSING:

May today be among the happiest days of your life. May you forget all that brings you sadness today. May God bless you.

94 "WHAT I HAVE SEEN TODAY – MAY GOD HELP ME"

But they that wait upon the Lord shall renew their strength; they shall mount up with wings as eagles; they shall run, and not be weary; and they shall walk, and not faint. (Isaiah 40:31)

When we moved to Valea Lui Mihai I had not imagined that I could have been among the very first black people to be seen by anyone. To me it will never feel unique as I have never changed into anything else ever since I was born. My race, as that of everyone else, is not modifiable.

In the mornings I used to do a different kind of school run with the children. At 9, Vuyo would usually walk to school and arrive within about 4 minutes from home. So he really did not need me to take him to school. He in fact preferred to leave home as early as he could so he could go and play with the other children before school started. We had to impose a time before which he could not leave home because he would not even eat otherwise. Vuyiso was still going to a pre-shool group. It took about 15 minutes to walk to her school while she cycled on her pink little bike with stabilisers on it.

Sometimes we both walked without taking her bike to school. On those walking days we incorporated a game of hide and seek along the way to her nursery school. I remember those moments all too well and I will always remember them in future. For her, I noticed, it was a bit of an adventure and fun to be treasured.

During one of our first days in town as we walked on the school run there were many other people around us going about their own business. There was a day or two in the week that were designated as market days. I think it must have been on those market days that some older people first saw us. I could never have known that they had ever talked about me or even what they had said if there had not been my wife's colleague's husband who happened to be close by.

One old lady apparently remarked out loud something like being so shocked that she had never imagined in her whole life that she would ever live to see people like us. She apparently expressed a prayer in Hungarian to God for Him to help her because of what she was seeing. She said that she did not know such people as us really existed and thought they were only found on TV. The man who knew us already quickly answered the lady's prayer by explaining that we had actually come to live among them. Thereafter the man greeted us but did not inform us of what had just happened. I only got to hear of it later on after his wife Alisz had told the story to my wife.

REFLECTION:

At the time of this incident I had started a new life. I was not to be grieving anymore but excited about my new life. How I truly wish it were that simple in reality. The reality was that I was acutely aware that grief was indirectly ultimately responsible for getting us to live in Valea Lui Mihai. Yet it was also evident that God had given me a new life, renewed my strength and that He had never left me alone.

BLESSING:

May God bless you today and direct your paths to a happier life.

95 A SWEET TRADE

And he said unto them, Out of the eater came forth meat, and out of the strong came forth sweetness. (Judges 14:14)

The place of worship that we attended much of the time when we lived in Valea Lui Mihai was in a different and larger town known as Marghita farther into the county of Bihor. This was because it was Erika's family's church and had been for many years. That was where I began to learn more about the people who were well familiar with Erika but who were new to me.

As we got used to each other people wanted to know what I spent my time doing while at the same time I wanted to know the same about them. I learned that it had been a big challenge for the Seventh-day Adventists during the years of communism to obtain their education. Many schools compelled the children to attend classes on Sabbath, which was not acceptable for Adventists. Consequently many of the men of my generation had not been through university. They did however all learn a trade, and for most of them the trade was a very sweet one.

Beekeeping is something that Romanian and Hungarian people do very well. It is also something that brings in a good sweet profit for many. The hot summer seasons of Romania and Hungary enable the blooming of flowers on acacia trees, sunflower and rapeseed plants. That makes it easy for the bees to harvest a lot of nectar from the abundance of these kinds of plants. It also makes beekeeping quite a lucrative business and one which many of the Adventist men do. By this they have independence and flexibility and thus are free to rest on the Biblical Sabbath according to the commandment and worship God their creator who in Exodus 20 commands, "Remember the Sabbath day to keep it holy".

At that time I had just set up an internet based international phone calls business that was giving me small but steady profits. It was pretty much self running and did not require much daily input of labour from me. So when I learned of beekeeping I was intrigued by the idea of learning the sweet trade.

My brother in law Beniamin and a new friend from church Lucian both donated two and three beehives to me respectively to get me started.

They both planned to train me by practically showing me how to take care of the bees. It turned out that my limited comprehension of Romanian and their own preoccupation with their own several tens of dozen of hives made it harder for me to learn fast enough. Nonetheless I bought a beekeeping suit, a smoker and other tools and did what I could. With a few bee stings on my skin, that summer I harvested close to 30kg of quality organic honey from my very own bees.

REFLECTION:

The joy of not needing to spend a penny on buying honey for an entire year while consuming top grade honey was just priceless. Even more delightful was the thought that the honey was from my own bees. I will remain forever grateful for the brothers who not only gave me bees but also taught me how to look after them. When circumstances of life unexpectedly change due to bereavement there are basically two ways to go. One way is a downward spiral through an out of control sadness deepening into depression. The other way is a sadness that does not consume the grieving person. In bereavement everyone must contend with either way of coping. My faith in God, my determination to be there for my children and also my new found love helped me to not get consumed to my own death by grief.

BLESSING:

The sun may or may not shine wherever you are today. Yet regardless of that I pray that the Son of God may shine in your heart today and give you the courage to keep on going with hope and life.

96 CARRY YOUR PASSPORT: A POLICE CONFRONTATION

But our citizenship is in heaven. And we eagerly await a Savior from there, the Lord Jesus Christ, who, by the power that enables him to bring everything under his control, will transform our lowly bodies so that they will be like his glorious body. (Philippians 3:20-21, NIV)

Whereas it was such a delightful thing to enjoy preferential racial privileges in Romania generally the border police officers seemed bent on doing the exact opposite. The biggest and most effective methods I discovered of getting them to leave me alone were to call them out on their racist behaviour, which embarrassed them thoroughly, and to appear connected to higher authorities.

My first few days in Valea Lui Mihai as a newlywed husband had me going to the flea-market early one morning with my wife. Erika was busy browsing away at the merchandise while I stood by her side. Suddenly there appeared an unfriendly looking border policeman with his "Politia de Frontiera" (frontier police) tag on his uniform. He came straight to me, the only black person in the entire market, and said a lot of things very quickly in Romanian which I did not understand at all. Erika started to interpret what was being said but I was not happy about it because it was not her job to provide interpretations for the police who are even hostile to me. Nonetheless she carried on.

It turned out that the policeman was eager to catch an illegal immigrant and border jumper. He demanded to see my passport. I assured him that I did have a passport and that it was at home just a few thousand yards away but for now he was harassing me as I was shopping with my wife. I showed him my driving licence as it was in my wallet. He rudely insisted that I should have a passport with me. I retorted saying that I was not travelling today and so I did not need my passport. I said that on the day I passed the border my passport was checked. He insisted that I did need to show him my passport. By now the people in the market who knew my wife as a teacher for their children at the local school were getting agitated by the policeman. Another policeman arrived in that moment. That was when I was now demanding the credentials of the first policeman so that I could file a complaint. I was saying that he needed to show me his own passport and identity documents because I was going to report him. The people in the market seemed to agree with me; even adding that the policeman probably did not even own a passport.

Erika then mentioned the name of one of the highest ranking officer whose child she was a teacher of and the zealous officer suddenly lost his enthusiasm and left still quietly muttering something about the need for a "pashapoti". The top officers of the border force were contacted by the school head later and told to inform all their staff to cease and desist from harassing me. I was not bothered by any police again in and around Valea Lui Mihai. That was not so though in Sacueni, which is also a frontier town, until they were informed of who I was and where I lived and knew also about my children who were playing and going to school with the children of the police officers.

REFLECTION:

By the time I was being harassed for a passport by the border police I had already lived in Romania for a while. So the police of the western frontier towns were not about to newly influence my opinion about Romanians. In fact the police further inland had never stopped me even once in all the time I lived in Bucharest. I think God was telling me not to become too comfortable in Romania and feel that everyone wanted me to feel special. In fact God was probably saying to me that I should not get too comfortable on this earth but look forward to the new heaven and new earth that shall be thereafter.

BLESSING:

Today may nothing and no-one ever make you feel as though you do not belong. This whole world belongs to God and is for you to belong to while preparing to go and live in heaven with Jesus. Be blessed as you go about your life today.

97 DRIVING THE WRONG WAY AND CAUGHT TWICE

For the eyes of the Lord are over the righteous, and his ears are open unto their prayers: but the face of the Lord is against them that do evil. (1 Peter 3:12)

When I was protected from being targeted by the border police for my race I was a pedestrian. The protection was not extended to include not being stopped by traffic police in the same town. It most certainly did not extend to those times when I could really have been on the wrong side of the law. I think every driver, even the most careful one, has been on the wrong end of the law at one point. Some of the legal traffic requirements can sometimes even be violated unknowingly.

The "villa" which we resided in was on Strada Kalvin Janos (John Calvin street) in Valea Lui Mihai. The street has a portion of it that by regulation is accessible by motor vehicles only in one direction. And this access restriction is clearly sign-posted.

At first I never drove into the street from the wrong direction against the no entry prohibition sign. However, living there quickly revealed to me that all residents of that street and police seemed to take no heed to that prohibition. They always drove in the direction that was opposite to the legal one of the one way street. Considering the distance it required to drive around and the length of the unpaved portion of the street that one had to drive to get to our house, it was much better to drive the wrong way in. The street was wide enough and not a danger to cars from the correct direction. Usually there was hardly any traffic on our street anyway.

Forgetting about my distinct foreign number plates on my car, I became bold enough to join the status quo. After all this was what everyone was doing. I even asked our next door neighbours and they told me that residents were exempt from the one way regulation. So I habitually started driving the wrong way home.

One Saturday evening after the end of the Sabbath I was returning home from church with my family as usual. I re-entered our street from the town end which was the shorter way home and which minimised the distance of travel as well as the length of dirt-road driving. I had driven roughly just 200 yards or so of the approximately 400 yards to our house when suddenly I heard a loud police siren sound and saw blue flashing lights in my rear view mirror. So I stopped the car.

A very clearly agitated policeman approached my car window from the passenger side as my car had the steering wheel on the right as normal British cars do. (My observation of traffic police throughout my time in Romania was that they always appeared irate in dealing with drivers). The policeman started talking to my wife about the wrong direction of driving on a one way street. She told him that she was not the driver. Then he tried the same on me but he was not going to get a quick response since I needed interpretation either way.

With the police car still flashing lights behind ours the neighbours needed no explanation to help figure out what was going on.

Nonetheless after learning that we live on the street and which house we live in the policeman himself stated the unwritten rule of the exemption and left us to reach home.

Roughly a month or so later some similar police pursuit occurred for the exact same reason. Again we as a family were just getting back home on a Saturday evening. This time however the gate of the house was open and I turned in and stopped on the driveway. The pursuing officer was not agitated as he approached me and quickly asked about why we were at his colleague's house. He still did talk about the one way street but advised that if any other police should ever trouble us we should mention the name of their decorated high ranking colleague in whose house we lived in. Again the policeman left us without any further ado.

REFLECTION:

On both occasions I was guilty of breaking the law. Yet some exceptions to the rules seemed applicable at the discretion of the officers. It also mattered who we knew and we were even advised to mention his name to avert trouble.

The trouble of grief can also be contained at the mention of the name of Jesus the Saviour in prayer.. This has been my constant help and continues to be so even whenever painful memories of loss flashback. God is ever listening for our earnest prayers and is ready at all times to answer us.

BLESSING:

May you experience peace from knowing and calling upon the name of Jesus today.

98 THE GOSPEL COMMISSION IN VALEA LUI MIHAI

And he said unto them, Go ye into all the world, and preach the gospel to every creature. (Matthew 16:15)

Behold, I send you forth as sheep in the midst of wolves: be ye therefore wise as serpents, and harmless as doves. (Matthew 10:16)

The little town of Valea Lui Mihai got me to think a little bit. As I learned that it was called the valley of Michael I thought it was such a beautiful thing. Michael in the Bible is the archangel (Jude 1:9, Revelation 12:7, Daniel 12:1) who is Jesus Christ himself. So I thought that the name of the town was very apt. I was convinced that it was from some Christian background that the town had such a name. I was told however that it was from a different Michael who had historical significance for the town. Still it did not discourage me from seeing Christ themed in the town. I recognised the name of the street I lived on was that of a reformer. Strada Kalvin Janos means John Calvin Street. John Calvin was a protestant theologian and reformer from France. He was the successor of the other great German reformer, Martin Luther.

Having just done my theological studies and being aware of the protestant reformation (which basically started with Martin Luther) I was intrigued by the coincidences of the town name and my street name too. The protestant reformation movement began when Luther posted 95 thesis on the church door at Wittenberg, Germany His sentiments resonated with the people and a big movement ensued. Luther stated that the Catholic church's selling of indulgences purporting to absolve sin was unbiblical. He also questioned why the wealthy pope did not use his own money to build St Peter's basilica rather than money from poor believers. I will not rewrite the history of the reformation here but I highly recommend that anyone who is not aware of it should study it or a least view a video documentary of it.

I had been well informed of how the people, including old people in the town were curious about me, a new black resident in town. I was ready to do something with the training I had just completed. Unfortunately I spoke neither Romanian nor Hungarian. Yet I thought that God could use me in this little town regardless of my language limitation barrier. So with my thoughts that I could be used by God, and the fact that people seemed curious about me but were not brave enough to stop me and talk to me or thought our languages would not permit us to talk I came up with an idea.

The local church pastor at the time was my good friend and pastor Adrian Belean whom I first met when I was visiting to preach in his church in Oradea. He was keen to do evangelism and Valea lui Mihai was a good place for it with several church buildings within a very close vicinity of each other (another reason for me to think the people around this town must really have loved God and prayer). I suggested my idea to him that we should run a series of evangelistic meetings where I could share the good news with the people and hopefully when they see my picture on posters around the town they would come and listen to me. He himself would be my interpreter for the series. I thought it was really a brilliant idea and I felt we could truly capitalise on the fact that people were keen and curious to see me on the street and now they would have a chance to formally meet me.

Posters were made and advertising was done around the town with my colour photo on the posters. The church prayed and prepared for the series and brass musicians were invited from Carei as well as other singing groups from Oradea and Marghita. The series went very well but we had only a handful of visitors from the community. Yet we were thankful to God for the fact that we did have some people coming to the meetings. How the seed of the gospel that we planted would fare we accepted was entirely a matter for the Holy Spirit.

REFLECTION:

I learned that the dominant Greek Orthodox religion in the area had a very strict priesthood. The members were not even permitted to go and hear what other denominations teach. I do not know how true that was but I left it at that. I was thankful for the blessed experience of sharing with those who did come.

One of my topics in the series was a Biblical explanation and exposition of what happens when people die. I saw many people frequent the graveyard just behind my backyard to bury their loved ones. Some came frequently to tidy up the graves and to put flowers on the graves. I was left frustrated that I could not give all the people the good news about the resurrection and I could not help to eliminate their pain of thinking of eternal torture because many did not come to learn from the series.

BLESSING:

May God give you the reassurance of the resurrection and the peace that those who died in Christ shall rise first to an immortal and an eternal life. Have a blessed day today.

99 WHY BLUE FLAMES?

Therefore shall her plagues come in one day, death, and mourning, and famine; and she shall be utterly burned with fire: for strong is the Lord God who judgeth her. (Revelation 18:8)

One chilly winter evening as we sat on some cosy and comfortable sofas around a crackling and relaxing fire that burned in the fireplace there was no doubting that everyone was pleased by the fireside experience. The effects of just sitting there brought about different ideas to everyone in the family who was present. I just felt like singing and worshipping. So I invited the family to join me in songs of praise, Bible reading and prayer. Erika wanted to play flute and so she did so while I attempted my hand at the violin. The kids also played their violins and altogether some simple but sweet music echoed through our living room.

After a while the playing discontinued but the thrill of the fireside experience endured. Just watching those red hot coals and hearing the crackling was nothing less than therapeutic. The experience of the awesomeness of the fire was not just for the grown ups in the room. The children too were enjoying more than the warmth and family togetherness time. They were also watching the flames. Mind you there was no distraction from any television sounds or sights[1]. So suddenly I heard a very thoughtful question from Vuyiso, which Vuyo also emphasised by adding, "Yes. Why daddy?" Vuyiso's question had been "Daddy, Why are the flames blue?"

When kids ask daddy a question then daddy needs to answer the question. Sometimes daddy does not really know the answers himself but he should try his best and not disappoint his kids who assume daddy knows everything. Of course there is nothing wrong with admitting that daddy does not know everything. In fact children must know that nobody knows everything, not even their daddy. But saying I do not know to all things does not inspire confidence and the quest to learn more by asking. I remember the question and the relaxed ambiance very well but I do not recall what answer I gave or if my wife quickly responded with an answer.

---

[1] We did not and we still do not have any television in our household at all.

REFLECTION:

The fire scenario is one that invokes a few significant aspects. Fire will be the agent of cleansing the earth, sin and sinners at the second resurrection. The Bible also talks about death being thrown into the fire (Revelation 20:4). Therefore if death is destroyed in the fire it means afterwards there shall be no more death.

Having suffered as much as I have as a consequence of death I just can't wait for the day death shall meet its fate of obliteration.

BLESSING:

Today I pray that God will lift up your spirits and make you go forth with cheerfulness and gladness.

100 HAPPY WITH OLD BUILDINGS OR GLOOMY WITH NEW

Go up to the mountain, and bring wood, and build the house; and I will take pleasure in it, and I will be glorified, saith the Lord. Ye looked for much, and, lo it came to little; and when ye brought it home, I did blow upon it. Why? saith the Lord of hosts. Because of mine house that is waste, and ye run every man unto his own house. (Haggai 1:8-9)

Having lived in the country and in different parts of it, I have my impressions about Romania. I think the country is rich with beautiful buildings which are among the world's best designed architectural structures. The country is endowed with the most amazing. castles and other buildings. Its parliament building is the second largest in the world after the USA's Pentagon building. It also has amazing mountains and plains as well as rivers and springs. Collecting drinkable crystal clear spring water from the mountains is one of the most popular things people do in Romania. Indeed Romania is a place to which people travel from all over the world for skiing, hiking, spa baths and the tranquility of rural living.

Within the country are also some not so fabulous looking edifices and roads. Regardless of how the roads and buildings may or may not have been I saw the flamboyant joyfulness of people in Romania. However the place may have been, be they rich or poor, most people did seem to be quite happy.

Contrary to this tranquillity found within a country in which not all the buildings and structures are the the most amazing are other places that have first class modern architecture and developments. By contrast, in those places I have met with and seen some of the most miserable people. They have all the wealth surrounding them but they are living gloomy lives. I wish that it were not so but sometimes people have had to choose between being happy with their old and unimpressive buildings and gloomy with their state of the art skyscrapers, central business districts and accommodation.

REFLECTION:

The country, as lovely as I know it, is a therapeutic destination for the mind. It was therapy for my soul just to be in Romania in my time of grief and without the means to fly to Africa which I would rank even higher for its beauty in nature as a destination, I would go to Romania for a healing break. There is more sunshine there, even in the sub-zero metre high snowy winter. The people are generally friendlier and the cost of living for those with a pound sterling muscle is fairly low. I would highly recommend it to anyone who needs to get away from their normal home to take their mind off bereavement[1].

BLESSING:

May the spirit of God make your day be a happy one wherever you today.

---

[1] As long as I am able, I would also be willing to give advice to anyone who needs it about where to go and who to contact.

101 SPECTACULAR CARAVANS ON OUR DOORSTEP

Some trust in chariots, and some in horses: but we will remember the name of the LORD our God. (Psalm 20:7)

When I first attended the theological institute at Cernica there were two main routes of accessing it when coming from central Bucharest. One of the ways drove over a railway bridge while the other way, the shorter of the two, had a level crossing of the railtrack that leads to Constanta[1].

While waiting at the level crossing I remember seeing, for the first time, some very old trains. These old trains were the likes of which I had only ever seen in movies about the past era of communism. The movies I remembered had depicted people being transported in such trains to concentration camps. That was way before I saw that the more elegant and modern trains also exist in Romania. In the same way I observed that Romanian police cars and taxis seemed to be mainly old dacia logan cars but yet they also have more modern cars too. Romania is a truly interesting place.

Now I shift back to the county of Bihor in the west of the country. The end of the unpaved Strada Kalvin Janos was also the start of the centre of the paved streets back in the Valea Lui Mihai town. That also was the location of the flourishing and highly popular weekly market. It was to this weekly market that the very fascinating rarely seen canopied caravans came.

The caravans were no more than horse drawn chariots with some kind of canvas cloth around and an opening at the back which was closeable. I was fascinated by these sort of chariots because I previously had only ever seen them in cowboy films. To wake up and find 6 or 8 of these lined up on my street and even outside my gate was very exciting and therapeutic for me.

Once, I took a picture of these caravans and posted it on Facebook. My friends from all over the world asked questions like, "Where is that? Is that

---

[1] Constanta is a very popular city for its beaches and seashore particularly in the summer.

a movie shooting scene?" Clearly I was not the only one delighted by seeing the good old caravans.

REFLECTION:

In the movies that I had watched before, I had seen how the lengthy caravans had been used to also carry someone's coffin. The mind can associate almost anything with what it dwells on the most. As such I had been asking God to help my thoughts to stay positive and hopeful. Thanks be to God I never veered into thinking about any coffins when I saw these caravans on my street. God was helping me by healing me slowly but surely. Thankfully, He never left me alone.

BLESSING:

May your thoughts remain positive today and may God give you peace.

"Blessed shall be the fruit of thy body, and the fruit of thy ground, and the fruit of thy cattle, the increase of thy kine, and the flocks of thy sheep." (Deuteronomy 28:4)

It was during our stay in Valea Lui Mihai in Romania that, as newlyweds, we got a confirmation that Erika was expecting. This was exciting news particularly because Erika had never experienced the joy of having her very own baby before. The moment of reading up all about baby development and trimester counts had just begun for her.

As the nearest city from where we lived was Debrecen, Hungary and also as Erika herself is Hungarian, a series of trips to a gynaecologist in Debrecen began. Initially some tests and checks were done which revealed that all was okay. They suggested that Erika's diet, who had never eaten meat in all her life, should just add millet because it is a complex grain that is good for vegans.

Placenta previa is the term they use to describe the situation in which the placenta lies low in the uterus and covers the cervix. The situation can and does usually correct itself in time but at times it does not. In that case normal delivery becomes risky to the life of both mother and baby. Placenta previa happens in 1 out of every 200 pregnancies.

As the pregnancy progressed, more tests and checks were carried out. On one occasion some rather disturbing results were given. The results of the latest checks showed Erika's pregnancy to be that rare one out of 200 to have developed into placenta previa. Also, her uterus was contracting as if she was already in labour and her cervix was also open. That meant that the placenta could be eliminated at any time, and that would have meant she would have bled to death if she did not reach a hospital quickly enough. The doctor therefore advised us to make sure that we always had some fuel in the car and so could get to the closest hospital quickly if needed because if Erika had started bleeding then she could even have died from the bleeding.

Distress and shock were upon me as I learned the news. My fairly recent experience of loss was not very helpful for putting my mind at peace.

REFLECTION:

For someone like I was, just recovering from widowhood, this was the kind of news I really could have done without. I sent out prayer requests to all the people that I could reach. I was so terrified of possibly losing my new wife and baby. I could not imagine how I would cope. But I still hoped and prayed that all would be well.

BLESSING:

Leaving all your cares to God, may you enjoy a peaceful day today.

103 IT NEVER RAINS BUT IT POURS

He is despised and rejected of men; a man of sorrows, and acquainted with grief: and we hid as it were our faces from him; he was despised, and we esteemed him not. (Isaiah 53:3)

When tales are told that culminate in a romantic setting, often they end with "Then they lived happily ever after." That suggests that the marriage began a new phase of life full of endless joy that saw no raging storms of life. What an ideal and a beautiful story ending which is also the most desirable one!

Unfortunately for some individuals like myself the reality of life is somewhat different from the fairy tale fantasies. The reality is that with the news that a child has been conceived comes also a real threat to life and limb.

The crossborder doctor and midwifery visits from Romania to Hungary had of necessity to become routine. The scans and checks were constantly required to monitor the unborn baby's growth and the already discovered placenta previa condition.

One afternoon as the Hungarian doctor finished doing his checks and scans he remarked that the unborn baby looked just like me. That was an amusing statement that was needed to bring humour to a situation that could be summed up by the phrase "a complicated pregnancy".

To reduce the chances of a placenta rupture and a haemorrhage, Erika was advised to be constantly bedridden. That was the only known way to greatly increase her safety.

REFLECTION:

I think it might be difficult for some to imagine my state of mind unless I tell them.

This prevailing situation happened in our very first year of marriage. The year that should have been the start of the happily ever after story became a year of the risk of wife loss. There was not that expected delight of fun with each other of newly weds because the wife had now become a patient. Why should my wives become patients? But only God knows that answer and I trusted Him to resolve things best who knows things best.

BLESSING:

Should you meet with any unexpected situation today I pray that you may see the hand of God throughout. Be mightily blessed today.

104 SHE WOULD NOT STAY IN BED

Yea, though I walk through the valley of the shadow of death, I will fear no evil: for thou art with me; thy rod and thy staff they comfort me. (Psalm 23:4)

Oh that my grief were throughly weighed, and my calamity laid in the balances together! For now it would be heavier than the sand of the sea: therefore my words are swallowed up. For the arrows of the Almighty are within me, the poison whereof drinketh up my spirit: the terrors of God do set themselves in array against me. (Job 6:2-4).

"Please pray for us and especially for my wife who has just been notified about a condition that could potentially put her life in danger. This is very serious." (My own Facebook post - July 4, 2013 at 7:20am) While I sent out prayer requests and stressed about the wellbeing of mother and baby, my wife took things too easy. The doctor's advice was for her to have bed rest due to the complications of her pregnancy that were a danger to her own life.

Erika was a biology teacher at the secondary school in Valea Lui Mihai. She continued being a teacher with as full teaching load as everyone else did. Often she walked to and from school daily. She was not about to stay bed ridden.

At some point I had travelled to the UK and from there I had driven back in a Mercedes Vito van. In the van were lots of personal effects. Part of the contents of the van were some bicycles for myself and for the children that we had left in Swindon. Erika also had a bike which her late father had bought for her from Germany. She was not going to be left out of the family bike fun. I serviced all the bicycles and ensured they were safe and usable.

One warm summer Sabbath afternoon we decided to roll out the bikes and all go for a little spin. We left our house towards the main road that leads into Hungary. Each of us from the youngest to the oldest was freely controlling their own bike. However we were all cycling in a single file. Everyone was having a lot of fun during the ride except me. The reason why it was not fun for me was because I was so terrified for the safety of the children. I kept screaming for them to stay in line and out of the road.

We cycled all the way to the border and looked over into Nyirabrany in Hungary which is where the border is located. We then cycled back towards Valea Lui Mihai, pausing a little for some photographs at the road sign welcoming people to Valea Lui Mihai. We also took some pictures in the wheat fields that run parallel to the main road. What fun we had on our biking out trip!

REFLECTION:

The demarcation between danger and safety is somewhat so thin that sometimes you cannot regulate for someone who feels strong to always lie down. I had to give up arguing about it and hope that the one who is pregnant could judge her own condition best. At least nothing perilous happened on that occasion. I still thought it was too much risk taking. She was really very brave!

BLESSING:

May you be protected from any harm and danger that could befall you today and may God bless you.

105 MY EMPATHETIC SON OR MY MOURNING SON?

For my life is spent with grief, and my years with sighing: my strength faileth because of mine iniquity, and my bones are consumed. (Psalm 31:10)

For in much wisdom is much grief: and he that increaseth knowledge increaseth sorrow. (Ecclesiastes 1:18)

The very first day of 2013 heralded some sad news for me. 2013 was already scheduled to be the year of a new beginning for me. Wedding plans were already at an advanced stage with all legal paperwork and announcements already done as required by law at the marriage registrars office in England. We were moving forward and happily so too.

Early on the very first day of the year I got a message to say that my grandmother had died at 4am that same day. I told everyone at home about it and showed them a picture of my grandmother. Vuyo asked me about my other grandparents. He wanted to know if they were still alive. When he heard that they had all died he started crying. But his crying was excessively painful. I asked him why he was crying so much and he said it was because I had no grandparents left. Trying to console him whose own mother died I told him that at least my parents were still alive, both my mum and my dad. I think he possibly now understood death as he had experienced the loss of his mum and felt the full force of grief but had suppressed it.

I never really observed my son to be someone who likes dolls. I know he did play with a few soft toys with his mother but I was not paying much attention then. As long as he was happy and playing I was satisfied. But when I was now solely in charge of looking after him and his sister I observed him cuddling a soft toy to sleep every night. That tended to bring a pain in my heart while it also made me happy to see that he had something he liked to hold as he went to sleep. When I played with him previously it was not with dolls but it used to be either hide and seek, cars or cycling. All those things had suddenly slithered away with my bereavement and I could hardly play anymore with the kids. Sometimes just looking at the kids made me feel like crying, especially looking at Vuyo. I must admit that does worry me a bit because I do not understand why I feel pain for the sake of the children which they themselves do not even feel.

REFLECTION:

Certainly, even children grieve! I could not really understand why my son got so affected by the news of my grandmother's death except that perhaps he now empathised as he got a bit older. When his mum died it took him a while to even shed his first tears. But even when he did it had not been so bitterly until about a year or so later. Yet when considering my own pain I have often felt that my deepest hurt was for the children's loss. Even years after their mother's death when I look at the children or see them experiencing unfairness and problems my pain returns about their loss and it hurts me so badly. Yet I am not the same as I was years ago. The reduction of pain certainly is huge with time, but I wish I could say that there is a complete elimination for all time and at all times - for now I still cannot.

BLESSING:

May God wonderfully guide your life and pour a double measure of His blessings on you today.

106 CHARIOT RIDES BUT NOT FOR MY WIFE

Some trust in chariots, and some in horses: but we will remember the name of the LORD our God. (Psalm 20:7)

In a village not so far off, perhaps around just 6 kilometres away from Valea Lui Mihai lived some unknown family. I have absolutely no idea just how the lady of the household found me on social media. What I do remember well from the time is that I was offering English lessons to people in the community and I think perhaps that was how I was so easy to find. Anyway she just began to struggle to talk to me in what I understand was not very good Romanian even on her part. At first the conversation was initiated in Hungarian then at my request moved to Romanian as English was out of question for the lady.

She just told me that I was very nice and that her son wanted to meet me. I understood that she was trying to be friendly as we were fairly new to town. I thought it was a good thing for local people to be curious about us and interested in being our friends. I told my wife about this new person who had just randomly appeared and started conversing with me. She was not so fascinated or intrigued about it. So the conversation carried on with the lady, Edina, asking when we could come to her village as a family. She would prepare food for us and give us melons from her garden since her husband was a gardener. In the end we arranged to go there as after all it was only a very short distance away.

We reached the very kind lady's humble household on a very hot Sunday afternoon. There she was with her husband and her son as well as her sister in law. They were all really very excited that we had come to their home. We were a real spectacle in the village and I think it is because black people were a very rare sight there if they ever had been there before. Even the neighbours, from the way they looked at us as they stood by their gates, seemed somewhat envious of this family that was entertaining some exotic guests.

We were treated to melons and corn on the cob before being shown to the back of the homestead where there was a chariot parked in the shed. It was an exciting sight for us to see and then the man asked if we wanted to have a ride on it. That was a thrilling offer that nobody could refuse, except my poor wife Erika who this time was really concerned for her own condition. I was sorry for her but she told me that she had ridden in chariots like that many times before. A quick call was made and someone else, another man arrived who harnessed the horses onto the chariot and guided us onto the chariot. Soon we took off on a quick grand tour of the village of Curtuiuseni.

We were not gone long as not all of us were riding. But as soon as we got back another offer was made to Vuyo and Vuyiso to ride on horseback if they wanted to. They did want to and the man in charge of horses got them to ride in turns. They had the day of their lives and we took pictures of them on horseback without any t-shirts on themselves since it was such a typical hot summer day in Romania.

In spite of not riding on the chariot, thankfully, Erika still enjoyed her visit too. Up until this day, Erika is still in touch with Edina and they remain friends even until now.

REFLECTION:

Some days of fun were planned by us but out of nowhere, a different day of fun was offered to us by people whom we did not even know. They were not even believers in the same faith as ourselves and I think they said they were Greek Orthodox Christians. God certainly does have his people in all the different faiths and we appreciated their kindness so much. The wisest thing that we can do is to love people the way that God loves us and that He loves them. In the Bible account of Luke 10:29-37 it was a Samaritan who rescued a dying robbed Jewish man when both the Priest and the Levites who were both high ranking church officials decided to go by another way.

BLESSING:

Today, in all that you may do and wherever you may go, may the good Lord cover you with favour as a shield and give you many blessings.

107 THE BUSINESS

And I have filled him with the spirit of God, in wisdom, and in understanding, and in knowledge, and in all manner of workmanship, To devise cunning works, to work in gold, and in silver, and in brass, And in cutting of stones, to set them, and in carving of timber, to work in all manner of workmanship. (Exodus 31:3-5)

As we enjoyed our lives in the little agricultural town of Valea lui Mihai, the expenses of the family were still heavy and needed an income to be injected to ease the burden. I was getting more convinced that my ministry goals were not going to be fulfilled fully while I was living in Romania. Whereas I was placed twice a month onto the preaching plan of Marghita and once a month on the preaching plan of Valea lui Mihai I was not doing anything much else. I tried to befriend as many people as I could while hoping some may be interested in learning more from me about my God but it appeared a slow process that required years to achieve. Yet I was not even employed and needed some income.

The circumstances demanded that I begin to think outside of the box, literally. My beehives boxes were only a startup idea without deep beekeeping skill behind them. Besides, the beekeeping financial results are only seasonal as is the intensity of the beekeeper's labour. I had to come up with something else. And I came up with an internet based international calling card business.

The setup of the business was a complicated affair to begin with. I needed some voice routing antennas and equipment to integrate phones and computers into a functional voice system. I also needed suppliers of the networks for communications and billing systems to control the costs and duration of calls. Then I needed to physically locate my systems in different countries. Then finally test the systems before advertising my services.

I sourced my equipment from China and from the UK and set up the complicated systems and then after testing successfully I began full operations. Everything seemed to be running smoothly and perfectly with minimum intervention from me. I was earning a small amount of income for each phone call that people made via my system and I was proud of my achievements so far.

One Sabbath evening after we arrived back from Marghita church where I had been preaching I sat down at my desk to read my emails. I found a message from my bank asking me to authorise a payment of about £800. I also got an alert message telling me my balance was used up for my business calls. Upon investigating I traced a hacker who had broken into my server from Lithuania. He had used up all my remaining credit of about £50 and then attempted to top up my credit payments by taking money from my accounts. Thankfully I had not activated any automated top up facilities. But my systems had now been compromised and there was no telling how aspects had been set to trap any further activities on my platform. There could even have been some keyloggers that my unwelcome systems visitor may have installed to still my passwords and ruin me further.

REFLECTION:

The effort of trying to restore my business and secure it better could not be justified by the tiny income I had been making for the months I did make money. After all it appeared to me that phone calls were now being superseded by free services like Skype and WhatsApp and Viber. So I cut my losses and boxed my equipment which I hoped for years to reuse again but never did. This was a huge blow to my efforts to adjust from a mourning period being superseded by a new marriage without the income that I had in my first marriage or the ministerial call for which I quit my last employment after being widowed. Yet I did not give up completely. I intensified my efforts to find students needing English tuition for a fee.

BLESSING:

May your anxieties be vanquished today as you enjoy a peaceful day with your God.

108 ENJOY THE TRIPS

Fear thou not; for I am with thee: be not dismayed; for I am thy God: I will strengthen thee; yea, I will help thee; yea, I will uphold thee with the right hand of my righteousness. (Isaiah 41:10)

One of the places that became a regular feature of our life in Valea lui Mihai, Bihor, Romania was Debrecen, the second largest city of Hungary. To get there took us just around 40 minutes if the border checks did not delay us with queues of cars. We often went to Debrecen for two main purposes namely shopping and music tuition for the children by a violin professor of the very big music school of Debrecen. The third major reason for going to Debrecen was the airport which linked us directly with London.

Tesco supermarket, in Debrecen was always open and for all 365 days of the year including Christmas day and New year's day. In the same location with Tesco was a whole lot of other shops such as the shoe giant Deichman and Natural Remedies and natural foods shop. Outside the same mall, which has a huge car park, there was a car boot sale every Sunday. Elsewhere in the city were several huge shopping malls like one called the Forum and others like Auchan. There was no shortage of reasons for my wife to say let us go to Hungary, with or without money to spend! Hungarian currency is surprisingly weak in terms of value when you compare it even to Romanian money. Firstly I had thought that Hungary does its trades in Euro currency but I was wrong. In Hungary they use Hungarian Forints for buying and selling. Sometimes goods are even marked in the shops with a Euro symbol but the shops never accept Euro cash money. Then to understand the currency is a challenge because most things are worth thousands of Forints. Adding to this complicated money was that all goods have Hungarian labels on them and all aisles in the supermarket have Hungarian signs telling shoppers where to find what they need. I soon learned, for instance, to look out for "ritz" when I wanted to buy rice.

Fortunately most of the time my Hungarian wife was right there with me to tell me things I did not understand. It also meant it was quite terrifying to even think about going shopping alone to Debrecen. Eventually it did happen but not with much excitement. It reminded me of my first months in Botswana where some people did not speak English and I had to tell taxi drivers directions to where I lived in the age before the GPS navigation systems.

One Friday afternoon just after crossing the border into Hungary for violin classes I remember saying this just out of nowhere, "Enjoy these journeys because one day they will be no more they will be just a memory some day". At that time I had no idea how soon or even where we would possibly move to next. But I was almost certain that unless I had managed to create for myself some good source of a generous income then our stay would not be sustainable for very long.

REFLECTION:

If you have only ever lived in just one place then it is probably not easy for you to imagine the challenges of adjusting. Now imagine all the moving I have done from Zimbabwe to Botswana then UK then Romania and add the complications of doing groceries in Hungary. Each time before going to Hungary I had to go to a local Romanian money changer to obtain Forints because otherwise the conversion rate within Hungary was never in my favour. Remember also that as all these things are happening I am actually a recovering former widower who has moved on but to whom complications bring an emotional strain and makes it harder to become fully restored. No wonder my wife used to say I looked depressed. I know I was not depressed but there was a lot to take in including the fact that her pregnancy complications were life threatening. As long as I remembered that God was in control and I prayed, was peaceful and life was good.

BLESSING:

May you feel happy and comfortable where you are today. May God give you peace.

109 DON'T SEND ME SHOPPING TO HUNGARY PLEASE

For we brought nothing into this world, and it is certain we can carry nothing out. And having food and raiment let us be therewith content. (1 Timothy 6:7-8)

When you are lost or stuck it can sometimes make it necessary to ask someone for directions. If you ever have a problem with your means of transport (assuming it is not airbound transportation) in a place where either your roadside assistance insurance cover cannot help you or where it does not even exist then your best help can come from the people around you. This is normally such a good thing when you are in a place with very kind and friendly people.

Once when I was living on the campus of the Institute of Theology Training near Bucharest I was alerted about someone, a young lady, who apparently was terrified of me starting a conversation with her. Apparently she used to either change her path or walk as fast as she could whenever she saw me because she was worried I would speak to her. Her biggest fear was not just that I would speak but it was about the language I would use if I did speak to her. She feared that she would not understand me in English and she knew that I could not speak in Romanian. Her friend could speak English and it was this friend who informed me of this phobia about me.

Back in the village town of Valea lui Mihai I found out for myself what this kind of phobia was like. I was not so scared of anyone wishing to speak to me in Romania because usually if they tried to speak in Hungarian I could have always said a few words in Romanian to let them know that I did not understand Hungarian. What I was afraid of was the need to speak to anyone when I was in Hungary who could not speak either English or Romanian.

When the frequent trips from Valea lui Mihai, Romania to Debrecen, Hungary began to require me to sometimes go without my wife then my fears were elevated. I thought of how if I needed to speak to anyone and I could not, then I would have a huge problem.

The border crossing was not so problematic anymore after a few delays which initially used to happen as soon as the border agents took my British passport and registration documents for my British registered car. They at first used to make me wait for so long until I complained of their unfairness and I challenged them that they were treating me that way because of my colour. I questioned why they had to keep delaying me each time I passed there when they had seen me so many times before in the same car and with the same passport while they let all other people go quickly past. I even told them not just my address but exactly where I lived which was very close to the border.

When I was now being sent to Hungary without the company of my wife my fear of speaking became real. I was now hoping I would be able to do all I needed to do without ever needing to speak to anyone who does not know how to speak in English. Sometimes, and mostly, the reason for going to Debrecen was for the children's violin lessons. But because I was going to be in Debrecen anyway there was always the, "while you are there" kind of request thrown in. It was those kinds of requests that I would say were sent to try me because I could either just accept or winge and little about my fear of the language. Ultimately I needed to do what I was asked to do whether I was terrified or not. Yet I can only recall just one incident about which I ended up with quite a group of different people each trying to help me with what I needed but having to call someone else who they thought could speak to me in English.

REFLECTION:

Throughout the time that we were all trying to speak, there was one thing that all the people had on their faces, in spite of our failure to speak a common language, and it was a very broad smile. How refreshing and reassuring for an anxious person who is worrying about language difficulties to meet the language of smiles. The smile is such a universal language which is also contagious because it is only mean-spirited people who frown back at those who smile at them. What a therapy it is also in a grieving situation, albeit an ageing one which though fading dimmer still flickers momentarily and intermittently. But God is the one who directs smilers to enhance our experiences of life as we need them.

BLESSING:

May God smile on you today and send you lots of smiles via the people you encounter today and may your day be a blessed one.

110 MY TIDY AND NEAT WIFE

Who can find a virtuous woman? for her price is far above rubies. The heart of her husband doth safely trust in her, so that he shall have no need of spoil. She will do him good and not evil all the days of her life. She seeketh wool, and flax, and worketh willingly with her hands. She is like the merchants' ships; she bringeth her food from afar. She riseth also while it is yet night, and giveth meat to her household, and a portion to her maidens. (Proverbs 31:10-15)

When we think about neatness and tidiness, my wife Erika has got to take the prize for the first position. Anyway as the well known proverb says, cleanliness is next to godliness. That should therefore place my wife right up high because not only does she like a super clean and tidy environment, she likes a spotlessly clean and tidy place too, as we all should.

If you can now imagine what it is like to live in a huge house referred to as a villa in Valea lui Mihai, Romania, and also have a passion for neatness and tidiness you may figure out a thing or two about our household. Now try to add the house size to the size of the children in the household, or rather to their very tender age. Picture their inability to clean up and then weigh that up against their ability to make a mess at that same age. Think that through for a moment.

Those who have met with my wife's wardrobe arrangement, kitchen arrangement of everything belonging to the kitchen plus dining room tidiness will understand it better. Even those who have seen her classroom cupboards and drawers will vouch for her precision in the placing and keeping of all items in order. You may be tempted to imagine that it runs in her family but that could be because you have not seen her siblings and their homes as I have. You have not also seen her mum as I have. Not that they are untidy in any way at all but Erika takes tidiness to a whole new level. She tells me that she imagines that God's angels would not be interested to come to an untidy place. I think she is right, but I think of her as an angel herself that was sent to straighten up our household.

Against this background you can then imagine the stress that Erika endures when things are out of place. Often she can be found staying up late to put things into the order that she likes, over and over again and night after night. Admittedly the results of her labour leaves the place very attractive and makes it a desirable dwelling place.

REFLECTION:

The importance of order and neatness for the calmness and tranquillity of the mind cannot be overemphasized. This is more true at a time when one is recovering from some long lasting emotional blow like bereavement. With the tendency to be distressed by the sight of the cemetery over the fence from my backyard I really needed to live in a tranquil and tidy place. I believe that God put Erika in the right place to ensure a super tidy atmosphere prevailed.

BLESSING:

May God give you a de-cluttered mind today so that you too may experience His peace and love all day long and evermore.

111 A FAINTING WIFE

Is not destruction to the wicked? and a strange punishment to the workers of iniquity? Doth not he see my ways, and count all my steps? If I have walked with vanity, or if my foot hath hasted to deceit; Let me be weighed in an even balance, that God may know mine integrity. (Job 31:3-6)

Imagine someone lying still and motionless on the floor. Imagine that how they reached that floor was not by purposefully bending and getting into position for a little nap. The person actually fell onto the floor due to feeling faint and blacking out. You have just imagined the situation that I did not have to imagine at all but a reality that I faced multiple times.

Now imagine me bending down and trying to talk to her on the floor. Imagine again that several times this trying to talk yields no response at all. Or sometimes a response which is unintelligible comes through. Then picture me taking hold of her head and putting it either over my shoulder or my arm, ensuring not to twist her neck. Then lifting her whole still body to take her upstairs to the bed or onto the couch in the living room. For me this is not just a mind picture of the imagination but a replay of actual events that did transpire. Mind you we are talking about a pregnant woman who is heavier than her usual self.

I myself cannot define the exclusive triggers of Erika's fainting episodes. What she says for herself though is that she always felt faint when terrified with stressful imaginations. A particular thing that caused her to be faint is when she went to a hospital or saw some badly injured person or people. Even a gory story such as me describing a surgical procedure by a dentist following a tooth breakage was enough to send her into fainting mode.

When she was pregnant, Erika would sometimes faint for no apparent reason at all. Several times the faintness just came upon her when she was standing and walking. Also, any distress that Erika ever got into left her so faint that she literally collapsed afterwards. That left me with the responsibility of picking her up and restoring her to peace and calmness again.

The bigger distress for me, in all the episodes of faintness was that Erika was not only with child but that her pregnancy had complications that were a threat to life and limb. How could I make her stay peaceful and without any stress in her mind? How could I reach her super high standards of cleanliness and tidiness and still be able to live a normal life within the same space of smartness? How, indeed, could she teach an old dog new tricks?

REFLECTION:

Some things God allows to happen can leave you with more questions than answers. I was happy to have moved on into a new happy marriage. But in just the beginning moments of a new married life came the fear of another loss. Feel the churning of my stomach as I pick up my fainted wife. What was God allowing to haunt me? When were my woes going to end? Why could I not enjoy life with my new wife without all this distress after all that I had just been through?

BLESSING:

May all of life's complications elude you today and may joy fill your day as God takes care of all your needs.

112 SERENITY AND TRANQUILITY FROM SIMPLICITY

It is of the LORD'S mercies that we are not consumed, because his compassions fail not. They are new every morning: great is thy faithfulness. (Lamentations 3:22-23)

As the months added up and the complications of the pregnancy of my wife progressed, we knew that it was not just the risks that were presented by the placenta previa and contractions conditions that we needed to contend with. With her repeated falling, I was now probably getting used to picking up and lifting my motionless and still fainted wife. Maybe my muscles were even getting strengthened by the lifting routine. But it certainly was not one of the most pacifying events of our household.

One Sabbath afternoon after we had just returned from church we decided to explore our surroundings a little bit and if possible commune with nature. We knew that we were close to countryside villages but yet we did not know what we could expect to find in or around those villages. So we all jumped into the car and set off on our expedition.

About 5 or so kilometres away we reached a village called Simian (pronounced shimiyarn with the "i" sounding the same as in indigo). It was a very small village and in a couple of minutes driving we were already on the other end of it. The road paving ended around the end of the village. But the unpaved road carried on. We followed the unpaved road a bit further and then we saw it! The best of the reasons why we had really needed to come out that day was right before us.

It was a more than average size body of water that is found at the end of the dirt road in Simian. The lake was just what we needed to see to fulfil our joy of being in nature on a Sabbath afternoon. We quickly found a spot to leave the car so that we could get closer to the lake.

Soon we were all sitting right on the edges of the banks of the lake. Immediately a song came to my mind and I invited my wife and the kids to join me in singing it. It was so wonderful to sing together, "We'll tarry by the living waters" in harmony. That singing that day started a new special and favourite song which saw us later presenting the song in different congregations as a special song rendered by the Khanye family. The visit to Simian lake became just one of many others that followed afterwards. The short trips to the lake provided a much needed contrast to the fainting spells of indoor confinement.

REFLECTION:

It was such a delightful thing even for the children to be able to run around and to throw stones out in the open area in nature. The lake provided such a healing serenity that brought tranquillity even for the expecting mother. With all the simplicity, the environment brought the much needed serenity that every human could enjoy. Nature is one of God's many ways of healing a burdened heart. Thankfully, it is useful for both the mind and the body's well being.

BLESSING:

May you feel refreshed today as you pay attention to nature's simplicity and potency in delivering God's mercies to you today.

113 A LOVELY ACCIDENTAL SABBATH AFTERNOON WALK

I am the rose of Sharon, and the lily of the valleys. As the lily among thorns, so is my love among the daughters. As the apple tree among the trees of the wood, so is my beloved among the sons. I sat down under his shadow with great delight, and his fruit was sweet to my taste. (Song of Solomon 2:1-3)

The only plan we had was to visit the building site of our friends' new home. We had been shown picture after picture on Facebook of the progress in the building development. One particular photograph that had been posted was of our friend, Mircea, pouring concrete mixture onto the ground to form a foundation slab. The picture had an inscription on it that read something like, "pouring money into the ground". It was an inscription whose pun had caused us to really laugh.

Fortunately for us our site visit was to transpire during a Sabbath afternoon, a time when there should have been nobody doing any labour. We had finished our lunch meal, which we had in Marghita that day, and we headed in the direction that we understood to have been provided. It would not have been long to get to the site, we thought, and drove off with expectation.

After taking all the turns we believed to have been correct we found ourselves facing some very odd looking area. The area was a bit too out of town to fit the description of what we expected. The road leading to the area had become a very rugged unpaved one too. We wondered how our friends would have chosen such a place to construct their dwelling place. But soon we would cease to wonder as we gave up the search for the building site and parked the car at some dead end of a bad road.

We got out of the car to have a little browse of the forest area that we suddenly found ourselves at. The forest was one good surprise for us that we had not even been searching for. It turned out to be a beautiful collection of trees and flowers with footpaths that hikers could follow. So we indulged ourselves a bit and edged in a little farther into the thicket, careful not to lose our way back. What a blissful moment it turned out to be for the whole party of four, including the expectant mother. In fact it was in this moment of being lost (I say lost just because we did not find where we were going) that Erika decided the place was too beautiful to miss the chance to take pictures. So pictures were taken which we still have as a memory of that impromptu, amazing accidental Sabbath afternoon walk.

REFLECTION:

We knew where we were trying to go that day but God knew where we needed to go on that particular day. He knew that Erika needed to have her picturesque moments of joy in the forest and to pick some flowers along the footpaths. He knew that the children needed to shout and hear echoes of their voices without being told to be any quieter. God knew that there had been too much going on for a recovering former widower turned muscleman to keep lifting his fainting wife as she fell. There was no surprise for the almighty and He had allowed us these moments of peace in the forest for a good reason. And we thoroughly enjoyed the view even though we had been on an unplanned detour.

Later on we met our friends who told us where we had taken the wrong turn. On another day we did reach the construction site we had intended to visit.

BLESSING:

May God direct your paths into areas you never imagined before and give you the blessings you need today according to His riches in glory.

114 SPEEDY RUSH TO HOSPITAL

As thou knowest not what is the way of the spirit, nor how the bones do grow in the womb of her that is with child: even so thou knowest not the works of God who maketh all. (Ecclesiastes 11:5)

As the months progressed towards the completion of the final trimester of Erika's pregnancy, the threat to her life had passed. The pregnancy was no longer at risk but yet the time of delivery still had the potential of complications as do all pregnancies. We were now living constantly on high alert and had put a plan in place for who would take care of the kids while we headed for the hospital in Debrecen, Hungary.

On the night of the 15th of December of 2013 Erika felt the frequency of the contractions to have intensified. Then while she was still trying to decide if she should be preparing to go to hospital or not she said she thought she had the ultimate evidence that the delivery process had now begun.

Indeed it was time to take the prepared little luggage and drive off. We were going to leave the kids sleeping but let someone go to the house in the morning to get them ready and take them to school. They knew about the plan beforehand.

We quickly jumped into the car and headed straight to the Hungarian border 6km away. Fortunately the immigration officers attending that night understood our rush and let us through very quickly. The BMW 318i vehicle we rode in was never driven as fast by me as it was that night. Neither was I even bothered by the speed limits on any police speed radars in Hungary. I just navigated my way to the delivery unit of the university hospital of Debrecen as fast as I could. Fortunately we had been there before to familiarise ourselves with the place during some previous routine check visits.

When we reached the delivery unit the patient was soaked and uncomfortable. But the Hungarian nurses assured her that they had seen far worse situations and that all was okay.

After all the rush and adrenalin from speeding and panicking all that happened in the hospital that night was an allocation of a bed for the patient and a seat for her husband to patiently wait. At least we had reached the hospital now and Erika and the unborn baby were being monitored.

REFLECTION:

Sitting in a hospital ward next to my wife's bed was not the most exciting place for me. It was somewhat reminiscent of when I was in a different hospital in England next to the bed of a dying wife. But I had to readjust my thoughts even though it was tough. A new day had dawned and this was a happy and healthy event not an end of life event. Here I was to wait in expectation of the inception of the new life of my own child. Truly God had been faithful and answered my prayers and of those whom I had requested to pray for mother and child.

BLESSING:

May your strength be renewed and may your life be recharged as you go about your day today. May God truly bless you.

115 THE MIRACLE OF CHILDBIRTH

For unto us a child is born. (Isaiah 9:6)

And it came to pass, when men began to multiply on the face of the earth, and daughters were born unto them. (Genesis 6:1)

The rush to the hospital in the middle of the night began to seem a bit like it had not been such a panicking issue. The wait in the hospital was longer than either of us had anticipated. I had literally sat through the night on a hospital chair. My wife was lying on the bed right next to me as she watched the monitoring systems that showed the contractions that were not enough to deliver the baby.

Having been present twice before in a delivery unit of a hospital when my other two children were born I found this Hungarian one somewhat different. Previously, in a different hospital I had heard agonising of mothers in the adjacent or nearby delivery rooms. Here in the Debrecen hospital I could hear absolutely none of that.

When morning came the time came for the doctors to do their rounds. A doctor attended briefly to my wife and then left her to wait for her usual doctor. Later into the day her usual doctor finally came and assessed the situation. He assigned oxytocin to make the contractions much stronger and thereby hasten the pace of the delivery commencement.

At some point later he came back and applied the epidural anaesthetic to stop the feeling of pain during delivery. That application was probably the reason why I was not hearing the delivery ward screaming I had heard in my previous encounters with delivery wards.

Later into the afternoon of 16th December, after an ordeal I will not be writing any details about, a beautiful healthy baby girl was born. Both mother and baby were safe and well. This was the most important thing.

REFLECTION:

Childbirth is a miracle; God enabling mortal humans to participate in the process of procreation! It is such a wonder and a blessing! Ecclesiastes 3:2 says there is a time to be born and a time to die and chapter 7 verses 1 and 2 says "a good name is better than precious ointment; and the day of death than the day of one's birth. It is better to go to the house of mourning, than to go to the house of feasting: for that is the end of all men; and the living will lay it to his heart."

Even as I rejoiced at the time my girl was born the reality is that at some point death shall come. I was there thinking that probably my very own death will one day likely bring pain to the same child who was just born. Also, I reflected on Psalm 103:15 which says "as for man, his days are as grass: as a flower of the field, so he flourisheth."

BLESSING:

May you face the day today with courage and hope. May you be blessed today with wonderful and everlasting memories.

116 BABY NAMED AND CELEBRATED

And out of the ground the LORD God formed every beast of the field, and every fowl of the air; and brought them unto Adam to see what he would call them: and whatsoever Adam called every living creature, that was the name thereof. And Adam said, This is now bone of my bones, and flesh of my flesh: she shall be called Woman, because she was taken out of Man. (Genesis 2:19, 23)

And Adam called his wife's name Eve; because she was the mother of all living. (Genesis 3:20)

The excitement of the arrival of the baby was well proclaimed. Photographs and videos of the tender little one were scattered all over social media platforms like Facebook and WhatsApp. We named the baby Myra Vuyisiwe.

Myra has several meanings to it. Biblically it is the name of a city and also means weeping and bitterness. It also means a sweet ointment and an aromatic shrub called myrrh in Greek. The arrival of Myra to our weeping family was sure to bring a sweet aroma among us.

Vuyisiwe means we have been made happy. The significance of her name is that it brings to light the fact that joy came into our family by the baby's arrival. Some in the family had suffered loss before and the months of pregnancy also had presented challenges that were stealing happiness from the family. At this point in time whatever unhappiness there may have been needed to go away because indeed we had been made happy by the birth of Vuyisiwe.

The Debrecen hospital's staff issued us with papers according to what names we told them for the baby. They told us that the papers were proof of the baby's birth and could be used to get the birth certificate. We were delighted to hear that we could take the baby to Romania the very next day. I on the other hand needed to go and look after the children who were left in the care of friends for the time being.

REFLECTION:

It is a privilege to be in the same place as Adam was at creation. Adam decided what names to call all the things that God had created. He named all the animals by whatever names he chose. He even decided to call Eve a woman. Everything was perfect at the time of creation. Everything is just nearly perfect too when a child is born and when we can give the baby any names we choose. Indeed God had a way of replacing sorrow with joy.

BLESSING:

May He whose name is exalted high above every other name fill your day with joy today.

117 A HUNGARIAN POLICE CHASE

And the watchman told, saying, He came even unto them, and cometh not again: and the driving is like the driving of Jehu the son of Nimshi; for he driveth furiously. (2 Kings 9:20)

A day after baby Myra was born, I left the Debrecen hospital late at night to go and relieve the friends who had remained looking after our other children. I was going to try to get some very much needed rest. With my children's Bible cartoon movies playing (that was just about all that was in the car at that time) I set off towards the Romanian border. The car I drove had screens just behind the driver and passenger's seats as headrests. So whatever I played on the DVD player also showed on the screens at the back.

Soon I was going to reach Nyirabrany which is the Hungarian side of the border with Romania leading to what is called Valea lui Mihai on the same border's Romanian side. I had joy in my heart as I expected to bring the baby home the next day. I was also looking forward to reuniting with the other two children. I was not in any hurry though and I was driving very carefully.

I had just driven through a little village town of Vámospércs and was now on the outskirts of it. Suddenly I saw blue flashing lights on my rear view mirror. The Hungarian police were following me and stopping me. I put my hazard lights on and stopped the car. One of the policemen came to my car to tell or indicate to me to pull over and get the car out of the road. I did as ordered and then asked what was the matter. We had a communication problem right away because the men could not really speak English well. Then one of them told the other one, "Angol" (pronounced Ongol and meaning English). However they managed to tell me that I was over-speeding. That I knew very well that I was not and even now, so many years later I know I was not over-speeding on that particular occasion that they stopped me. So I contested the allegation and defended my innocence in the matter.

They looked around my car and asked where I was coming from and where I was going to. I told them I was going to Romania to my children and that I was from the hospital where my wife had just had a baby in Debrecen. They saw the aforesaid Biblical cartoon characters still playing on the screens behind the front backrests. Then they told me to go well and be careful. Whatever their motivation, I think they were persuaded to be gentle and nice to me because of my story of a baby in hospital and children waiting for me. But that was really one of the strangest things I have ever experienced in all my driving life of over 25 years at the time. I was accused of speeding, which truly I have done at other times, but on this particular occasion I was actually not even over-speeding.

REFLECTION:

Sometimes, in foreign countries, vehicles have been targeted by the police for no other reason than the fact that they are foreign vehicles. The registration number of a British registered car late at night in Hungary could have attracted the attention of the police and they may have decided to make up an excuse to stop the car and make up an over-speeding allegation as a reason. Whatever motives they may have had I really do not know. All I know is that I was not guilty of their accusation. In life there may be some false accusations that can occur out of literally nowhere. God sees all of these things and sometimes allows them to happen for reasons best known to Himself. We are not to lose our faith due to these hiccups of life but to continue to trust that God allows things to happen for a reason. These things may well be a test of our faith in God.

BLESSING:

I pray that today if there is any test upon your faith that you may conquer and continue to trust in God to order your ways and help you to overcome.

118 ATTEMPTING TO SMUGGLE OUR BABY HOME

And the children of Israel went into the midst of the sea upon the dry ground: and the waters were a wall unto them on their right hand, and on their left. (Exodus 14:22)

The day finally came on which the expected hospital discharge was pronounced by the doctors for mother and baby to go home. The papers for the baby to prove where she was born and her given names had been signed and stamped by the hospital authorities. By the time all was done and ready it was already night time. Two things were missing though that could be thought to be valid travel documents for the tiny little baby. These were a birth certificate and a passport. All of our enquiries about obtaining these documents suggested that it would take no less than a few weeks for these papers to become available. How on earth were we going to get her out of Hungary and into Romania without either of these two documents?

We decided to pray and then set off in faith. God was going to make a way somehow. So, placing the baby in her infant's car seat we strapped it onto the back seat and headed for the Nyirabrany border.

As soon as we left Debrecen the baby fell fast asleep. She did not even stir or make any sound at all the entire journey to the border. We even now hoped that with a blanket concealing her little seat her very presence could be unnoticed. So a blanket was flung over her seat so it may appear like some luggage on the back seat.

As we reached the border gate, the reduction of speed and the coming of the car to a stop caused a shaking that immediately woke the baby up. At that moment we were now meant to produce our passports and show them to the immigration officers at the border. They saw our two passports, a Hungarian one and a British one. But they also heard the third human being in the car who when she entered Hungary a few days before had not needed a separate passport since she was inside the womb of her mother. They wanted to see the passport or the papers for the little passenger in the back-seat.

We showed them the papers from the hospital but they said these were not enough for passage at the border. They needed a passport or other travel documents and at least a birth certificate. It was a very stressful moment and the baby cried even more, which helped soften hearts.

The border officers from Hungary then said they could let the baby go as no papers could be done now. It was up to the Romanians now. (At this border officials of both countries are usually together working side by side) The Romanian officers had a man who recognised my wife as a teacher of one of his children and me as the father of his children's friend and classmate. This was the angel sent to the rescue. The officers ultimately just waved us into Romania with all their blessings on the baby which in Romanian is transliterated "much health" to the baby.

REFLECTION:

God had opened up the red sea for us. Where in the world do border staff allow anyone across the border without relevant papers? This was the very same border where I previously had suffered unnecessary delays. This time we got a blessing and personal recognition at night as though God was saying these are my children. Thus saith the LORD, "Let my people go, that they may serve me". (Exodus 8:1)

BLESSING:

May today be a day on which your faith in God is enhanced. May you receive many blessings today.

119 A BABY NAMES DATABASE IN HUNGARY

Behold, I have graven thee upon the palms of my hands; thy walls are continually before me. (Isaiah 49:16)

He that overcometh, the same shall be clothed in white raiment; and I will not blot out his name out of the book of life, but I will confess his name before my Father, and before his angels. (Revelation 3:5)

Some things that are done in certain countries may not be known about unless a situation arises to highlight them. Before 2014 I would have never known that Hungary has a list of names from which baby names can be chosen. The list is not even of optional choices as an alternative to any other names but a definitive list of the only names that are permissible by law in Hungary.

Having my daughter born in Hungary meant that I had to find out about the law of restricted baby names. It also meant that I was either going to accept whatever I was being told to be the law of the land and give up my wishes or confront the issues head on. I had to explore all possibilities and deal with all the challenges that came with seeking exceptions.

Firstly I was informed that unless my marriage was registered in Hungary then the baby's name would not only have to be selected from the database list but only the mother would be recorded as a parent for the child. That sounded weird and very awkward. So I needed to register the marriage in Hungary and obtain a Hungarian marriage certificate. Doing the registration process was not cheap or straightforward. It cost over €100 plus several trips to Hungary from Romania. But thankfully in the end it was completed.

The next critical issue was that of obtaining the birth certificate. The birth registration officers seemed to keep changing the explanation of the requirements of the procedures depending on the individual we spoke to. Ultimately my wife embarked on a process of research into the matter. Armed with emails from the head office and also with details of Hungarian law of birth registration we visited the Debrecen officers.

I had to prove that I was a British citizen and also certify that the name I was registering for my child did not have a vulgar and unacceptable meaning. I also had to bring my own Hungarian to English interpreter, who was not my wife, to the office. Again I also had to pay for the several trips to Debrecen. It was certainly not an easy but not an impossible task. Thanks be to God we finally got our baby a birth certificate, with the names of our choice and not from a database list, 3 months after she was born.

REFLECTION:

God in His wisdom had helped us take the baby out of the country quickly before the struggle to register her birth. Who would have imagined that the process would drag on for 3 months?

Dire circumstances might persuade many a people that they need to give up certain plans or ideas that they want to carry out. In many instances that has not been the case for me. I have faced many situations that on the surface, seemed impossible. But I have not got the mentality of assuming that difficult means impossible. Or the mentality of giving up anything just because someone suggests that I should give up. I believe in a God of the impossible and one who makes many miracles happen even in this day and age. Many times my God has come through for me, which helped me face the next seemingly impossible thing.

BLESSING:

May your name be found in the book of eternal life. May peace be with you now and always.

120 A DELAYED FLIGHT AND BUS

I have heard thy prayer, I have seen thy tears: behold, I will heal thee. (2 Kings 20:5)

I was due to travel to Swindon, England. I found and booked a Wizzair flight from Debrecen to London Luton airport whose return price was probably less than £30 inclusive of taxes. I think one way tickets were just £13. My business going to the U.K. had something to do with the house that needed some work done. I was really low on cash and could not afford to hire anyone to do the work. So I had to come and do it all myself.

Money was really tight so to keep the cost of travel low, I had booked a seat on the bus from Luton airport to London Victoria coach station. There I would take the underground train to Paddington station from which I would then take the train to Swindon. This was the most cost effective way for my journey.

All my travel tickets were pre-booked and prepaid. All I needed to do was just show up and travel. I think my train fare was £23 including the underground. On the day of travel the plane from Hungary was delayed for about half an hour. When I finally got into the easy-bus the time was already late. Then something else happened, the normal road to central London was closed and the bus driver went around in circles trying to find alternative ways. When he finally figured out a new route I was now running about an hour behind schedule for my trains.

When I reached the underground train station to take the train to Paddington I was way too late. But the kind officials let me through. In the Paddington station my ticket failed to unlock the gate to the platforms. The security guards sent me to the customer services desk for help. But the only help I was offered was to buy a new ticket for about £36.

I did not have that kind of money with me. I did not even have any contact with anyone who could help me. So I explained the reason why I was that late and that it was caused by my bus and flight before. The man told me to just buy a new ticket and then claim compensation from the bus company or from my travel insurance. The trouble was that I could not even afford to buy a new ticket. Also claiming back would have been next to impossible since I was not residing in the country anyway.

I tried to explain to the man but he wanted me to leave so he could serve other people. I told him that I could not leave as I could not go anywhere now so I really needed help. He now became unkind and rather aggressive with me and I told him to call the police to remove me from there. He quickly rang security as I stood by waiting.

Soon a pair of metropolitan police officers appeared and they were told some distorted story about me. Then turning to me they asked for my side of the story. Then I told my story in detail. As I carried on with the story a tear began to flow from my eye and the officers immediately summoned a train conductor and asked if he would take me onto his train on my existing ticket. He took me with him and for the first part of the journey I sat in first class before he later moved me to the economy cabin.

REFLECTION:

My distress about my train journey brought back the reason why I was now so poor that I could not afford to buy a new ticket. I had quit my job and so had minimal income. But bereavement had caused me to choose to forego my job and my income. This bereavement situation was what made tears to flow so easily when I had tough situations to confront. God saw my tears and he softened hearts so I could be helped.

BLESSING:

May you meet with merciful, kind and compassionate people today. May today be a joyful day for you.

121 HIDE AND SEEK ALL THE WAY TO KINDERGARTEN

He hath made his wonderful works to be remembered: the LORD is gracious and full of compassion. (Psalms 111:4)

I remember the days of old; I meditate on all thy works; I muse on the work of thy hands. (Psalms 143:5)

I never thought much of it at the time and frankly I only did it to entertain my daughter. It was an idea that just suddenly popped into my head one morning. I was walking Vuyiso to her kindergarten one morning. When I say walking her I really mean that I was walking next to her. She herself was not walking but cycling.

The normal routine was for me to take her to her "school" while she cycled. Then when I reached the school I would take her bike and walk back home while pushing it alongside myself. Later in the day I would roll the little bike along to go and fetch her back. On exceptional days when the weather was too adverse I would use the car to take her.

It was on one of the normal days that I had this idea to make the walk a bit more fun and a bit quicker too. I ran a few meters ahead and hid behind one of many trees that lined the main road in Valea lui Mihai. Soon enough Vuyiso caught up and I shouted "boo" as she laughed happily while quickly riding past. I ran ahead of her and repeated the process over and over until we reached her kindergarten school.

The hide and seek school runs were just one of the things I knew I could play that were fun for Vuyiso before she went to start her year 1 schooling. As I say, they were for her to have fun but yet surprisingly they left an indelible mark on my own memory. Incidentally, I have memories of my own father playing with me in my childhood that I still remember till this day.

REFLECTION:

Making lasting memories is achievable only by making lovely present day activities. Today's pleasant events will become tomorrow's priceless memories. Even things done for the delight of another become tomorrow's pleasant memories of the one doing them for the sake of others.

BLESSING:

May the things that happen today in your life form some of the most cherished and pleasant memories in your future. May you be blessed today.

122 MOVE OUT THEN LATER COME BACK

**And if a stranger sojourn with thee in your land, ye shall not vex him.
(Leviticus 19:33)**

As we continued our stay in one of the largest homes we ever lived in we received a message from the landlord. They were planning to come back from Belgium for a period of just two weeks. But they were bringing guests with them and altogether they would make a group that would be too big to go and live in a hotel for that period.

The only thing that the landlord decided was best to do was to reclaim their home from us. They told us that we would need to evacuate their house for two weeks. We as a family of 5 together with our infant baby needed to leave the home we were renting and paying our rent faithfully every month. We were to go wherever we could go then after two weeks come back and bring our things back to retake our tenancy

We made arrangements about where we would go. But at the same time we made it clear that we would not return. Where in the world can the tenant be kicked out of their home even for a day just because the landlord needs their property back? I thought it was one of the most appalling behaviours ever known to mankind. Yes the rent was low but we deserved some respect not to be so despised and treated like destitutes.

REFLECTION:

Some occurrences in life can be surprising. One would have thought the landlord would appreciate a tenant who pays their dues faithfully and helps them with their loan repayments. But this turned out to be not the case on this occasion. To try to withhold our deposit money they even tried to insinuate that the house needed professional cleaning. But we had left the house even cleaner than we found it.

The situation was another lesson to show us that in life we will not always meet with reasonable people. Sometimes people can be self centred. Yet our trust in God should never waver. For our own sanity, we need to forgive even people who hurt us in ways like this.

BLESSING:

May you be blessed today and may you deal with honourable and reasonable people.

123 A HIGHER CALLING

Them hath he filled with wisdom of heart, to work all manner of work, of the engraver, and of the cunning workman, and of the embroiderer, in blue, and in purple, in scarlet, and in fine linen, and of the weaver, even of them that do any work, and of those that devise cunning work. (Exodus 35:35)

My telephony[1] business had been hacked and I had no zeal to rebuild it. I frankly did not have my old enthusiasm for computing systems that I had in the past. When I was working with Information Technology previously I was doing so with such excitement because I simply enjoyed my work. I was getting paid because I was doing my job yet it really was my hobby that I was being paid to enjoy. But the thrill certainly was gone now. Yet I needed to generate income to support and sustain my family.

I started looking for IT management and Systems Analyst and Systems Administrator jobs again. The prospective employers invited me to job interviews. They paid for my flights and overnight hotel accommodation to attend the job interviews. Twice I went to Oxford university for such interviews and once to Cambridge. But it seemed like something was just not right anymore somehow because I was not being picked.

In the past I had been so confident that whatever organisation I applied for a job from which offered me an interview would certainly offer me the job after the interview. I was always that sure. I had a family which supported me with prayer in all the times I was seeking new employment. They would even all be praying during the exact times that I was being interviewed because I notified them of the exact dates and times. I knew that when my mother and father were praying for me as well as my sisters then I would triumph in my job quest.

It had happened in Botswana where at Botswana Housing Corporation they wanted and even specified in their adverts that they preferred a citizen of Botswana for the job. After interviewing 10 of us candidates they were offering the job to me who was a foreigner. They said I was their best candidate. My parents had been praying.

---

[1] Telephony, not telephone, is the correct word for the type of business

Meanwhile I had been head-hunted by Botswana Accountancy College to a job I had not even applied for and offered a very high paid job with benefits that I could never have refused. These included high cost accommodation payment, car loans and interest free settlement loans on top of a very lucrative salary. The housing corporation tried to match the package offer but as a parastatal could not reach what the college had for me.

These many years later, nothing had changed much about the prayer support network as I did my interviews. Nothing had changed about my many years of previous job experience in senior and well paid positions either. The only thing that certainly was not the same was me. I was not the same anymore. I could not impress anybody with my thrill and excitement for the job. It seems like my lack of enthusiasm showed itself. The fact is that I was now looking for a job to earn money not a career to enjoy working in that was also a hobby as was in the past.

REFLECTION:

I would have been happier if the jobs were about serving God and helping people. I wanted to work in pastoral ministry work. I had a higher calling and desire to be a servant of God. I had quit computing even mentally and my mind seemed to know it. But there was a need to do something now. And I could not even understand why God was not providing what I believed He had called me to do. I wait patiently to get into God's ministry while I do other things to feed and sustain my household.

BLESSING:

May the good Lord give you the desires of your heart today according to His will.

124 MOVING TO SCOTLAND

But the God of all grace, who hath called us unto his eternal glory by Christ Jesus, after that ye have suffered a while, make you perfect, stablish, strengthen, settle you. (1 Peter 5:10)

Something was not right somewhere in spite of how excited I could have been to be with and live among the wonderful Romanian people. My family and I had enjoyed the special treatment by Romanians as well as life in Transylvania. I however still needed to provide the bread and butter for our survival. And under the prevailing circumstances it did not seem to be about to improve anytime soon. Losing the huge house had not helped us to live in comfort either. So the best remaining solution was to move farther afield.

Moving however always came with a lot of pain for us all. I for one liked Romania very much for how Romanians had treated me. The children were sad to have to part with their friends. My wife was also unhappy to have to leave her country and live far from her family.

The tough adjusting process saw us ultimately living in Irvine, North Ayrshire, Scotland. The children enrolled into the local school close to where we lived and began to make new friends there while the toddler stayed home with her mother.

Why Irvine of all places? One may ask. Well the simple answer is that firstly it appeared to be a lovely area to live. Then more importantly it was a cheaper part of the country to move to and relaunch our life from. One additional key element was that it was close to where some old friends lived. So it would be a good thing to move so that we would live close to our friends and to a cheaper part of the country.

Among the Scottish people we felt welcome and at home. We settled in well and met many wonderful and lovely people with whom we formed new friendships. Such has always been the case with being part of a global Seventh day Adventist family. Wherever we go in the world we just fit in quickly with the people from the local church immediately taking us as a part of them. I recall that in Irvine some of our new church friends even gave us some plates and cups to help us settle.

REFLECTION:

I had absolutely no idea about the possibility that I would move around homes so many times following widowhood Only after experiencing it did I eventually learn that it happens to many widowed people. Though not all widowed people end up moving homes, chances of that happening are very high. Moving is sometimes part of some difficult but necessary adjustments. Even in this, God certainly never left me alone.

BLESSING:

May you be calm and peaceful today and may God bless you.

125 BECOMING A CARER

And, behold, the courses of the priests and the Levites, even they shall be with thee for all the service of the house of God: and there shall be with thee for all manner of workmanship every willing skilful man, for any manner of service: also the princes and all the people will be wholly at thy commandment. (1 Chronicles 28:21)

Living in Irvine had some advantages over where we had just been before. But the advantages were not massive because I still had not found the pastoral ministry role I was waiting and hoping for.

Whilst living in Irvine, I enrolled for the diploma in Holistic Nutrition course. Through contacts by one of the church elders in Irvine I also got a little bit of work repairing laptops for a computer shop in Saltcoats. Still income was not adding up well.

One Sunday I attended a church officers event in Crieff, Perthshire. While there I had the pleasant surprise of meeting with one lady, Mrs Joyce Chengeta, with whom my late wife had become very close to. She owned a care agency and I knew as soon as I saw her that my financial difficulties were going to be reduced. I even told her that I knew that my troubles were now over because I had found her. I had no idea she was living in Edinburgh. I told her all about my situation and she immediately offered to train me as a carer and give me a job in the areas around Glasgow.

The training as well as the staff uniform and badges which were normally given at a cost to the trainee were given to me all free of charge. Thanks to Mrs Joyce Chengeta.

I was soon working and earning a fairly useful and much needed income.

REFLECTION:

I had excitedly taken the carer job thinking that in addition to helping the clients and earning an income I would have a chance to also share the good news about Jesus and salvation. I had also thought I could help the clients with my natural remedies and nutrition knowledge but I had no idea that it would be completely impossible. Nonetheless I was still thankful for having a job and some income.

BLESSING:

Today may all your decision making be blessed and inspired and may joy always be yours.

126 AN EMAIL FROM ROMANIA

"For the wisdom of this world is foolishness with God. For it is written, He taketh the wise in their own craftiness." (1 Corinthians 3:19)

After residing in Irvine for just over a year, as a family we were getting used to Scottish life. We had now established certain routines and our daily life was now more or less predictable. We were now fully integrated into our church community and could now identify with Irvine as our home.

A few years before I had completed my studies in Romania. I was left only with taking either the comprehensive 6 hour exam covering several modules of the program or writing a thesis. There was no hurry to do either of the two as there also was no demand for the full qualification papers. Everywhere that I had contacted about my completion and readiness to serve for one reason or another did not seem ready to take me. So I had very little incentive or motivation to rush the thesis or exam sitting action.

In my relaxed state, lacking any urgency, I one day received an email from the MA program's Secretary. The email was written to warn and advise me of the fact that the years allowed to complete my degree were now running out. I had to do my thesis or take the exam immediately or lose some of my courses. The longer I left it would mean that I would lose more and more of my courses that I had paid for, studied and completed. So I replied and asked for the dates of the next comprehensive examinations.

The response I received was a rather shocking one. I was told that the degree issuing university in Michigan, USA had stated that the courses that had been used from my first degree as prerequisites had not been sufficient. I was informed that I needed to do 4 more courses before I could either take the examination or write my thesis. That was a real blow to me.

REFLECTION:

I was not bothered by the fact that I had not yet received my MA diploma and I had no sense of urgency about it. I still wanted to work in gospel ministry work but I was under the impression that I may not be useful anymore due to my lack of Romanian language skills in the case of Romania. I also thought, based on what someone had told me, that the UK would have no use of my training since I had not studied in the UK and they preferred UK graduates. So I was kind of resigned to doing anything really. But when I was told about losing my courses I was really disturbed and wanted to resolve the situation and at least get my completion papers. But somehow I knew God was still in charge even though I did not understand the situation at all. He who never left me alone in my grief was not about to leave me now.

BLESSING:

I pray that today God may make you appreciate His work in you and help you celebrate your accomplishments so far in your life. May you be blessed in all you do.

127 HOLIDAY IN ROMANIA
WITH A SURPRISE

We will go three days' journey into the wilderness, and sacrifice to the LORD our God, as he shall command us. (Exodus 8:27)

During the school summer holidays we as a family decided to take a now familiar long trip by car to Romania. While it is a long and tiring journey for the whole family and particularly for me as the sole driver, it is a trip that is quite picturesque and scenic. The whole family likes to go on the trip through 7 countries.

So we set off from Scotland with an established day of return. We drove down to Dover, Kent, England and enjoyed the car ferry crossing the English channel part of the sea. On the ferry crossing segment of the journey I must always sleep due to exhaustion. So I was sleeping as usual on the deck as the ferry sailed us to Dunkerque, France. Through Belgium and Netherlands we drove before reaching the famous German autobahn on which there is mostly no driving speed limit, much to the delight of my son. Upon finally reaching Austria and paying the vignette road tariffs we inched closer to Hungary. After a night of rest in the castle at Bogenhofen college in Austria, we then passed through Hungary and finally entered into Romania.

While enjoying our rest within Romania I began seeking for some information about where I could be useful in the country since I needed to come back to do a number of courses spread across the year. As providence would have it I learned about a privately owned Adventist Christian school just over an hour away from the theological seminary. I learned that the school was looking for staff and so I contacted them. The excited owners of the school invited us to meet with them in Sovata, a lovely tourist resort area, for a discussion.

The result was that a new plan was born from the meeting. We were to soon go back to Scotland and wind up our stay then head back to Romania again where I would become a volunteer English teacher at the school at which our children would also be attending. I would also be able to take time to attend the 4 extra courses the institute had said I needed to.

REFLECTION:

The path of life in recovery from grief can be long and winded. I could not ever know what would happen from one phase to the next. I think in all the phases God had something significant for me to learn. Things may not have been going as I wished or expected but God was still in control. After all I was no longer in mourning and the adjustments were essential for the moments they happened in. I needed to be still and watch God in action. Yet to suggest that it was easy, for me or my family, would be misleading.

BLESSING:

May you have calmness of heart and of mind and watch God in action in your life today. May He richly bless you.

And I have also established my covenant with them, to give them the land of Canaan, the land of their pilgrimage, wherein they were strangers. (Exodus 6:4)

At last we were clearing out our Scottish home in Irvine in readiness for travelling to Romania. We had said our farewells to our friends from church. We had shed a few tears of parting and promised to keep up communications. We also planned to visit and also invited friends to visit us in Romania.

Some of our friends had ultimately come to help us de-clutter and lighten our baggage. I felt the pain of sending a tall and fully functional fridge freezer (though 10 years old I had bought it brand new from Currys) to the recycling plant. We sold some of our furniture at give away prices. Prices that were far lower than we had paid for them not so long before. For items that we could not sell we either gave them away to whoever wanted them or we threw them away. We had been reassured that we did not need to bring anything because all we could ever need was there already.

All the clearing and packing of things away was neither easy nor fast. The plan had been to depart on either Monday or Tuesday. But we ended up failing to empty the house, pack and leave on our planned time.

We had 2 cars in our household and I had tried but failed to sell one of them quickly enough. Then we thought of towing one car behind us using an A-frame. An A-frame is a metal "A" shaped bar that can be used to tow a driverless car. I bought an A-frame but had to quickly return it since I learnt that in mainland Europe by law, I would not be allowed to use it.

Next, still within the week, I had to look for a car transporter trailer. I found one and bought it for £750. My plan was to sell the trailer in Romania as well as the second car. The price was good if I would sell because in Romania such trailers cost a lot more. But I also needed to buy heavy duty belts to strap and secure the car onto the trailer and that added another £200 cost. The towing car needed a tow hitch installed at a price of £275, yet another cost. The expectation was that it would be easy enough to sell all these things in Eastern Europe.

Finally, the car trailer was loaded up with a fully packed car. The house was empty and clean at last. We gathered together and with nostalgia said our very last prayers in that home before leaving.

REFLECTION:

Packing and moving house is now probably one of the least desired activities for my family. Yet by its recurrence it is also one of the things that have consistently reminded me of the misfortunes of grief. Even when I was not mourning anymore I knew deep in my heart that all the moving had its primary cause as the loss of a human being's life. Yet even this was also in God's hands. Should it happen also to you, just remember that God is still in charge and sees you through it all.

BLESSING:

May your life be joyous and stable. May you appreciate the stability God gives you and may you be filled with joy.

129 THE ACCURSED THING

Did not Achan the son of Zerah commit a trespass in the accursed thing, and wrath fell on all the congregation of Israel? and that man perished not alone in his iniquity. (Joshua 22:20)

It was very late on Friday night when we finally started off. It was almost midnight when we pulled out of Irvine, North Ayrshire towards England. My wife suggested that we spend the night at the church but I said it would be too complicated and I deposited the church key back where I was meant to.

So, leading my family against the 4th Biblical commandment, "Remember the Sabbath day to keep it holy" (Exodus 20:8), I drove the VW touran with a heavy trailer behind, on the A76 road towards East Ayrshire. As it was raining, and had been for a while before we set off, the fully loaded vehicles did not make it any easier to drive away. It was also not very useful that it was my first time to drive such a massive load.

We had passed Mauchline then Sorn and were on the B743 road heading towards Muirkirk when we faced quite a steep ascent. I could feel that the car was struggling to go uphill but I hoped it would still pull through. Gradually the car failed to keep ascending and ultimately ground to a complete halt. I thought to allow the car to roll back down a bit before trying to drive back up faster. As soon as I rolled backwards the trailer crossed the road so that now I was blocking both lanes of a two way traffic road.

Keeping my foot hard on the brake pedal I asked my wife to go and look for stones to place behind the trailer wheels. I feared that the trailer would pull back both vehicles downhill and crash. She tried but could not find any, and she was too scared to go further as it was dark and wet. Then she remembered that the trailer had a handbrake. I asked her to pull it and she tried but failed as it was too hard for her. So we had to swop our feet on the brake pedal so I could go and apply the trailer handbrake. That was successful and at last we could let go of the brake pedal and deal with waving down passing cars to slow them down and then redirect them onto the grassy verge of the road.

In the end we removed all the luggage stacked up on the driver's seat (of the car on the trailer) all the way against the front windscreen and put it all on the ground next to the road. Then I reversed the mazda premacy car down from the trailer onto the verge because the trailer was not straight on the road. After that I attempted to start the VW engine so we could pull up the trailer straight onto the left side of the road again. But the battery was now dead after hazards and parking lights had been on for more than an hour. Trying to jump start using the mazda which had been on the trailer resulted in it getting stuck in the mud! We had to find sticks and branches to get the car unstuck.

Finally we pulled the car trailer straight onto the road and I drove back into the nearby Sorn village to leave the mazda while we drove the VW onwards towards the motorway. But I was now too sleepy to carry on driving so I pulled into a safe area beside the road and slept a little on the seat of the car as everyone else in the family.

REFLECTION:

I believe that like Achan, my decision to commence our journey into the Sabbath hours had the same effect as his taking the "accursed thing". My family suffered because of my actions. I believe that God was not happy with me for purposely doing what I knew to be wrong. In my life I have always experienced what I feel is God's painful correction for breaking His commandments, including the Sabbath commandment. "To whom much is given, much is required" (Luke 12:48). I certainly cannot blame grief every time I get into problems. Yes there was a problem with the car's diesel injectors I found out months later. But I think traveling on God's Sabbath made me feel the pain of God's wrath as I missed out on fellowship and prayer as a result of the breakdown.

BLESSING:

May you walk in the light of God as you understand His commandments for yourself. May His word be your strength and your shield as you go through your day today and be blessed.

130 KINDEST MUIRKIRK PEOPLE

He loveth righteousness and judgment: the earth is full of the goodness of the Lord. (Psalm 3:5)

Our original planned first stop was in Middlesbrough. As I woke up in the car on Saturday morning along the road, I imagined that it was still possible to reach Middlesbrough. I thought that there we would still be able to fellowship and worship with other Sabbath keepers in a church building.

So I resumed driving towards Muirkirk. It was still in the early hours of the morning when we reached the little village town of Muirkirk. But as we drove through the high street a very loud squeaky sound could be heard coming from our car. I immediately looked for a lengthy parking space for both the car and the trailer so that I could investigate the source of the noise.

As I walked around the car searching for the problem, a man appeared from a nearby shop. He had been smoking outside the shop and had seen our car approaching. He pointed me straight to the nearside trailer wheel that was almost dangling off. He said as we were driving the wheel was wobbling so hard that it seemed as if it was about to come right off. A closer examination showed that a few wheel nuts had already fallen off. The remaining ones were not holding much anymore.

Fortunately the trailer had a total of 6 wheels altogether with a pair on each side at the rear. But the nuts could not be tightened anymore as the threads had been ruined already. Removing the remaining nuts so as to drive on was a huge challenge. I did not have many tools to use. I tried to hit the nut off using a wheel spanner but I was not successful. A man suddenly came where I was and asked what was wrong and where we were going. He then left and went to his house and brought me a hammer and chisel. He told me to keep the for myself after using them.

The other man who had been smoking went back to his shop and filled a bag with crisps, biscuits and water and gave them to my family. He asked if any of us needed to use the toilet and offered us the use of the toilet in his shop, which was normally for staff only.

A woman who owned a beauty salon outside of which we had parked also came and befriended us. She too offered the use of her toilet facilities and brought a pack of liquorice sweets and crisps.

We were stuck for a while but in the end I managed to get the wheel off and place it and strap it onto the trailer. We then drove off towards Douglas where we would join the motorway at last.

REFLECTION:

God's justice is always mingled with mercy. It was a horrible night and an unpleasant morning to wake up to another breakdown after what we had already been through. Yet this was only a portion of what was still awaiting ahead of us. My wife even began to say that it seemed that God was not happy with us going to where we were heading to.

BLESSING:

May your joy be full today as you meet kind and loving people. May your mind shut off any stressful news and events as you enjoy the peace of God.

131 ANOTHER BREAKDOWN – IN A CARPARK

Then called I upon the name of the LORD; O LORD, I beseech thee, deliver my soul. (Psalms 116:4)

We finally left the village town of Muirkirk with the limping trailer on 3 instead of 4 hind wheels. It was not long before we joined the M74 motorway Southbound. But the smoother the ride became on the motorway the faster I became drowsy again. I could not even drive very fast because of towing a trailer, and a limping one at that.

As soon as I spotted some motorway services I decided to pull in for a little nap. The little nap lasted for more than a whole hour. When I finally awoke it was time to have one of our in-car journey meals.

After the sleep and the food break it was time to return onto the motorway. Turning the key to start the car however failed to start it. Instead several dashboard warning lights came on. One of them said "Emissions Garage". I did not know what to do but I knew that if i kept cranking the engine I would soon have no battery power left. So I invited my family to say a prayer with me for God to help us.

After praying I sent several text messages to a few of my friends who could potentially advise me on what to do. The chances of any of them responding were quite slim because they were likely to have been at church or to have their phones turned off for the Sabbath. After a couple of minutes, however, I got a call from a mechanic friend who lived in Portsmouth.

My friend asked me a few questions to determine how best to resolve the problem without needing a breakdown recovery service. He ultimately suggested that I try disconnecting the battery terminal and wait for about half an hour for the car's computer memory to reset itself and delete its existing errors. I had no other option but to do as suggested.

After waiting half an hour I put the connector terminals back on the battery. I tried starting the car again a few times and cranked it for longer. Lo and behold the car started again and the emissions warning disappeared. What an instant answer to prayer that was!

There was only one incidental problem left. We had been stuck in a car park that had a maximum stay period of 2 hours and I only saw a sign reminding me of this as I left the car park to rejoin the motorway. I think we had been there for around 4 hours but that was the least of my problems for that moment. The only trouble was that the car park owners would not know why we had overstayed in their car park. At the same time we were not going to be able to know if they were unhappy with us for overstaying since we were on our way out of the country. Any communications about our parking would have had to follow us overseas, and we did not receive any communications while we were overseas.

We reached Middlesbrough around 8pm on Saturday. We parked the trailer just opposite to the shop in front of the house. We removed all the bits of luggage that we had strapped onto the trailer and left only the wheel whose rim had been ruined. Finally, almost 24hours after we started off, we could sleep inside a house.

REFLECTION:

It is very easy to fall into a situation that demands reaching out to others for help. In fact it forces one to swallow their pride because they must ask another for assistance.

Reading back as I write the dramatic things we experienced sounds almost like fiction to me now. Even the family finds the stories, which they were part of quite a fascinating reminder of what God brought us through. And yet the dramatic and stressful events had only just begun!

BLESSING:

May your day be a stress free one. But should anything go wrong today, may God keep you calm and restful in His care.

132 AN UNPLEASANT DISAPPEARANCE

Which now of these three, thinkest thou, was neighbour unto him that fell among the thieves? (Luke 10:36)

After all the drama and events of the journey so far, it was time to rest for a while. I now frantically tried to find a second driver with whom I could go back to rescue the Mazda left in Sorn, Scotland. You would think that surely the worst had already happened and no more dramatic events would still occur.

A friend and brother from the local Middlesbrough Adventist church responded to my appeal for help. The truth is that I really hardly knew the man but he had been kind and friendly when we first met. He was not even from the same country as me but from Rwanda. No other person had even replied to my message which requested help. There was not even an acknowledgement from others to say they had got my message but could not help. I guess they were either busy, they did not get my message or they did not realise how desperate our situation was.

With my kind Rwandese friend and brother, we drove off towards Scotland around 1.30pm on Sunday afternoon. About 45 minutes later I got a call from my wife. I wondered what she wanted because she knew I was traveling.

The purpose for my wife's call was to ask me where I had put the trailer. I told her that I had not moved it from where we had left it overnight. She said she thought I had put it somewhere safer because it was no longer where I had left it.

The thieves of South Bank, Middlesbrough had wasted no time in helping themselves to my property! I had bought the trailer using borrowed money! Now I was left with no money and no trailer neither.

I phoned the police immediately to report the theft. They asked for some details and for whom I suspected could have done it. That was pretty much the end with the police and the last conversation with anyone who could even try to look for it. I guess for them it was too cheap and not worth spending time and money on looking for the thieves.

We found the Mazda safe and intact and drove back One car behind the other to Middlesbrough with my good new friend. God bless him!

REFLECTION:

Sometimes in life we learn lessons we may not even be expecting to learn. I learned not to have too much expectation from all people. Only one person whom I had least expected to respond to my request for help actually did respond. God inspired this particular brother whom even beyond that day I have thereafter seen to be consistently always there to help whenever needed. This was exactly the same trend in my bereavement. I had people that I hardly even expected showing me compassion and comforting me. Be attentive to this aspect and you may discover the same to be true for you also.

BLESSING:

Today may your cup of blessings overflow. May you take the overflowing blessings with thankfulness and delight.

133 ANOTHER TRAILER ACQUIRED

Restore unto me the joy of thy salvation; and uphold me with thy free spirit. (Psalms 51:12)

With the car transporter trailer gone and the journey having only just begun a new and urgent solution was needed. The anxious owners of the school in Romania kept calling to ask us when we would be arriving.

A day after the trailer theft we had one of those "are we there yet" kind of calls. We just had to report the sad news about the stolen trailer. At that point there clearly was reason to worry by the people who were waiting in anticipation for our arrival in Romania.

The next day we got another call by the man who wanted to drive a van from France, where he worked, to come and fetch our baggage. The trouble with his idea was that he had never been to England before. Even worse than that was the fact that he could not speak any English at all. So talking to border officials would be very difficult for him.

When the idea of coming to collect our things seemed not to be feasible another idea emerged. We were to search for another trailer, a box trailer this time and the man would lend us money to buy it. A trailer of that sort, we reasoned, should be easy enough to sell in Romania. We would try to sell the Mazda in the UK, albeit for a lower price.

We found and acquired the new trailer from Hartlepool. The man sent us the money via Western Union money transfer. We loaded the trailer on the very same night and parked it chained to the car overnight. We also made a reservation with DFDS Seaways, a car ferry company, to cross the English channel to France.

The Mazda was not sold. So we left it with our friend who had gone to help us bring it from Scotland. He would continue trying to sell it for us.

REFLECTION:

After the turmoil of the events since starting off from Scotland it seemed like some calm was now returning. We were now all looking forward to an easy going steady journey. Little did we know that it was not all over yet. God was still going to show us more of His providence in our distresses.

BLESSING:

May you enjoy God's providences in your life today. May your day be a happy one today.

134 BON VOYAGE, AT LAST

They that go down to the sea in ships, that do business in great waters. (Psalms 107:23)

At long last the younger members of our traveling party's prayers were answered. They had been repeatedly asking the question, "When will we go?" It was a lot harder for them to appreciate the difficulty of resolving our logistical issues.

Two of the children's bikes could not fit into the trailer. This was in addition to many other items that had fitted well before in the Mazda that was on the car transporter trailer. Some things actually had to be left behind since the capacity of the box trailer was quite small. So I strapped the bikes outside the front of the trailer and behind the boot of the car for the long journey.

On our departure day we rose up early in the morning and headed down the A19 then A1/M then M1 motorway towards Dover, Kent. The speed was a bit too slow for my liking as it was being restricted by the load in the trailer. I think the slowness was also equally tiring as boredom also set in. As such we had a number of comfort breaks as well as our family famous journey picnic foods. Since our diet is mostly on the plant based side as well as non-fried foods it is always easier to make our own provisions whenever we journey than to buy.

When we reached the sea port of Dover we showed our British and Hungarian passports to the British and French immigration officers. They asked us where we were going and checked each of our names by reading them aloud for us to respond individually. After this they gave us back our passports and waved us on.

Next we went through a customs search area. They did not seem keen on checking our load this time and so we drove around to the DFDS Seaways check-in gates. They again checked all our passports before giving us a lane number to go and queue in. The queue we were assigned to was that of cars with trailers and motorhomes.

We finally drove into the vessel. With a length of 186metres and width of 28metres, the ship had the capacity of holding 250cars and 1000 passengers. It was such a beautiful hotel-like vessel with a number of dining venues, a café, play areas, a shop, a money changers shop, private lounge and even facilities for commercial drivers. Many heavy goods vehicles were also on board.

The doors or gates were shut and the huge vessel undocked as we set sail towards Dunkerque, France. At last we were on our way out of the UK into mainland Europe.

REFLECTION:

The very first time I rode in a huge vessel with trucks, cars and people on board I could not enjoy the ride at all. My grief was too much to think of the splendour of the vessel.

At the time described above I was not in mourning anymore. In time, God does heal even hearts that are full of grief and we can once again appreciate beautiful things. But heaven is the place of ultimate splendour that God has made for us who love Him. I certainly do not plan to miss heaven!

BLESSING

May all happiness be yours today. May God bless you.

135 THE BELGIAN EXPERIENCE

But when they in their trouble did turn unto the LORD God of Israel, and sought him, he was found of them. (2 Chronicles 15:4)

This chapter was called 'the Belgian experience' I said when I finally got the trailer facing the opposite direction and now with some cash euros in my pocket. My wife quickly pointed out that we may still have more trouble if we ran out of fuel and it was too early to close the chapter on Belgium! What we learned in Belgium was that it is impossible to walk into a bank with cash and exchange its currency and walk out with another currency just like that.

The night before. On a ferry over the English channel enroute to France we had already secured some cash in euros before my wife said that the rate of exchange used had been so bad! I asked her what a good rate would have been before I decided to go back to the onboard currency exchangers. They happily returned my pounds and stated that they too would never change their money in their own bureau of exchange on the ferry!

We had enough fuel to go through France and exchange cash the next morning at any bank we figured. With this in mind, and after passing by the city of Antwerp which was congested with traffic we got off the motorway and about 10km later found a bank. The bankers told me that they could only credit my account if I had one with them but they would not give me cash in exchange. They suggested I return to the city of Antwerp and try to get cash there. Of course being me never giving up easily, I tried another bank which was a different one! Meanwhile we went into some huge shopping complex where someone told us we would find a bank. There was no bank at all there, but just some very clean and tidy bathrooms which the whole family needed so desperately after being confined overnight to a vehicle environment! We drove away to another area still away from Antwerp where the same was said by other banks.

Ultimately getting instructions and a printout of how to get to the money changers in the city, we reluctantly drove our low-on-fuel-car back to Antwerp to search for the said currency exchange bureaux. In Antwerp, we were sure that we had reached the train station near to which would be currency people. So leaving the family in the car about a mile away where we had managed to park our extraordinarily long vehicle (including the trailer) I went to seek the money changers.

I walked to so many places, including the post office and I even reached one bank where I was only told that they had just closed for lunch at 12! In the end I had to take my family and drive to another area of town where there was the central train station not the Antwerpen Berchem station I had gone to before! The traveling time lost so far was about 3 hours.

When we finally found the money changers I was surprised find no parking space in a dead-end street that had been closed by construction work! My car and trailer with family remained in a place where clamping costs for illegal parking were about 120 euros. I took the risk and very quickly I rushed back with cash after finally succeeding to change it with a good rate too.

Then came the stress of trying to reverse the car out of the dead-end road. It was such a task that set us back another whole hour. The end of the task came only because one merciful woman watching from a shop nearby decided to open the gates of a space next to her shop so I could reverse the trailer into it. Moments later we were driving away normally as I exclaimed, "That chapter was called the Belgian experience". A stranger felt sorry for us and helped by letting us into their gate! Thank God for lovely strangers that help anyone!

Fuel stations were not as easy to find after this as they had been before we had money to buy fuel, and fuel from the car was running out fast! Thank God we finally got to a fuel station in the end, before the tank was completely empty!

REFLECTION:

Some issues that just surface out of nowhere like this desperate currency search in Belgium make no sense at all. The only apparent use of the event is maybe to teach us patience. But trying to understand the reason why everything happens may drive us insane. We just have to accept that we will never understand every single thing in life. Only God knows all things.

BLESSING:

May your blessings be multiplied today right where you are.

136 ANOTHER MISHAP, IN GERMANY THIS TIME

Do not boast about tomorrow, For you do not know what a day may bring forth. (Proverbs 27:1)

After driving tired for a while, as my family slept I could not contain my own tiredness and sleepiness. So I parked at a layby to rest a little, but the little rest turned out to be a few hours. When we all awoke along the German autobahn (motorway/freeway) I pulled into a filling station to fill up the tank and proceed on our journey. I noticed the air on the tyre of the trailer seemed too low and I naturally felt inclined to resolve the situation. So I added some air to the tyre and was satisfied that it was now ready to carry the heavy load of the trailer.

It was also a good time to use bathrooms and have some food before resuming our journey towards Austria. After we had intervened when the satnav had attempted to take us Northward to some very long route we were now back on track and heading where we knew to be right. All was well on a bright and lovely and warm sunny summer day. Who would think that anymore bad thing was about to happen on such a pleasant day that was so ideal for traveling.

We were just outside the city of Nuremberg and now picking up speed (as much as could be done with a trailer behind us). By then I had learned to go a bit faster than when we first started our journey. But this time I had just made a huge mistake. The worst thing, I found out the hard way, that I could have done on a heavily laden trailer wheel was to inflate it hard. I suddenly heard an explosion and felt a slight shake as the rear right trailer tyre that I had only just inflated gave way to heat and weight above it and popped.

Logical reasoning would likely suggest that I would now just need to get the spare wheel and change and carry on with the journey. But there was no spare wheel anywhere on the trailer, inside it or in the car drawing it. The biggest blow had just happened in a country where we had nobody we could call and at a time I had not subscribed to any roadside assistance cover by motoring associations. Only God could get us out of this mess now! It was time for another family prayer. After the prayer I took off the dead wheel, and left a reflective warning triangle behind the car as I said goodbye to the family and walked backwards towards the off-ramp that was about half a mile behind us. I was going to try to stop any car and ask them to take me to the city to get another tyre.

There were so many cars going fast and it seemed as though nobody was going to stop for me. But with the trailer wheel in my hand to hint I was needing help, I kept trying to wave them down. Suddenly, about twenty minutes later, a silver-gray BMW 320d saloon full of passengers stopped. A man came, rolled down his window and in English, asked me what had happened. I explained as quickly as I could so he would not lose his patience. Then he told me to go back to the car and tell my family that I had found someone to help us and also to reassure them that I would be back since we did not have any way to keep them updated by phone.

REFLECTION:

By this time in my life I was careful not to try to make people feel too sorry for me. Though I still felt sorry for myself many times I had progressed from where I had been when I was bereaved. I now felt almost embarrassed that I should need to seek help from others. I think that is some form of pride which really never helps anyone. Wanting to live independent of other people in this world is, in my view, taking away the social closeness that humans should enjoy. It is much more pleasant to help others and it makes the world a better place when people live together in harmony.

BLESSING:

May you enjoy blessings today as you think of doing good for someone else. It is more blessed to give than to receive and so may you enjoy more blessings today, particularly from giving to another.

137 STRANGERS HELP ON THE GERMAN AUTOBAHN

And on the morrow when he departed, he took out two pence, and gave them to the host, and said unto him, Take care of him; and whatsoever thou spendest more, when I come again, I will repay thee. (Luke 10:35)

He told me his name was Oliver. He said he was on his day off and going with his family to some water sport. He said generally nobody in Germany stops to help anyone on the motorway. He added that it was not because I was black but that my race definitely did not help the situation very much!

After he stopped to help me all the same. His wife moving to the back-seat to make the front-seat available for me, and illegally take 4 passengers in the back-seat he told me he would help me and take me to a tyre company in the city but I would have to take a taxi back to this motorway where I was so terrified I would never find my broken down trailer with the family at the car!

In the end Oliver took me back to the car after about 3 hours of driving around (his family trip was cancelled due to my family's emergency situation). Advancing me some needed emergency finance, he had bought a brand new tyre and its rim because the UK trailer tyre and rim was not compatible with the German ones. When all was done, after spending a total of €90 for me Oliver asked me, 'Do you have enough money to carry on with your journey?' He wanted to lend me some more money. And all he took was my email address.

REFLECTION:

"Which now of these three, thinkest thou, was neighbour unto him that fell among the thieves?" (Luke 10:36) I had been trying to stop different cars for help for about 20 minutes. I think my neighbour was Oliver. A German man with his kind family.

BLESSING:

The biggest blessings I pray today and always upon Oliver and his wife and children for sacrificing their day out and giving up their fun trip for me and my family. I pray a blessing also on all who read this extraordinary story. May God give you peace.

138 TAKE THE FERRY IN PASSAU

And I have led you forty years in the wilderness: your clothes are not waxen old upon you, and thy shoe is not waxen old upon thy foot. (Deuteronomy 29:5)

"Turn right and take the ferry!" said the TomTom satellite navigator (satnav) device after making us travel for about 20 minutes in the magnificent city of Passau, Germany. As Wikipedia describes it, Passau is a town in Lower Bavaria, Germany, also known as the Dreiflüssestadt ("City of Three Rivers") because the Danube is joined there by the Inn from the south and the Ilz from the north. Well known for its gothic and baroque architecture, Passau was home to Adolf Hitler and his family from 1892 to 1894. Indeed it is one of the loveliest cities that I have seen in daytime or nighttime.

I had put the settings on the satellite navigator to allow us to use ferries whenever needed. But I had not imagined that it meant that at some point we may have to leave the car and all our luggage and go by ferry to another place.

We were hoping to quickly get to the border with Austria but rather than use the motorway (at a cost in Austria), we were trying to use secondary roads with satnav guidance. The very last thing we all expected was that we were being taken to a standing boat after hours... whose destination we know not!

"Take the ferry" repeated the satnav, much to our amusement! Normally the satnav does not repeat its instructions. But as if it could hear our laughter and shock, the satnav repeated this weird instruction when we least wanted a ferry!

We turned away from the ferry dock and followed the road signs into Austria. Fortunately we managed to travel the rest of the way without any further noteworthy incidents till we reached our favourite place of rest, Bogenhofen College. We proceeded from there through Hungary but as we drove into the night, my tiredness got the better of me again. I had to stop and take a rest again before awakening too late to reach the baptism of my wife's niece.

After spending the night and part of the day in Bihor, Romania we then proceeded to Baicoi. Traveling the rest of the day we finally reached Baicoi late on a Sunday night to begin work on Monday, the very next morning.

REFLECTION:

God has some humour and I guess He wanted to cheer us up a bit after all we have been experiencing lately in our sojourn to the promised land! We were getting closer to our destination even with each incident along our way. There were some difficulties we faced but none of them were catastrophic. So when we look back and think about what we went through it is like an adventure. But when it was happening it was a lot more stressful. Still the stress weighed in more after the situations were resolved. So the point to note in this is that there is always an end to situations. As my mind keeps ringing the words of one friend, "Everything will be fine in the end. If it is not yet fine, then it is not yet the end!". When God shall bring all things to a close He shall indeed bring all bad things to an end.

BLESSING:

May you endure till the end and may the promised blessings from God be yours.

138 THE EARTHQUAKE

So likewise ye, when ye shall see all these things, know that it is near, even at the doors. Verily I say unto you, This generation shall not pass, till all these things be fulfilled. Heaven and earth shall pass away, but my words shall not pass away. (Matthew 24:33-35)

Just two weeks after our arrival in Baicoi we went to sleep as usual on a normal Friday night. Our apartment was on the top floor of a three-story building from where we had a view far into a lovely distance of nature. The weather had been quite still and calm on a fairly warm summer evening as we went to bed. Suddenly I woke up on a shaking bed at around 2.12am on September 24th, 2016! The door of the room was also shaking and rattling loudly! The entire building indeed was shaking like a train in motion! I was terrified but I did not want to show it to my wife who awoke and asked, "Is it an earthquake?" I quickly answered, "'NO, it is a very strong wind." I just wanted her to be calm and go back to sleep. Fortunately the tremor lasted but just a few minutes and everything returned to normal again. The sleeping children did not even wake up from their sleep and had no idea what had happened while they slept.

In the morning we saw from other Facebook users and also heard from other people around us that there indeed was a violent earthquake in Bucharest that shook the earth with effect felt up to about 94km from the city! Where would you run to when an earthquake happens where you are? Indeed where could we go but to the Lord?

There was not another time I appreciated the rising of the sun and its beauty and splendour as early that Sabbath morning. I even took a photograph that I kept and cherished until this very day.

REFLECTION:

Even as we sleep, death could be knocking on our door. Many people do die in their sleep.

We have no abiding city here in this world. It remains a possibility that one day we could indeed be consumed by the earth in an earthquake moment. May we be right with the Lord if such a thing should happen to us. We can then look forward to the first resurrection and live eternally with Jesus in a new earth where no sin or pain exists.

BLESSING:

May the King of kings say to you one day, Come ye blessed of my Father, inherit the kingdom prepared for you from the foundation of the world[1].

---

[1] Matthew 25:34

139 CAR REGISTRATION TIME IN ROMANIA

And other sheep I have, which are not of this fold: them also I must bring, and they shall hear my voice; and there shall be one fold, and one shepherd. (John 10:16)

I woke up early in the morning and went to the queue at the police station located at Strada Vasile Lupu Nr. 60, Ploiesti. This was my second day of trying to process the registration of my UK car in Romania. The previous day I was told that I needed to come early and join a queue of people that would be issued with queue position numbers. After the said numbers were given to the people then the people would wait until their number was reached. Only a certain number of people were served on any given day and that number was only of those who were around at the time of the issuing of numbers as the police station opened in the morning. I only understood all this information after speaking to several different people who were around there. I had to build the meaning of what they were saying to me from the bits of Romanian I could now understand, combined with some bits of English that some of the Romanians had tried to tell me in.

I got a ticket number for the queue and was advised that service on my number would not likely be reached that day. I could wait but my chances of getting helped were not very good. Yet, they continued, I should still remain for some hours or come back a bit later because around midday they were going to redo the queue number issuing for the next morning. I remained there until they finally redid the reissuing of numbers at around 1pm. Now I could leave and return the next morning to see if my number would be any closer to being served the next day.

It turned out that I finally got to be served on the third day. But yet I was served because I pretended not to understand when I was being told to go away and come back again on the next day. I just went past people and into the building where someone at the front of the queue who tried to repeat what I was being told before suddenly decided to change what he meant. He spoke to me in some English then he took me straight to the officers at the number plates issuing desk and told them that I was a British citizen who needed their help. He told them that they should respect and serve me because I was a foreigner (all this he said in Romanian and I had no interpreter needed to tell me what he was saying!)

After I got the temporary red number plates for my car I was meant to go to get my car and trailer checked at Registrul Auto Roman RAR (Romanian Vehicle Registry). RAR was at a completely different location altogether. There they also had some huge bureaucracy to follow and lengthy bookings for the vehicle inspections and payments. That was when a sister from my church, Corina asked if I had been successful in getting anyone to help me with the registration process. I had not really gone very far and I was struggling although making some progress by pretending to not understand anything when frustrated. Her husband, Costel, could not speak English either but he came to offer to help me with dealing with the remaining processes.

It would entail several visits to RAR and even appealing for assistance from the director of the department because the legality of my red numbers was limited. Costel travelled several times to the city of Ploiesti to meet me at RAR. Finally both the car and the trailer which needed to have its own registration book according to Romanian regulations, got clearance to be registered. I could then return to the police station on an appointed date to collect the numbers without the days of drama in the crowd that was called a queue.

REFLECTION:

Costel was not a Seventh-day Adventist member, but his wife Corina was. Costel said he was Greek Orthodox but not practicing. He did not understand much about religion but did believe that there was a God. I was keen to discuss what the Bible teaches, with him, but he was a very busy man and we never got much of a chance to do this. I very much appreciated his kindness and sacrifice. I found him to be one of the most selfless and altruistic people I have ever met.

BLESSING:

I pray that God may give you a joyful day and miracles of your own when you need them as I did. May God also bless Costel and all people like him.

140 WINTER BLESSINGS NEAR THE UKRAINE BORDER

And it shall come to pass, that from one new moon to another, and from one sabbath to another, shall all flesh come to worship before me, saith the LORD. (Isaiah 66:23)

The time I got closest ever to Ukraine was in January 2017. It was in a little Moldovan village of Romania called Vulcanesti. A very quiet and calm place where practically everyone who lives there knows everybody around them. Blizzards and very chilly winds in that region remain engraved in my mind as I recall my week in the area.

One good friend and colleague from the theology program, pastor Gabriel Stefanita together with his lovely wife Crina had extended an invitation to me to come to their district. Unfortunately, through our pastor Dorian Sisu, my local church in Baicoi had already long asked me to run a four week series of Revelation seminars in Baicoi. That left me with just one week that I could spare for the Vulcanesti seminars before rushing back to Baicoi. With Gabriel Stefanita as my interpreter, the seminars turned out to be such a tremendous blessing for me. I felt the genuine love and warmth of God's people as I fellowshipped nightly with them. I learned new songs that I had never heard sung elsewhere before. I particularly loved the song about the end of time titled "Sfârșitul Veacului Trăim" (The End of the Age We Live In) and learned and sung it with the people with inspiration. The song talks of the end of the age of bad things being near and that Jesus is coming soon. I felt the people's hope for the second coming of Jesus in their singing, praying and general conduct.

The people braved snowy and dangerously icy roads to attend the programs. There were attendees who were Christians from other faiths than the Adventist faith and it was a real blessing to fellowship and praise God together with them. They were very happy too and excited to learn explanations from the Bible in ways they had never had before. Some of their questions which they could not find answers to or had been told they should not ask were addressed in the seminars. It was such a blessing indeed.

As our own vehicle, the Volkwagen Touran that had come all the way from the UK had broken down. I could not use it for the journey.

Nonetheless the owner of the school, had kindly given me use of his minibus for me to go and do God's work of preaching. That vehicle formed a part of the memory of going to Vulcanesti. We often rode to the meetings with other people from the village who needed a lift. Our accommodation and delicious food was kindly provided by the lovely and kind Felea family. They made fire in the furnace to heat our room for the week. They also heated water for us to take our daily baths. Most notably they kept us well fed at all times. It was a wonderful experience to be their guests.

REFLECTION:

The first evening I was asked to present myself and my background and origins as well. I was asked to explain the circumstances under which I ended up in Romania. That enabled me to connect with the people and for them to accept me as one of their own. They too had experienced loss and some were actually caring for loved ones who were facing death. Experiencing the warmth of the people of Vulcanesti left gave me a reassurance of God's enduring love that followed me wherever I went.

BLESSING:

I pray that today you may experience the love of God from all the people who surround you.

141 THE PRODIGAL RETURN

And when he came to himself, he said, How many hired servants of my father's have bread enough and to spare, and I perish with hunger! I will arise and go to my father. (Luke 15:17-18)

After being away from the UK again for another couple of years and having no clear vision of a future going forward in Romania it was time to think of returning to England. With my thesis delivered and defended and my MA degree certificate now in my hands I could perhaps become useful in England. The Romanian church did make good use of me and I was among the most blessed people there but there was no prospect of me getting employment with my limited command of Romanian.

The biggest of my problems was that I had no financial reserves when we were meant to arrange to travel back. I had not received any more than a meagre rent income from property in the Uk for months. I was truly fending for myself and for my family. I had acquired a vinyl cutting machine that I was using to generate income by making arts and craft items like t-shirts and wall and car signs and stickers. But my market was very competitive and saturated. I also faced the challenge of language limitations.

It so happened that I spoke to one of the elders of the church. He was called Gabriel Jica and he asked for details about how I was planning to arrange to send my family's effects back to England. We always referred to him as brother Jica. He was ever so kind and gentle and always smiling. He always appreciated the lessons from all the sermons I preached in his church. I was always blessed to preach in Baicoi.

The plan and idea that I had was very sketchy. I was considering leaving much of our things behind in some storage arrangement until the time I could afford to transport them to the UK later. Brother Jica spoke to his cousins who owned a bus transportation business. They agreed and offered to transport all of our items to the UK completely free of charge. All we needed to do was to pack and label our baggage into boxes and load them into a trailer.

In the end that was exactly how our things came to England while we drove back in our VW Touran as family.

REFLECTION:

The way God works is a mystery. But I continuously see His mercy upon me and His continued providence over and over again. The man of God came out of nowhere to ask me about my plans. Then without me asking for his help in any way he hacked out a plan to bail me out. That is how I have continuously experienced new mercies from God. At the time that I am at my lowest, He just sends me another solution in unexpected ways. God's help is not only for the sad and lonely and grieving but also for any who need help. I will forever praise God for how he has seen me through. I will forever be thankful for those whom God has used to show me such love and unmerited kindness.

BLESSING:

May God's love and kindness flow your way. May you be blessed beyond measure.

142 A KINDLY BROTHER

By this shall all men know that ye are my disciples, if ye have love one to another. (John 13:35)

I would like to share a specific experience that touched me towards my final days in Romania. It is about one brother that I met at church. We could not speak too much during my days in his town as my Romanian was not very good and he spoke no English at all. He had recently hurt his back during work and he was not meant to do any physical work including lifting. Yet, to my surprise, the man who came to my biggest aid during my time of packing and moving things to the trailer for the return journey to the UK was my brother from the Baicoi church, Mircea Schiopu. When I had to load up my car and drive to the trailer, Mircea availed his estate car and loaded it to the full. Notwithstanding his back injuries, I think he made at least four trips with boxes full of our things to be shipped to the UK.

He and his wife Irina knew that we were preparing for our departure from Baicoi. They were among the many kind and loving members of the church group we fellowshipped weekly with. They were also aware of our little business of making and selling t-shirts. Up to this moment I had not imagined that they were even remotely interested in any of our products at all. Then one day I heard Mircea saying that he wanted to buy some t-shirts from us for memory's sake since we were now leaving. He asked if we still had any t-shirts left.

Mircea came and took just a couple of t-shirts from the ones we had left but the money he gave me for it was way too much for the price we were selling them for. He said it was because he wanted to help us with fuel for the journey back to England. I was tearfully moved by his kind gesture and thanked him. I think he did not even know that my finances were not at their best at the time.

REFLECTION:

After we reached England, Mircea renewed my car's Romanian insurance during the time before I could get the UK registration back. He used his own money to buy the insurance and sent the papers for it by registered post to England. I reimbursed him later but there are not many people who would have acted as swiftly as he did. I had missed about a month of insurance without realising the insurance had already expired when I quickly contacted him for help. I know I have a friend and a brother in him. God sent one who took my troubles upon himself and made efforts to help me for no personal gain. God never left me alone!

BLESSING:

May God hear you when you call and may He see you and rescue you in your time of need as He did see and rescue me.

143 THE END SHALL COME

Then came there unto him all his brethren, and all his sisters, and all they that had been of his acquaintance before, and did eat bread with him in his house: and they bemoaned him, and comforted him. (Job 42:11)

He healeth the broken in heart, and bindeth up their wounds. (Psalm 147:3)

The last enemy that shall be destroyed is death. (1 Corinthians 15:26)

Many people are familiar with the story of a man in the Bible whose name was called Job. He was befallen by a myriad of calamities the magnitude of which is only ever found in his life story and nowhere else. While his was an extraordinary case there are times when some people may think that theirs are the worst problems.

If this is your first time to learn of this story then I highly recommend that you read it from the Bible, in the book of Job, for yourself. You may find that your problems pale in comparison to those of Job.

Why am I ending my personal life stories with that of Job's life? The answer is simple. There are a number of parallels in my own life as in the suffering I see in Job's life. Like Job I did experience deep pain from loss. But my loss was nothing compared to that of Job's.

The end of the book of Job records his friends still coming to comfort him. Everything he had lost is replenished and multiplied. But yet the Bible says that his friends came to comfort him. They had wronged him and he had forgiven them. But they still came to comfort someone who was now considered to be now healed.

The healing from grief for a loved one will never bring you back to where you were before. You will certainly feel better and better as time goes by. In your whole lifetime you will never be the same person you were before the loss. The wound left by death is often so deep. This does not mean that God cannot heal. It just shows the gravity of the result of sin that is death. And the Bible says that death is an enemy that shall be destroyed in the end.

What should certainly bring you comfort and hope is that God's angels are always by the side of those who grieve. Yes the pain of grief is present and real. It is worth knowing that the Lord never leaves us alone. "The Lord is nigh unto them that are of a broken heart; and saveth such as be of a contrite spirit." (Psalm 34:18)

REFLECTION:

How I long for the day that death shall be destroyed. The day that God Himself shall wipe all tears from our eyes. Sin and suffering shall be no more. Cruelty, meanness, craftiness, deception, suffering and loneliness will be gone forever. Peace and harmony and endless joy and happiness forever shall be ours as we reunite with all our loved ones who died in Christ.

BLESSING:

I pray that one day you shall walk on the golden streets together with your loved ones singing praises to God. May God bless you most abundantly and eternally!